Urban Police Patrol Analysis

The MIT Press
Cambridge, Massachusetts, and London, England

Urban Police Patrol Analysis

Richard C. Larson

363.2
L 33 u

MN

Library of Congress Cataloging in Publication Data

Larson, Richard C   1943–
  Urban police patrol analysis.

  Bibliography: p.
  1. Police patrol. 2. Police patrol—Mathematical models. I. Title.
HV8080.P2L37   363.2′32′0184   72-274
ISBN 0-262-12052-6

Contents

Preface

In the Fall of 1965 I was indirectly the victim of a grand larceny. In the course of trying to track down the perpetrators, I met a number of people in Massachusetts law enforcement agencies who freely discussed some of the criminal identification problems they experienced. My lack of success at locating the larcenists was more than offset by the encouragement of these individuals to study automated fingerprint recognition and related problems that seemed suited to the skills of an engineer. Soon thereafter my graduate advisor at M.I.T. learned of my newly acquired interests but suggested that I consider broader systems issues in police work that were receiving little attention at that time.

I had just begun a Master's thesis with him on the police response system when a unique further opportunity appeared. The Director of the Science and Technology Task Force of the President's Commission on Law Enforcement and Administration of Justice invited me to join that task force. This experience (during 1966 and 1967) led to a deep interest in operational problems of criminal justice agencies, one result of which was a Ph.D. thesis at M.I.T., "Models for the Allocation of Urban Police Patrol Forces," (September 1969). This book is a direct outgrowth of the thesis and work done earlier with the Boston Police Department and more recently with the New York City Rand Institute, in conjunction with the New York City Police Department.

Some of the material presented here has appeared in different forms elsewhere. For instance, several of the results of Sections 3.2, 3.3 and 4.1 appeared in "On the Modeling of Police Patrol Operations," *IEEE Transactions on Systems Science and Cybernetics*, vol. SSC-6, no. 4, October 1970, pp. 276–281. A very general overview appeared in "On Quantitative Approaches to Urban Police Patrol Problems," *Journal of Research in Crime and Delinquency*, vol. 7, no. 2, July 1970, pp. 157–166. Parts of Section 3.5 were first reported in "Response of Emergency Units: The Effects of Barriers, Discrete Streets, and One-way Streets," New York City–Rand Institute R-675, April 1971, supported by the U.S. Department of Housing and Urban Development (HUD). Certain topics of Sections 3.6 and 8.1 were first discussed in "Measuring the Response Patterns of New York City Police Patrol Cars," R-673-NYC, July 1971, also sponsored by HUD; this report also contains the analysis of a patrol data gathering experiment that is not reported here. Approximately half of the material in this book appeared in a preliminary version in M.I.T. Operations Research Center Technical Report No. 44,

"Models for the Allocation of Urban Patrol Forces" (adapted from the Ph.D. thesis), which is now supplanted by this book.

During the past six years I have met and worked with many people whose thoughts and conversations have influenced the writing of this book. Certainly primary responsibility for encouraging such a flexible graduate career in applied operations research from 1965 to 1969 belongs with Alvin W. Drake (Associate Professor, Electrical Engineering Department, M.I.T., and Associate Director of the M.I.T. Operations Research Center) who supervised my master's and doctoral theses. Special acknowledgment must also be given to Alfred Blumstein, former Director of the Science and Technology Task Force and now Director of the Urban Systems Institute, School of Urban and Public Affairs, Carnegie-Mellon University, who enhanced my interest in administration of justice and provided continual encouragement since the days of the Science and Technology Task Force.

In the Boston Police Department, it is a pleasure to acknowledge Superintendents John Howland (now Director of the Command Training Institute at Babson College) and William Taylor, and Deputy Superintendents John Bonner and John West for providing many hours of informative discussions during 1965–1967 and, more recently, to Commissioner Edmund McNamara and Mr. Steven Rosenberg (Director of Planning and Research) for providing the opportunity for implementing some of the techniques developed in this book.

In the New York City Police Department, I am grateful for the cooperation in various data gathering experiments of Captain Howard E. Anderson, Deputy Inspector Harry Burns, Captain William Devine, Deputy Inspector John T. O'Brien (now Public Safety Director, New Brunswick, New Jersey), Captain Donald Rowan, former Chief of Patrol Harry Taylor, Inspector Stephen Walsh, and the patrolmen and officers of Divisions 8 (southeastern Bronx) and 16 (eastern Queens).

Both the Boston and New York City Police Departments were very cooperative in allowing me to spend more than 100 hours in the rear seats of patrol cars and a comparable amount of time in central dispatching rooms.

I owe a great deal to the organizations that supported most of the work reported in this book: the National Science Foundation, through grants to the M.I.T. Operations Research Center; the U. S. Department of Housing and Urban Development, through contracts to the New York City Rand Institute; and the Ford Foundation, through a two-year postdoctoral fellowship.

Extensive reviews of an earlier draft were provided by James Kakalik (Rand Corporation) and Mr. Keith Stevenson (a doctoral candidate at the M.I.T. Operations Research Center), both of whom I would like to thank for greatly influencing the final form of the book. I would also like to thank for useful comments on certain parts of the book Alfred Blumstein, Jan Chaiken (New York City-Rand Institute), Alvin W. Drake, Joseph Ferreira (Assistant Professor, M.I.T. Department of Urban Studies and Planning), Saul Gass (Mathematica, Inc.), John Jennings (New York City-Rand Institute), Amedeo Odoni (Assistant Professor, M.I.T. Department of Aeronautics and Astronautics), and Sorrel Wildhorn (Rand Corporation).

In addition, I would like to express my gratitude to Ann LeMieux for her patience in typing two drafts of the manuscript and to Douglas Lazarus and Laura Wiener (both of the New York City-Rand Institute) who drafted the original illustrations, many of which are used in this book.

Finally, it is with a special pleasure that I thank the M.I.T. Operations Research Center for providing a "home" for this work.

All computer computations, exclusive of data analyses, were performed at the M.I.T. Information Processing Center.

Richard C. Larson
Cambridge, Massachusetts

To Susan and Boris

Urban Police Patrol Analysis

Introduction

Police and fire departments, emergency ambulance services, and emergency repair services are maintained in most cities to provide citizens with rapid and competent emergency service when needed. Indeed, lives and property are often dependent on the effective performance of these systems.

The costs of providing emergency services are considerable. For the police and fire departments alone, New York City budgeted approximately $1 billion for fiscal 1971–1972. This figure follows a "human resources" category ($2.3 billion) and education ($2 billion) as the third-largest item in a $10 billion budget.[1] As an industry, emergency services may be one of the most labor-intensive, undercapitalized in the country. with employee salaries and fringe benefits consuming over 90 percent of the budget in most cities. At present salary levels, the cost of fielding one two-man police patrol car around the clock ranges from $100,000 to over $200,000 annually.[2]

Coupled with a pressure toward increased salary levels, there has been a marked increase in the amount of service demanded by citizens. In some cities over the past 10 years the number of requests for service has increased at a rate of 15 to 20 percent per year. Although budget levels have grown considerably, the manning levels have often not kept pace with rising demands. The result in many cities has been a reduction in the quality of service provided.

A citizen may perceive degraded service in the following ways:
Lengthy delays of 30 minutes or more until arrival of an ambulance,
Excessively long ringing of an emergency telephone before answering by a clerk,
A refusal of the police department to respond to certain types of calls,
Only a cursory examination of a crime scene, once patrol officers are on the scene,
A reduction in the amount of equipment available to be sent to a fire,
Criminals escaping from a crime scene due to an excessive response time of patrol units,
A diminished frequency of patrols past one's residence.

Such reductions in service can have lasting side effects. For example, a police department that appears not to care about open fire hydrants may cause citizens to become apathetic about reporting other more serious kinds

1. *The New York Times* (May 2, 1971) p. 70.
2. To fill one post 24 hours a day, each day of the year, requires approximately five individuals (considering days off, vacations, and sick leave). Thus, one two-man post such as a two-man patrol car requires approximately ten individuals. Conservative estimates of salary and direct benefits yield an annual cost exceeding $10,000 per officer in most cities, thereby giving a total annual cost per patrol car in excess of $100,000.

of conditions in their neighborhoods. If a citizen's only direct contact with city government comes as a result of requesting emergency service, a poor response could negatively effect his attitude toward the entire city government. From the point of view of potential criminals, a police department saturated with service requests poses little deterrent threat of apprehension. If performance is noticeably worse in some sections of the city than in others, citizens may correctly perceive inequities in distribution of services, perhaps leading to alienation. The reader can easily continue such a list.

Thus the "costs" of poor service extend far beyond just monetary costs, incorporating many diverse social costs that are difficult to quantify.

Where does this book fit into the picture? First, throughout the years a standard response of administrators of emergency services to increased demands for services has been, "We just need additional personnel." Such a response would often come *after the fact* of congestion, indicating a lack of planning.

Until recently there has been remarkably little effort expended on identifying and evaluating means for improving service other than that of simply adding personnel. Exact figures are difficult to find, but it could be safely assumed that less than one-tenth of 1 percent of the budgets of these agencies have been devoted to research.[3] This compares with research amounts of 2 to 4 percent in industry and 10 to 13 percent in defense.[4] Therefore, one primary focus of this book is on the identification and evaluation of alternative means of improving performance.

Second, why the focus on *urban police patrol analysis*? The methods proposed and developed here are not limited to police but can be applied (perhaps with modification) to any urban emergency service. For instance, similar

3. This statement should probably be modified following the passage of the 1968 Omnibus Crime Control and Safe Streets Act, which has provided external funds for research in police departments.
4. Over the decade of the sixties, private industry funds allocated to research and development as a percentage of net sales ranged from 1.8 to 2.4 percent; additional federal support of private research and development increased these figures to 4.0 to 4.2 percent [National Science Foundation, "Research and Development in Industry, 1968" (Washington, D.C.: U.S. Government Printing Office, 1970); National Science Foundation, "Industry Research and Development Spending" Science Resources Studies, 70–47, (Washington, D.C.: National Science Foundation, January 22, 1971)]. Over the comparable period, the obligations for research and development in the Department of Defense as a percentage of its total budget ranged from 10 to over 13 percent; during the period fiscal 1967–fiscal 1971, the figure stabilized near 10 percent. Charles L. Schultze, "Setting National Priorities, The 1971 Budget" (Washington, D.C.: The Brookings Institution, 1970); The Budget of the U.S. Government Fiscal Years 1960–1970 (Washington, D.C.: U.S. Government Printing Office, 1970) p. 154.

methods have been successfully used by the New York City Rand Institue to study fire operations in that city.[5] *Police* are chosen here partly because of the author's acquaintance with law enforcement and administration of justice, originating with the Science and Technology Task Force of the President's Commission on Law Enforcement and Administration of Justice,[6] and partly because the police are the most costly and complex of the urban emergency services.

We focus on *urban* police because the problems of congestion, delay, and limited patrol resources are most noticeable in large urban police departments. But the techniques can be readily applied to any size of municipal police department. Not included in this study are state police, private police agencies, or federal law enforcement agencies.

Patrol is selected as a focus because the patrol force constitutes the largest single class of police personnel, usually consuming 40 to 50 percent of the total police budget. Also, the activities of the patrol force (for example, arrests) give rise to the need for other types of police personnel (detectives and supervisors) as well as personnel elsewhere in the criminal justice system. However, attention is not limited to patrol. Other personnel such as radio dispatchers and emergency telephone operators (complaint clerks) perform important related functions within the *police emergency response system*. These personnel, and related technologies to improve their performance, will also be included in this study.

Analysis as a focus implies that attention is given to the following classical steps:
1. Define the problem.
2. Specify the objectives.
3. Define criteria relating to the objectives.
4. Specify alternatives.
5. Analyze alternatives.
6. Compare alternatives.
7. Present results.

Indeed, one is hard-pressed to suggest a preferred alternative to analysis.

Within the context of the seven steps, our focus will be on the development and interpretation of mathematical models of operation. These are most rele-

5. The New York City Rand Institute, *First Annual Report* (New York City Rand Institute, 1970).
6. The work of the task force is summarized in *Task Force Report: Science and Technology, A Report to the President's Commission on Law Enforcement and Administration of Justice* (Washington, D.C.: U.S. Government Printing Office, 1967).

vant in Steps 3 to 6, although to some extent they are useful in each of the seven steps. By concentrating on mathematical models, we necessarily limit ourselves to aspects of operation that are quantifiable and conducive to abstraction. This obviously directed focus is not sufficient when implementing changes. For instance, command judgment, which derives from many years of experience as a police officer, is not likely to be replaced by any mathematical formalism. On the other hand, the consequences of altering operating policies may be too complex to tract mentally, even with many years of experience. Then, mathematical models of operation come into play to help develop correct intuition and to provide insights into operating behavior not readily obtainable from other means.

Third, the book is an attempt to introduce two historically separate groups —agency administrators and quantitatively trained analysts—to each other's vocabularies and to indicate that some agency problems can be usefully approached form a quantitative viewpoint. Although we select a wide variety of problems to study, by no means are all problems of patrol addressed. Indeed, we are only scratching the surface—both in the scope and depth of the problems of police patrol. For the problems addressed here, much further work is needed in generalizing model assumptions, testing validity of assumptions, and testing feasibility of recommended changes resulting from analysis of the models. The same can be said for most problems not addressed here, because the analysis of police operations is still in its embryonic stages. To indicate other related work in the field, we have included an annotated bibliography.

The fact that two audiences are addressed has complicated the writing of this book. On the one hand, we have the objective of convincing the police administrator that quantitative models can be useful in his planning and management process. On the other, we must develop the technical results and indicate to the quantitative community that there are many rich and unsolved, yet relevant, problems in police patrol. To these ends, we have written Chapters 1 and 2 in a nontechnical manner to provide descriptions of the system being studied, the problems addressed, the type of insights obtained, and the type of activity necessary to implement quantitative techniques successfully.

In Chapter 1 we first describe the police emergency response system and problems encountered while processing calls for service. Then we describe a typical 8-hour tour of duty for two patrol officers. Given these system descriptions, we attempt to identify meaningful measures of system effectiveness and compare these to traditional measures.

Chapter 2 presents a self-contained application of the techniques of Chap-

ters 3 through 8 to Simtown, a hypothetical city with a resident population
of approximately 200,000. The chapter traces the progress of a joint study
group partially supported by funds provided under the 1968 Omnibus Crime
Control and Safe Streets Act. Focusing on patrol and dispatch operations, the
study group is composed of individuals from the police department's planning
and research staff and from a local consulting firm.

Over the first 18 months of this joint effort, the group analyzes a number
of important operational innovations, including
A shift from precinct-wide to division-wide dispatching.
A formal priority structure for dispatching.
Allowing interruption of service on low priority calls.
Designating certain patrol units as specialists in preventive patrol.
Evaluating the benefits of car location information.
Designing overlapping sectors.
Training certain patrolmen in handling family dispute calls.
Adding ambulance calls.
Revising the tour structure.

The advantages and disadvantages of each innovation are analyzed prior to
implementation by use of the analytical and simulation models of the later
chapters. As a result of these initial analyses, some innovations are discarded
by the study group and others are implemented on a trial basis. Results of
such trials feed back to improve the predictive capability of the models and
to suggest improvements in the proposed innovation, thereby increasing the
chance of successful city-wide implementation.

After the first 18 months, the group has already implemented several city-
wide changes and plans a comprehensive, continuing program of evaluation,
test, and implementation.

Chapters 3 through 8 are written for a technical audience with a background in introductory calculus and probability theory. Central to many of
the developments in this part of the book is the role played by probabilistic
reasoning. The application of probabilistic analysis to criminal justice problems is not entirely new. In the early nineteenth century, the famous mathe-
matician Laplace applied probability theory to the determination of the number of judges required in a tribunal so that verdict "error probability" would
be acceptably small.[7]

The need for probabilistic analysis in police operations can be illustrated by

7. P. Simon, Marquis de Laplace, *A Philosophical Essay on Probabilities*, republished
(New York: Dover Publications, 1952).

a simple example. Suppose calls for service are generated from within a patrol sector at an average rate of one call per hour. For simplicity, we assume that all calls are serviced by the *single* patrol unit assigned to the sector; any calls that occur while the unit is busy on a previous call are entered in a queue that is depleted in a first-come, first-served manner. In addition, let us assume that the average time to service each call is one-half hour and the spread about the average (as measured by the standard deviation) is $\sqrt{2}/4 \approx 0.354$ hour. In this illustrative example we are ignoring complications due to meal breaks, patrol-initiated action, and possible time-varying demand rates.

Now, deterministic reasoning, which is not uncommon in present planning procedures, argues that this sector is *not* overloaded because the unit is busy on calls for service only 4 out of 8 hours. After all, the unit is being utilized at only one-half "capacity." The same reasoning argues that since the patrol unit services calls twice as fast as they arrive, any queuing delay incurred by arriving calls should be negligibly small. Finally, using deterministic arguments, one should expect the number of calls generated during an 8-hour tour to be very close to the average, eight.

Switching to probabilistic arguments, it would be reasonable to assume that a random process[8] generates calls for service, with an average rate of one call per hour. The probability that a certain number of calls are generated during an 8-hour tour is given by a well-known formula and is tabulated in the accompanying table. Note that the probability of *exactly* eight calls arriving during the tour is only 0.1396. For nearly 20 percent of the tours, the number of calls generated will be less than or equal to *five*. For nearly 19 percent of the tours, the number of calls generated will be greater than or equal to *eleven*. The *average* workload per tour, measured in hours required to service all calls, is indeed 4 hours. But one can show[9] that there is considerable dispersion about this average; as one measure of dispersion, the standard deviation of the workload is $\sqrt{3} \approx 1.73$ hours. Finally, using a well-known result of queuing theory,[10] one finds that fully 50 percent of the calls arrive while

8. A very good model for the process generating police calls for service is the Poisson process, whose properties are described in most introductory texts in probability and random process. See, for example, Samuel Karlin, *A First Course in Stochastic Processes* (New York: Academic Press, 1966), pp. 13–16; Emanuel Parzen, *Stochastic Processes* (San Francisco: Holden-Day Publishing Company, 1962), pp. 118–159; B. V. Gnedenko, *The Theory of Probability*, B. D. Seckler, trans. (New York: Chelsea, 1968), pp. 346–353.
9. Alvin W. Drake, *Fundamentals of Applied Probability* (New York: McGraw-Hill Book Company, 1967), p. 111.
10. L. S. Goddard, *Mathematical Techniques of Operational Research* (London: Pergamon Press, 1963), p. 97.

Probability that n Calls Are Generated during an Eight-Hour Tour*

$$P(n) = \frac{(8)^n e^{-8}}{n!}, \quad n = 0, 1, 2, \ldots$$

n	$P(n)$	Cumulative Sum of Probabilities
0	0.0003	0.0003
1	0.0027	0.0030
2	0.0107	0.0138
3	0.0286	0.0429
4	0.0573	0.0996
5	0.0916	0.1912
6	0.1221	0.3134
7	0.1395	0.4530
8	0.1396	0.5925
9	0.1241	0.7166
10	0.0993	0.8159
11	0.0722	0.8881
12	0.0481	0.9362

*One hypothetical sector; average call arrival rate is one per hour.

the unit is busy and thus have to be stacked in queue; the *average time* spent in queue by these calls is 45 minutes. These insights illustrate the usefulness of a probabilistic analysis.

In order to implement the results of a probabilistic analysis, it is necessary that operational objectives be stated in comparable terms. For instance, the following types of policy statements exhibit probabilistic points of view: "Allocate sufficiently many patrol units so that *85 percent* of calls for service can be answered without dispatching delay," or "Allocate sufficiently many patrol units so that the *average travel time* does not exceed *5 minutes*." Although such explicit policy decisions may be difficult to make, operating systems evidence *implicit* decisions that could be quite unacceptable if presented to an administrator.

The following paragraphs provide a brief tour of the problems addressed using probabilistic analysis. Chapter 3 focuses on probabilistic models of travel time, addressing the following types of questions:

How does average travel speed affect response?

How does sector geometry—rectangular, diamond-shaped, or elliptical—affect travel times?

If travel speeds vary according to direction of travel, how does this influence sector design?

What are the dispatching strategies available to a dispatcher who is not provided with car location information? What are the properties of each?

How does travel time increase as the fraction of time units are unavailable increases?

What are the effects on travel time of an impediment to travel such as a railroad, a river, or a park?

What is the relationship between travel time and the street mileage in a sector? Is sector street mileage or sector area a more important determinant of travel time?

How is travel time increased by one-way streets?

Are there easily implemented experiments to test the validity of the travel time models?

How does the travel time of a patrol car compare to that of a helicopter?

If travel distances are recorded in an experiment, do the odometer truncations to the nearest mile bias the results?

If the number of patrol units were increased by an increment, what would be the approximate percentage decrease in travel time?

The results of the chapter lead directly to Chapter 5, where travel time models are used with other models in a command-by-command allocation algorithm; to Chapter 7, where many of the above questions are reexamined assuming the dispatcher has accurate car location information; and to Chapter 8, where certain formal types of intersector cooperation are shown to modify earlier results.

Chapter 4 focuses on preventive patrol activity. Although preventive patrol often consumes 50 percent or more of a patrol unit's time, questions relating to objectives and performance criteria are still poorly defined. Thus, the results of this chapter should be viewed as preliminary steps toward a much-needed comprehensive study of preventive patrol. The chapter addresses the following questions:

Is street mileage a good indicator of preventive patrol workload in a sector? Are there better indicators?

What are the properties of *random patrol*?

How can we predict the frequency of patrol at particular points in a city?

How is patrolling strength diminished by other activities such as responding to calls, meals, maintenance, and so forth?

How can we predict the probability that a patrolling unit will intercept a crime in progress?

What factors are important in allocating limited preventive patrol strength?

Why are linear hazard formulas inadequate for the purposes of preventive patrol allocation?

The chapter concludes with a list of questions that require further work—both experimental and analytical.

Chapter 5 incorporates the results of the previous two chapters in a resource allocation algorithm. The algorithm is used to address the same question traditionally answered with hazard formulas: "Given a certain total number of patrol units, how should they be distributed among commands in the city? And how should this allocation depend on time of day, day of week, or season of the year?"

The proposed algorithm requires police administrators to specify a number of policy objectives for each command. These are stated in terms of constraints. For instance, for a particular command it may be decided that the average travel time for urgent calls should not exceed 4 minutes. Other objectives can involve preventive patrol, administrative considerations, or any other factors thought important. Then the algorithm determines the minimal number of units required in each command so that *all* objectives are fulfilled. If the total number of allocable units is insufficient to satisfy objectives, the algorithm computes the deficiency and requires a more modest set of objectives. If there are additional units to allocate, beyond those needed solely to satisfy constraints, they are allocated to commands in order to fulfill some city-wide objective (for example, minimization of average queuing delay at the dispatcher's position due to patrol force congestion). The method is illustrated with data from the New York City Police Department.

The remainder of the book examines modes of patrol and dispatch operation that are different from those commonly in use today. Chapter 6 describes a general simulation model that can be used along with analytical models to analyze the new alternatives. Many of the results for Simtown reported in Chapter 2 were obtained with the simulation program described in this chapter. By facilitating the detailed investigation of alternative operating policies, a simulation model provides a valuable planning and research tool. As a training instrument, it increases an administrator's awareness of system interactions and often suggests new criteria of performance. It provides a consistent framework for evaluating new technologies and new administrative procedures. And, by limiting a great deal of the "experimentation" to the computer, it reduces costs of implementing new programs, both direct dollar costs and indirect costs involving police personnel and the citizenry.

Given such a general-purpose tool, the uses to which it is put are limited only by the imagination and ingenuity of the user. One potential application that we are likely to see in the future involves public education. As an example, a police department may be contemplating redesignating their patrol cars *division cars*, rather then *precinct cars*. Under the contemplated plan, cars would be prepositioned about the larger division, rather than the individual precincts, and, should the need arise, each car could be assigned to a call anywhere in the division. Given the proposed plan, local citizens' groups might object to such a "step toward precinct consolidation," stating that they desire to retain police at the precinct level. However, if all parties could agree to one or more measures of effectiveness of patrol operation, simulation models could then be used to predict the extent of improvement (or deterioration) in operation that would result from the change. It may happen that under the old plan, precinct level congestion would cause citizens to wait an average of 15–60 minutes for a patrol car to arrive at the scene of an incident. Under the new plan, which transforms five separate multiserver queues into one queue with a large pool of servers (patrol cars), one might discover that average response time would be sharply reduced (say to 5 minutes, or less). If this behavior is predicted prior to implementation, citizens can be shown that a plan that they thought would reduce police service would actually improve it considerably.

The past few years have seen increased interest in applying new technologies to police operations. Given the labor intensiveness of police operations, one would be surprised if certain technological innovations could not be supported at least on a cost basis. Since one additional 24-hour two-man patrol unit costs in excess of $100,000 annually, a new technology that improves operation by the same amount as a given number of additional patrol cars can be argued on cost grounds if its annual cost is less than that number times the unit cost of patrol.

Car locator systems have recently been justified on this basis. Such systems would provide the dispatcher with up-to-the-minute estimates of the positions of all patrol units, thereby increasing the chance that the most appropriate unit is dispatched to the scene. Such improved information leads to smaller travel times. By computing the number of additional patrol units in the current system needed to achieve equivalent travel time reductions, one can compute the relative *cost-effectiveness* of the car locator system. Thus, for instance, if a car locator system reduces travel time in a city by the same amount as six full-time two-man patrol units each costing $150,000 annually, then the car locator system is said to be *cost-effective* if its equivalent annual cost is less than $900,000.

In practice, the analysis is not nearly so simple. Changes in operation involve other improvements (increased officer safety, increased administrative capabilities, and more flexible methods of patrol allocation) and they involve degradations in performance (decreasing an officer's identity with his sector by increasing the amount of cross-sector dispatching).

The purpose of Chapter 7 is to use the simulation model of the previous chapter along with analytical models to develop a knowledge of the varied effects of car locator systems. The following types of questions are addressed:

How accurate should a car locator system be?

What is the extent of improvement possible by implementing a car locator system?

How does dispatching the closest car increase cross-sector dispatching?

Does the size of the command have an effect on the value of car location information?

If cars were assigned to overlapping sectors with car location information used to dispatch the closest car, how would the operating characteristics of this system compare to those of traditional systems?

No recommendations for or against car locator systems are presented. Instead, the focus is on developing a methodology that allows the patrol administrator to explore each of the effects of a car locator system, thereby providing him with better information upon which to base a decision.

Chapter 8 concludes the book with an examination of various forms of intersector cooperation that may involve the movement of one or more available units to other areas to cover for busy units. Although we have labeled such movement *repositioning*, other terms are heard such as *moveup*, *relocation*, and *redeployment*. Such actions are common in fire department operations where one large fire would leave an area of the city void of fire protection if other available units were not repositioned into the area to anticipate other possible fires. Repositioning is not so common in police operations, perhaps because congestion in an area usually occurs as the result of many small incidents rather than a single large one (such as a fire). The discussion in Chapter 8 simply touches on some of the factors involved in repositioning and then lists important further areas of work. Staff at the New York City Rand Institute have developed several useful procedures for repositioning in fire department operations,[11] and these should provide insights into analogous problems in police operations. The chapter addresses the following types of questions:

What are the distinctions between local repositioning among nearby sectors

11. See, for example, P. Kolesar and W. Walker, "A Relocation Algorithm for the MICS," unpublished mimeograph (New York City Rand Institute, 1971); A. Swersey, "Dispatching, Deployment and Relocation of Fire Engines," paper presented at the 37th National Meeting of the Operations Research Society of America, Washington, D.C., 1970; W. Walker and S. Shinnar, "Approaches to the Solution of the Fire Engine Relocation Problem," unpublished mimeograph (New York City Rand Institute, 1970). This work is summarized in J. M. Chaiken and R. C. Larson, "Methods for Allocating Urban Emergency Units," R-680-HUD/NSF (New York City Rand Institute, 1971).

and wide-scale repositioning among commands? What are the advantages of each type of repositioning?

For what fraction of dispatches can a unit expect to travel to sectors other than its assigned patrol sector?

How is the amount of cross-sector dispatching influenced by time-varying demands and nonuniform workload distributions?

What are the travel time savings of having sectors paired together as cooperating units, with the free unit repositioning to cover for its busy partner?

How is sector design influenced by intersector cooperation and repositioning?

What are possible signals indicating the need for wide-scale repositioning?

In operating systems, what are the chances of a command becoming saturated?

How should large-scale repositioning be accomplished?

Several results in the chapter can be applied in contexts not related to repositioning. One example involves a model predicting the amount of cross-sector dispatching. Patrol administrators are often heard to argue in favor of assigning patrol units to nonoverlapping sectors in order to establish a *sector identity* on the part of the patrol officer. This identity, which derives from patrolling and from citizen contacts made while responding to calls for service, is supposed to cause the officer to feel responsible for public order in the sector. However, given nonoverlapping sectors, a model of operations (Section 8.1) shows that the physics of patrol force operation often causes a patrol unit to cross sector boundaries to respond to calls in nearby sectors. In police circles, this phenomenon has been labeled *flying*. The model predicts that the fraction of dispatches that are cross-sector dispatches usually *exceeds* the average fraction of time units are unavailable for dispatch. Thus, it would not be unusual to observe 40 to 70 percent of dispatches being cross-sector dispatches. As Chapter 8 indicates, these predictions have been verified in practice.

The fact that so many dispatches are intersector assignments raises questions about the underlying philosophy of nonoverlapping sectors and sector identity. It also sheds some light on citizens' complaints about not knowing their sector's police officers. This use of an analytical model indicates that much can be said about system operation *prior* to collecting detailed data. It also indicates that quantitative models can provide insight into problems traditionally thought nonquantifiable, such as some of the sociological aspects of sector identity.

1

System Description, Objectives, and Performance Criteria

This chapter focuses on the first three steps of the analysis process: (1) a system description that reveals operational problems; (2) a delineation of objectives; and (3) a selection of performance criteria that relate in meaningful ways to system objectives.

1.1. Police Emergency Response System

To address the problems of police patrol, it is important to view the patrol force within the larger police emergency response system (Figure 1.1). This system is activated whenever a citizen (or alarm system or other detector) communicates the need for police service to the police communications center (or command and control center). In order to describe the generic operation of this system, as well as to indicate some of its complexities, the path of a call for police service is traced through a typical system as follows:

1.1.1. Incident Occurrence

Assume that at time $t = 0$ an incident commences, such as a robbery, vehicular accident, or fire that requires on-scene police service.

1.1.2. Incident Detection

At time t_1 the incident is detected by a person or device that will report the incident to police. The detector could be a crime victim, a witness, an automatic detection system, or a patrolling police officer. Particularly with respect to this last possibility, it is important to note that the police patrol may enter at the *detection stage* of the system as well as later in the *delivery of service stage.*

1.1.3. Initial Attempt to Communicate to Police

At time t_2 the detector, say a citizen, attempts to call the police. In the case of witnesses or victims, the magnitude of the delay $t_2 - t_1$ would depend on the proximity of working public telephones or police alarm boxes. Or, if detection is by an automatic system, this delay would be negligible if the information is communicated directly to police headquarters. For burglary alarms, because of the high rates of false alarms, the direct route is usually to a private alarm company that may dispatch its own units to the scene or notify the police or do both. On the other hand, victim-triggered robbery alarms are often wired directly to police headquarters, and such alarms are given top priority. If detection is by police patrol, the officers may require additional assistance. In this case the delay $t_2 - t_1$ is the amount of time to

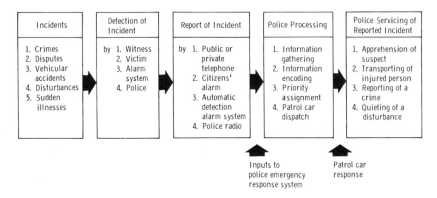

Figure 1.1 Aggregated flow diagram of the police emergency response system.

return to the patrol car in order to communicate via radio or to reach a call box or telephone.

1.1.4. Contact with Police

The police are successfully contacted at time t_3. For the case of a citizen calling via telephone, the delay $t_3 - t_2$ represents time waiting in the telephone queue; the caller simply hears a "ringing" telephone. Although this delay is often negligible, the author has observed saturated systems operating during Friday and Saturday evenings when up to 40 percent of the calls incurred delays of 30 seconds or more.[1] Such delays are particularly bothersome, because call priority cannot be determined until after initial conversation with the caller; it is a perverse property of calls to police that nonurgent calls typically require two to three times as much conversation time on the phone as do urgent calls, thereby greatly contributing to saturations of the switchboard facility.

The magnitude of the average telephone queuing delay depends on the rate of incoming calls, the rate at which they can be effectively serviced, and an important decision variable, the total number of complaint clerks assigned to answer calls. From city to city, all of these factors can vary widely. Small municipalities may need only one complaint clerk at all hours of the day. New York City, on the other hand, often receives over 1,500 calls per hour during evening hours, requiring more than 40 complaint clerks to process calls.

1. R. C. Larson, "Police Emergency Call Operations: A Preliminary Operational Study" New York City Rand Institute (unpublished mimeograph, 1968). Also, "Improving the Effectiveness of New York City's 911," in *Analysis of Public Systems*, A. W. Drake, R. L. Keeney, and P. M. Morse, eds. (Cambridge, Mass.: The M.I.T. Press, 1972).

The manner in which unanswered calls are selected for service (that is, the *queue discipline*) varies with department. The system in operation in Boston until recently required that each complaint clerk, when he finished servicing one call, manually switched in a call waiting in queue. Lines on which callers were waiting were indicated as blinking green lights on the switchboard in front of the clerk. Since it was very difficult for clerks to remember the order in which lights started blinking, most *switch ins* were performed without regard to the call arrival order, thus reflecting a nearly random service discipline. It is well known in queuing theory that a random discipline increases the dispersion about the mean (that is, variance) of the in-queue waiting time, reflecting a greater chance of a very long wait.[2] Recently Boston, New York City, and a number of other cities have each installed an automatic call distributor system that assigns calls in the order in which they arrive (first-come, first-served), thereby minimizing the chance of lengthy waits.

Incidents may also be reported by police over police radios. In these cases, the delay $t_3 - t_2$ is the amount of time to obtain a radio channel and reach the dispatcher, a delay that may be considerable in times of congestion.

1.1.5. Information Gathering

The communicated information must be recorded and interpreted by personnel at the communications center. We assume this activity is completed at time t_4.

For the case of citizens calling via telephone, the complaint clerk must gather information about the incident (for example, type and address of the incident, names of those involved, name of caller) and ascertain the priority of the call. If the caller speaks a language other than English, there may be additional time spent transferring the call to a bilingual complaint clerk. If the clerk decides that the incident does not require the dispatch of a patrol car, he may choose to terminate the call at that time, or to transfer the call to a backup board of operators specializing in nonemergency matters, or to refer the caller to some other part of the police department or to some other agency.

The important decision that the caller does not require on-scene police assistance involves possible high costs of error. On the one hand, several cases have been publicized in which the caller actually required urgent police service, but the complaint clerk either terminated the call or assigned it low priority; the cost of such an incorrect decision can include serious injuries,

2. See, for example, Thomas L. Saaty, *Elements of Queuing Theory* (New York: Mc-Graw-Hill Book Company, 1961), pp. 243–249.

property loss, or perhaps even loss of life. On the other hand, if too many calls are accepted as requiring on-scene service, the patrol force would become saturated, thereby diminishing preventive patrol and increasing the time required to get a patrol unit to the scene of an actual urgent call.

The average time required to gather information from a caller who actually requires police service is typically 20 to 30 seconds. The time required to terminate a phone conversation with other callers is typically 40 to 120 seconds.[3]

For the case of police calling the dispatcher over police radio, the time to gather the necessary information from the calling officer is usually much less than the corresponding time for a civilian.

1.1.6. Information Conversion and Recording

The reported street address must be converted to a code indicating the patrol command (for example, "precinct" or "district") and patrol sector of the incident. This activity terminates at time t_5.

In manual systems most of this activity is performed after termination of the telephone conversation. The address conversion usually entails a manual table look-up operation, after which the relevant information is recorded by hand on a "complaint ticket" or "incident slip." The ticket is then time stamped and transported to a dispatcher (often via conveyor belt). The delay $t_5 - t_4$ is the "complaint clerk address search and information recording delay."

In semi-automated systems the complaint clerk may type the information as received from the caller into a computer console. Provided the software of the system is reasonably flexible (so as to allow easy editing of errors and to correct street misspellings, for instance), the real-time computer capability can immediately signal infeasible addresses, indicating to the clerk that the caller must be requestioned as to the address. Also, the computer performs the task of address conversion to patrol command and sector number. By multiplexing the clerk's activity, the computer can reduce valuable seconds from the total complaint clerk service time ($t_5 - t_3$).

If the call is to the dispatcher over police radio, analogous information recording and processing activities, either manual or semi-automated, are performed by the dispatcher.

1.1.7. Transmittal to Dispatcher

The information recorded by the complaint clerk arrives at the dispatcher's position at time t_6, the time $t_6 - t_5$ being the complaint clerk to dispatcher

3. Larson, "Police Emergency."

transmittal delay. For manual systems involving conveyor belts, this delay is usually 5 to 10 seconds. For semi-automated systems, once all information is typed and verified, the computer directs the information to the appropriate dispatcher, for instance displaying the information before the dispatcher on a cathode-ray tube; for such systems the delay $t_6 - t_5$ is negligibly small. Of course, this delay does not occur for calls received directly by the dispatcher from the patrol force.

1.1.8. Entrance to Dispatcher Queue

Once the reported incident becomes known to the dispatcher, it has joined the *dispatcher queue*. In manual systems this queue is a physical stack of complaint tickets, or incident slips, that the dispatcher may hold in his hand— perhaps as a deck of cards, arranged by assessed priority. In automated systems this queue is an array in computer storage, and the dispatcher may or may not have the capability to peruse the queue to keep refreshing his memory as to its contents. The incident report leaves the dispatcher's queue at time t_7, when the dispatcher starts broadcasting the dispatch order to the selected patrol unit. The delay in queue is $t_7 - t_6$.

There are basically two sources for delay in the dispatcher queue. The first is caused by *dispatcher saturation*, which occurs when incident reports simply arrive in a flurry, faster than the dispatcher can physically process them. Delays associated with dispatcher saturation typically vary from a few seconds to a few minutes, but they rarely exceed 10 minutes.

Much more important is the second source of delay, that caused by *patrol force saturation*. In most cases, once a dispatcher examines the information describing an incident, he will only dispatch a patrol unit immediately if within the command of the incident there is an available patrol unit judged to be sufficiently close to the incident. Otherwise, the patrol force is found to be saturated, with all eligible units busy at the scenes of incidents reported earlier. In such a case, the incident slip remains before the dispatcher unserviced in a queue. This queue is depleted as units complete servicing previous calls and report dispatch availability to the dispatcher.

The importance of this patrol-related queuing mechanism is clearly shown by the magnitudes of the delays that can be incurred. In many cities, it is not unusual to observe delays exceeding one hour, not only during weekend evenings when they are most likely but also during daylight hours and weekday evenings.[4] During these periods the dispatcher queue delay may com-

4. Larson, "Police Emergency"; R. C. Larson, "Measuring the Response Patterns of New York City Police Patrol Cars," R-673-NYC/HUD (New York City Rand Institute, 1971).

prise 90 percent or more of the total police response time, thereby dominating all other delays in the response system. At other times, incident reports may be processed with *no delay* incurred in the dispatcher queue.

Because of the importance and complexity of the queuing mechanism related to patrol congestion, its properties will be examined following the completion of the discussion of call tracing.

1.1.9. Dispatch of Patrol Unit

As the incident report is removed from the dispatcher queue at time t_7, the dispatcher selects a unit to assign to the incident and broadcasts the incident's address and other pertinent information to the unit. The responding unit then affirms, or verifies the dispatch instructions via radio. This activity is completed at time t_8, the interval $t_8 - t_7$ representing the dispatcher decision-making and broadcast time. This entire interval typically lasts only 10 to 15 seconds, although it can be much longer if suspect descriptions or other lengthy verbal information is broadcast.

1.1.10. Arrival at the Scene

The assigned patrol unit then responds to the scene, traveling at a speed that reflects the urgency of the call. The unit arrives at the scene at time t_9, the interval $t_9 - t_8$ being the *patrol travel time*.

During uncongested periods, the travel time is usually the largest single component of the total police response time $(t_9 - t_2)$. Travel times typically fall in the range 4 to 7 minutes. But their values depend strongly on urgency of the incident, the dispatcher's success at locating a nearby available unit, the distance traveled, the driving officer's awareness of street patterns, traffic conditions, and a host of other factors.

For instance, should the unit assigned to the sector of the incident already be busy, then the dispatcher selects an out-of-sector unit to respond. His ability to select the most appropriate unit greatly influences the time required to travel to the scene. In extreme urgencies, he may either poll all nearby units as to their locations, or he may broadcast a general alert, resulting in the response of several units. But such extraordinary response usually only occurs for officer-in-trouble, felony-in-progress, or other extremely urgent and relatively infrequent calls. Since polling patrol units consumes valuable radio time on already congested channels, it is usually not feasible to implement that procedure as standard practice. Also, if general alerts were broadcast for any sizeable fraction of calls, the dispatcher would have even less knowledge of the whereabouts of particular units, thereby increasing the chance that large parts of the city could be left void of patrol for intolerable lengths of time. Thus, for most out-of-sector responses, the dispatcher selects that available unit he believes to be closest, usually estimating the positions of available units to be near the center of their respective sectors.

As these considerations indicate, the dispatcher plays an integral role in determining the performance characteristics of the police emergency response system.

1.1.11. Completion of Service

At time t_{10}, the dispatched patrol unit completes service at the scene and reports dispatch availability. The total service time depends strongly on the type of incident and the amount of follow-up work (for example, arrest and booking). Typical service times fall in the range 25 to 45 minutes.

A summary of the processing times in the police emergency response system is given in Table 1.1.

1.1.12. Additional Complexities

However complex the description of call processing may appear, many complications have been omitted. For instance, for certain urgent calls, some cities provide the capability to transfer the telephone call directly to the radio dispatcher, interrupting his current activity so that one or more units may be assigned while additional information (for example, suspect description) is

Table 1.1 Delays Incurred in the Police Emergency Response System

Symbol	Definition
t_1	Time until incident detection
$t_2 - t_1$	Time from detection until initial attempt is made to contact police
$t_3 - t_2$	Time from initial attempt until successful contact (telephone queue waiting time in the case of telephone contacts)
$t_4 - t_3$	Time to gather information about the incident
$t_5 - t_4$	Time to record information and convert street addresses to patrol sectors
$t_6 - t_5$	Time to transmit information to the dispatcher
$t_7 - t_6$	Delay in dispatcher queue
$t_8 - t_7$	Dispatcher decision-making and broadcast time
$t_9 - t_8$	Patrol travel time
$t_{10} - t_9$	On-scene service time
$t_9 - t_2$	Total police response time

collected. Occasionally the dispatcher may assign the unit he believes to be closest to the scene, at which time another unit that is actually closer than the one assigned may volunteer for the assignment. For certain special types of calls (for example, family disputes) the dispatcher may give more importance to the particular individuals assigned than the rapidity of response; for instance, a unit whose officers are trained in family disputes may be given preference over the closest unit, provided the estimated increased travel time does not greatly increase the chance of assault or injury to the parties involved.

In addition to these complexities, the time of service completion t_{10} is not always clearly defined, because the last five to 15 minutes may require paperwork that could be deferred if an urgent call were reported requiring immediate service.

During periods of large-scale emergencies (for example, airplane crash, flood, civil disorder, or earthquake), the entire operation of the system is revised according to comprehensive contingency plans. Such special operations are not included within the scope of this study.

1.1.13. Dispatch-Patrol Interactions Revisited

As the description indicates, the dispatcher plays the role of primal decision maker in the emergency response system. His actions greatly influence the magnitude of the delay in the dispatcher queue, the time required to travel to the scene, and the quality of service provided at the scene. Almost without exception, the sum of the dispatcher queue delay and the travel time comprises over 50 percent and often as much as 90 percent of the total police response time. Thus, the dispatching operation will receive a good deal of attention here.

Although many smaller cities and municipalities have only one dispatcher, larger cities have instituted various multidispatcher arrangements. Usually a single dispatcher's responsibility does not include more than 50 to 70 radio-dispatchable units. The region of responsibility for each dispatcher is usually given a name, such as *division* in New York City. That city has 17 divisions with 77 patrol commands (*precincts*) and over 700 radio-patrol car sectors. Although police departments differ in many respects, from department to department this method of successively dividing the city into finer and finer partitionings has been remarkably similar. For New York City the complete hierarchy of partitionings is city, borough command, division, precinct, and patrol sector. Their spatial relationships are depicted in Figure 1.2. Unfortunately, although the general idea of partitioning is the same in many cities,

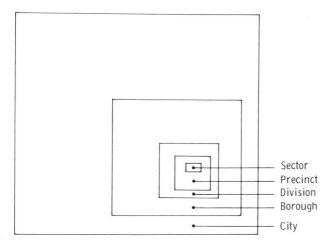

Figure 1.2 Successive partitioning of a city into smaller geographic units.

the names assigned are not. Such lack of standardization results in *sector* being called beat, district, or area. At the next higher level, *patrol commands* (in addition to precinct) are called districts, areas, or regions. For consistency, New York City's labeling is adhered to here except that precincts and *commands* are used interchangeably.

A less frequently occurring arrangement for dispatchers involves assigning two or more dispatchers to the same (overlapping) geographical region, perhaps with each dispatcher specializing in a particular activity. This was done in Boston in an interim system that has now been revised to three nonoverlapping zones, each with a separate dispatcher.

As will be seen, the administrative decision defining commands (or precincts) and divisions (or dispatching zones) plays a key role in determining the performance of the system.

When the dispatcher is deciding whether to assign an incident or to enter it in queue, the following considerations are important:
1. The current activities of the patrol units in the command of the incident,
2. The estimated priority of the incident,
3. The other unserviced incidents in queue,
4. The estimated locations of the incident and patrol units "near" the incident.

Taking 1 and 2 together, some dispatchers will hold an incident report, judged to be low priority, until the unit that patrols the sector of the incident becomes available for reassignment. More frequently, however, a dispatcher will immediately dispatch the patrol unit judged closest to the incident, as long as there is at least one available unit somewhere in the command of the incident. Intercommand assignments appear to occur rarely, and only for very high-priority calls. Thus, the dispatcher queue is in fact several queues, one for each of the commands in his division. It is not unusual to see one command backlogged with incident reports while patrol units may be available nearby in an adjacent command. Thus we see the importance of the administrative decision defining commands; in many cases, apparent congestion could be relieved simply by revising these administratively drawn boundaries.

A patrol unit is usually considered *unavailable* if it is servicing a previous incident, regardless of the importance of that incident and almost regardless of the importance of the current incident. That is, in most systems, one does not usually find units being interrupted (preempted) on one type of incident to be dispatched to a higher priority incident. If exceptions occur, they usually involve an urgent incident being reported when all units in the command are unavailable; then the dispatcher may broadcast a plea, "Any units in command x that can respond to a type y incident located at this address?" A unit can also be unavailable because of other activities, including a meal break; a patrol initiated action, of which the dispatcher may or may not be aware; a temporary return to the command headquarters (for example, a precinct station house); a fuel stop; and auto repairs or maintenance. Occasionally a dispatcher may attempt to assign units he believes to be available, only to find them unavailable for one of these reasons. It is more likely that a high-priority incident would preempt one of these lower priority activities.

Few departments have implemented explicit rules for considering priorities of incidents, but it is clear that an implicit priority structure exists. As an example, Table 1.2 contains statistics on response delays by incident type for a seven-day sample from the Boston Police Department. The tabulated response delays are

$t_8 - t_5$ = time from completion of complaint clerk processing until dispatch of a patrol unit;

= dispatcher processing and queuing time.

$t_9 - t_8$ = patrol travel time.

$t_{10} - t_9$ = on-scene service time.

The first entry in the table, Vehicular Accident, has the lowest mean dispatcher processing and queuing time (1.05 min) and successive entries each have larger mean times. This ordering and the fact that the rank ordering of

Table 1.2 Response Time Data from the Boston Police Department

Incident Type	Elapsed Time from Termination of Telephone Conversation until Dispatch of a Patrol Unit		Time Required for Patrol Unit to Travel to Scene of the Incident		Service Time at the Scene of the Incident		Sample size
	Mean	Standard deviation	Mean	Standard deviation	Mean	Standard deviation	
Vehicular Accident	1.05	1.00	3.98	3.09	54.25	25.97	44
Medical Case	1.73	3.01	5.35	3.38	40.38	24.74	225
Other Offense	1.74	2.04	5.41	4.03	22.68	18.19	97
Drunk	2.31	3.83	5.34	4.26	25.31	25.89	71
Burglary	2.39	4.24	6.45	5.05	51.76	31.36	33
Investigation	2.61	5.23	5.94	4.53	31.30	23.56	509
Larceny	2.79	4.34	7.58	5.52	31.74	15.57	38
Vandalism	3.42	5.85	6.90	4.40	36.14	24.23	118
Minor Disturbance	3.46	6.11	5.95	3.64	24.39	18.56	406
Auto Theft	4.83	8.08	7.09	4.35	35.54	21.87	94

Note: Delay units are minutes. Data were collected at the Boston Police Department over the seven-day period June 6–12, 1966.

average travel times is almost identical to that for processing and queuing
time clearly indicate that an implicit priority structure exists. (Mean service
time at the scene does not appear to be related to priority in any simple way.)
The assessment of priorities in most departments allows very great flexibility
on the part of the individual dispatcher; the same sequence of incidents over a
given time period might be handled quite differently by two different dispatchers.

With regard to position information in dispatching units, first it is important to note that even though an incident's exact location may be known, the
dispatcher may act as if he only knew the sector of the incident. For instance,
the semi-automated dispatch system in New York City, SPRINT (Special
Police Radio Inquiry Network),[5] provides the dispatcher with an ordered list
of recommended patrol cars that may be available to dispatch to an incident.
The list is generated considering only the sector of the incident and not the
location of the incident within the sector. As an example, an incident may be
reported from the northwest corner of sector George. The computer might
suggest trying to assign car George, if available; if not available, the computer
would suggest an ordered sequence to try, say Ida, Bob, Nora. Yet sector
Nora may have the most points in close proximity to the northwest part of
sector George. The ordered sequence is generated from long-run statistical
averages, which more or less place incidents and cars in the center of activity
(or *center-of-mass*) of their respective sectors. Although this makes good
sense for patrol cars, whose positions are unknown except for the fact that
they are within their sector boundaries, more accurate travel distance estimation techniques can be derived by considering the exact position of the incident. Even further accuracy can be obtained by implementing an automatic
car locator system[6] which would provide the dispatcher with up-to-the-minute position estimates for each car.

Although the SPRINT system probably represents the most formalized of
current dispatching procedures, the same considerations apply to strictly
manual systems.

---

5. "Communications Center, May I Help You?" Report published by the New York City
Police Department, 1969; and T. A. Puorro (Project Manager), "SPRINT Functional
Specification" (Gaithersburg, Md.: Federal Systems Division, International Business
Machines Corp., 1969).
6. See, for example, E. Knickel, "Electronics Equipment Associated with the Police
Car," *Task Force Report: Science and Technology, A Report to the President's Com-
mission on Law Enforcement and Administration of Justice* (Washington, D.C.: U.S.
Government Printing Office, 1967), Appendix E.

1.2. An Eight-Hour Tour of Duty

Because the focus of this study is on the patrol force, it is useful to describe
here a *hypothetical* eight-hour tour of a patrol unit. Tracing a typical tour
from the patrolmen's point of view helps to pinpoint possible problems as
well as indicate complexities of operation.[7]

Focus attention on two patrolmen, Ekard and Wheeler. They arrive at the
command stationhouse at 3:45 P.M., in time for the 4:00 P.M. roll call.
During roll call these two officers are assigned to sector Ida and briefed on
recent crime occurrence in that sector. For the past few months, Ekard and
Wheeler have worked as a team. They are both on the same squad and have
the same yearly schedule of tours to be worked (as shown on their "duty
charts"). About 80 percent of their patrol assignments have included sector
Ida. Occasionally, when there are insufficient men to staff all sectors, the
adjacent sector George is also assigned to them. At other times, due to special
conditions elsewhere in the command, their sector assignment would not include Ida.

A residential sector in the northwest corner of the command, sector Ida
generates a below average amount of radio runs but requires patrolling attention particularly for housebreaks and car thefts. A fair amount of the call-
for-service workload experienced by Ekard and Wheeler has been in nearby
sectors with shopping and entertainment areas.

At 4:00 P.M. as they report on the air to the dispatcher, they are immediately assigned from the stationhouse to a report of past burglary case called
in from sector George at 3:58 P.M. Requiring ten minutes travel time, they
arrive on the scene at 4:10 P.M. Victim interviews and report taking are completed at 4:30 P.M., at which time the dispatcher is again notified of their
dispatch availability.

During the next hour or so, the two patrolmen in their car patrol the streets
of sector Ida, paying particular attention to houses reported temporarily
vacant by vacationers. This continuous patrol is interrupted three times, first

7. The description given in this section is derived from my own experience in the rear
seat of patrol cars in Boston and New York. Also see F. Wiseman, "Law and Order"
(Cambridge, Mass.: Osti Films, 1969); "Patrol, Patrol, Patrol," New York City Police
Department, *Spring 3100*, July–August, 1960 [Reprinted in Samuel G. Chapman,
Police Patrol Readings (Springfield, Ill.: Charles C Thomas, Publisher, 1964), pp. 29–
38.]; and President's Commission on Law Enforcement and Administration of Justice,
Task Force Report: Police (Washington, D.C.: U.S. Government Printing Office, 1967),
p. 15. Another much more detailed and realistic depiction of a patrolman's life is pre-
sented in the novel: Joseph Wambaugh, *The New Centurions* (Boston, Mass.: Little,
Brown, and Company, 1970).

to give a traffic citation, second to assist an elderly woman across a crowded intersection, and third to refuel the car.

At 5:49 P.M. a brush fire is reported near a school (located in sector Ida), and the Ida car responds to guide traffic around the area and to keep on-lookers a safe distance away. This activity is not completed until 6:45 P.M.

At 7:00 P.M. the Ida car leaves the air for a one-hour evening meal break. The meal hours for the cars in the command are assigned by the patrol ser-geant and are staggered from 6:00 to 9:00 P.M.

Resuming patrol at 8:00 P.M., the patrolmen find that the volume of radio activity has picked up throughout the command. In fact, there is a report of noisy group call from sector Nora that has been waiting in the dispatcher queue for 15 minutes. The Ida car is immediately assigned to the incident, arriving at the scene at 8:10 P.M. A relatively harmless game of street stickball is found in progress and the players are asked by Ekard and Wheeler to re-strain their verbal enthusiasm. The officers explain that the caller, who lives in a nearby house, was recently bedridden and requires quiet for sleep.

The car is again available for dispatch at 8:20 P.M. The dispatcher im-mediately reassigns the unit to an incident in sector George involving theft of a television set from an automobile. Crossing into sector George en route to the incident, however, they come across a middle-aged woman who has just been stricken with what appears to be a serious epileptic seizure and is hemorrhaging. As a crowd quickly gathers, the officers radio for an ambu-lance. However, the closest available ambulance will require an estimated 20 minutes' travel time; the officers place the woman in the patrol car and drive her directly to the nearest hospital.

During the past month there had been several incidents of lengthy ambu-lance delays, and the crowds at the scenes had blamed the police officers for the delay. Although the police always have the alternative of transporting the injured person in their patrol car, this cannot always be done because of possible additional injuries to the victim and lack of experience and special-ized training on the part of the officers. Ekard and Wheeler arrive at the hospital emergency entrance at 8:40 P.M., at which time the hemorrhaging appears to be nearly stopped and the woman in relatively good spirits. She is advised to remain at the hospital for observation. The officers report dispatch availability directly from the hospital at 8:50 P.M.

There are no calls waiting for service in the command at that time, so they return to their sector to resume patrol. Again, they pay particular attention to unoccupied residences of vacationers. At 9:22 P.M. they notice people inside one of the supposedly vacant houses. After reporting the situation to the dispatcher, both Ekard and Wheeler go to the door to investigate. They discover that the family had terminated their vacation one week early but forgot to notify police. The car was again available for dispatch at 9:30 P.M.

At 9:55 P.M. the George car, in the adjacent sector, was still at the scene of an auto accident. A regular Friday church meeting of elderly men and women was due to be completed at 10:00 P.M., and it had become a standard practice for the George car to go to the church to help provide safe passage for those walking home to a nearby apartment complex. Prior to this protection provided by the George car, there had been several purse snatchings and muggings of individuals leaving the meeting. Through the dispatcher, the George car asked the Ida car to replace it at the church. Ekard and Wheeler stayed at the church until 10:30 P.M., at which time they again reported available for dispatch.

Once back in their own sector, the officers at 10:45 P.M. heard a general alert reporting an officer in trouble with a berserk patient in the psychiatric ward of the hospital. They sped toward the hospital, using siren and lights. But before reaching the scene the dispatcher notified all units that the situation was under control, at which time (10:55 P.M.) Ekard and Wheeler returned to sector Ida.

The final dispatch of the tour for the Ida car occurred at 11:22 P.M., at which time it was sent to sector George on a disturbance call. Arriving at the scene at 11:30 P.M., they found a husband and wife dispute that had escalated to a point where both parties were suffering lacerations and the wife was bleeding profusely. Ekard applied first aid to curtail the bleeding while Wheeler called for an ambulance. The ambulance arrived at 11:40 P.M. and took both parties to the hospital. Neither wished to place formal assault charges against the other.

Ekard and Wheeler returned to the stationhouse at 11:50 P.M., completed some reports, and turned their car over to the next two officers for the midnight to 8:00 A.M. tour.

Summarizing the tour, one notes that the Ida car was unavailable for 193 minutes on six jobs, including burglary report, brush fire, noisy group, injured person, officer in trouble, and disturbance. Only one of these jobs had been in sector Ida. Another 60 minutes was spent off the air on a meal break and another 43 minutes removed the car from the air because of two patrol initiated actions (investigation of people in a house and surveillance of a church area). Thus, of the total of 480 minutes during the tour, the car was unavailable for dispatch 296 minutes, or 61.6 percent of the time. The other 38.4 percent of the time was spent on preventive patrol in sector Ida. The six jobs required 40.2 percent of the unit's time, the average job requiring about 32 minutes (including travel time and service time at the scene).

Contrasting to other cars in the command during the tour, the adjacent George car had handled 11 jobs, spending less than 10 percent of its time on preventive patrol; the Nora car handled only 2 jobs, spending nearly 65 percent of its time on preventive patrol. Others fell between these two extremes.

There were no crime-in-progress calls from the command during the tour, although there were several non-crime-related incidents requiring rapid response. There were no patrol arrests of crime suspects during the tour.

1.3. System Objectives and Measures of Effectiveness
The descriptions of the police emergency response system and a typical eight-hour tour of patrol duty only hint at the complexities of police operations. It is probably not possible to construct a model (either verbal or mathematical) that will allow for every possible operational contingency; any set pattern of operation can be easily broken by an apparently exceptional situation. Also, each situation seems to be accompanied by its own operational constraints and objectives, some of which may be conflicting.

Some examples from the hypothetical eight-hour tour (Section 1.2) illustrate the interplay of objectives. The quieting of a stickball game was necessary for the bedridden complainant, but care had to be taken in explaining the situation to youths who might otherwise view the intervention as unwarranted police harrassment. Since citizens often perceive ambulance delays as the fault of the police, taking the hemorrhaging woman to a hospital in the patrol car was motivated in large part by the need to maintain satisfactory police-community relations; yet, there is the risk that such transport may further aggravate the patient's condition. Maintaining surveillance near a church at the end of a meeting is required to deter potential criminals from attacking those walking home and to assure the community that protection will be provided when the need is apparent; however, such conspicuous fixed-point patrol leaves vulnerable other nearby areas. The response to the disturbance call indicated the need for improved classification of calls as they are reported and the fact that reported incidents can escalate in seriousness prior to police arrival. Also, there is often no sharp dividing line between a public service type of call and a call involving criminal action.

Traditional police administration texts have cited the overall purposes of the patrol force to be[8]

1. The prevention and deterrence of crime,
2. The apprehension of criminals,
3. The performance of certain public services.

However, as the above examples illustrate, it is often not clear which of the possible actions are most appropriate to best fulfill these objectives.

In this book the focus is *not* on the idiosyncrasies and complexities of individual police responses. Instead of a clinical, or case-by-case point-of-view, a more aggregated statistical approach is taken, examining a number of planning and management problems that require workable solutions within operational, legal, and budgetary constraints. Most of these problems too are interdependent in terms of their impact upon fulfillment of the stated police objectives. For instance, both the addition of a radio channel and the implementation of new patrol strategies would have some effect on the deterrence of crime, the apprehension of criminals, and the performance of other public services.

Ideally we would like to transform the overall objectives of police into a complete set of performance criteria. Then alternative operating policies could be systematically analyzed within a unified framework in which the desirability of each possible outcome is known. Information presently available is too limited to define and solve police operational problems within such a global structure. However, useful results can be obtained from several interrelated analyses, each of which focuses on a particular part of the system and a particular operational problem. This is the approach throughout the book. Thus, rather than attempt large-scale optimizations, the focus is on analysis of local descriptive models that may reveal certain trade offs, or a range of policy options, or other properties of system operation.

There are many criteria for evaluating performance of the police response system, including

System response time,

System error probability,

System cost,

Amount of preventive patrol,

Probability of criminal apprehension,

8. O. W. Wilson, *Police Administration*, sec. ed. (New York: McGraw-Hill Book Company, 1963), p. 228; V. A. Leonard, *Police Organization and Management* (New York: The Foundation Press, 1950); Samuel G. Chapman, *Police Patrol Readings* (Springfield, Ill.: Charles C Thomas, Publisher, 1964), pp. ix, x.

Citizens' subjective opinions, and

Workload imbalances among police officers.

Each of these bears some relationship to the fundamental objectives of police. We briefly consider each in turn in the following paragraphs.

Total system response time, which is the elapsed time between requesting police service and the arrival of that service, is an important measure of police accessibility and responsiveness. Decreased response time is likely to have beneficial effects in terms of saving the life of an injured person,[9] or apprehending a crime suspect,[10] or improving citizens' attitudes. The recognition that response time is an important effectiveness measure is not new. For instance, in 1916, after implementing a telephone booth system for notifying patrolmen of calls for service, the New York City Police Department noted that "the time necessary for a patrolman to reach certain points has been reduced from 45 minutes to from six to eight minutes."[11] Even earlier, in 1888, the Cincinnati Police Department reported that "the *promptness* of the (telephone) service, . . . freedom from errors, while not all that could be wished, are . . . a source of great pride to the Department" (emphasis added).[12] More recently, the importance of response time in apprehending offenders has been discussed by the Science and Technology Task Force of the President's Commission on Law Enforcement and Administration of Justice.[13] However, one is not likely to obtain exact production functions relating response time to more fundamental objectives. Thus, for many calls response time serves as a limited but useful proxy measure of effectiveness whose reduction is widely accepted as a desired goal. As a measure of effectiveness, response time has the desirable properties of being measurable, being partially controllable by policy decision, and being easily interpreted (both by the public and the police). Response time can also be used to study possible inequities in delivery of police service.

9. R. B. Andrews, *Criteria Selection in Emergency Medical System Analysis* (University of California, Los Angeles: Report EMS-61-1-W prepared for Emergency Medical Systems Project, Graduate School of Business Administration, 1969).

10. A preliminary study by H. Isaacs [President's Commission on Law Enforcement and Administration of Justice, *Task Force Report: Science and Technology* (Washington, D.C.: U.S. Government Printing Office, 1967), Appendix B] conducted in the Los Angeles Police Department provided evidence that faster response would result in more apprehensions (arrests) of suspects.

11. E. D. Graper, *American Police Administration* (New York: The Macmillan Company, 1921), p. 128.

12. Cincinnati, Ohio Police Department, *Annual Report of the Police Department of Cincinnati, Ohio, 1888* (Cincinnati: Commercial Gazette Job Print, 1889), p. 33.

13. Isaacs, *Task Force Report*.

System error probability can refer to many types of occurrences, including
The complaint clerk misinterpreting the address of an incident;
A patrolman misinterpreting an address given by the dispatcher;
The dispatcher failing to redistribute or relocate forces in order to "cover" a busy section of the city, resulting in excessive queuing delays or travel times.
The dispatcher interpreting a patrolman's response as verification of a dispatch order when it is not.
The dispatcher assigning a car distant from the scene when there is an available one much closer.
An arriving patrolman arresting an innocent bystander as a crime suspect.
Each of these occurances should be carefully considered when implementing new procedures or revising current procedures.

System cost is usually considered in terms of dollars. Dollar costs are not insignificant, the annual cost of a round-the-clock two-man patrol car being $100,000 to over $200,000. But dollar costs alone are not sufficient for comparing alternatives. Other social costs accrue because of fear of victimization, on the one extreme, the perceived loss of freedom resulting from excessive police presence, on the other. These and other not easily quantifiable costs make cost-effectiveness analyses of alternative police programs very difficult to perform. Any such analysis that emphatically claims to have derived an "optimum" solution should, at the very least, be given careful scrutiny.

Preventive patrol constitutes touring an area, with the officer(s) checking for crime hazards (for example, open doors and windows) and attempting to intercept any crimes while in progress. By removing opportunities for crime, preventive patrol activity is supposed *to prevent* crime. By posing the threat of apprehension, preventive patrol is supposed *to deter* individuals from committing crimes. But agreement on how to achieve the objectives of prevention and deterrence is noticeably lacking in police circles. One recurring debate centers around the issue of marked vs. unmarked cars, the marked cars supposedly deterring crime by presenting a visible presence, thus influencing the *perceived* threat of apprehension; the unmarked cars supposedly deter crime by increasing the actual chance of intercepting a crime in progress.[14] This and other unsolved issues stem partly from a lack of even a commonly accepted set of effectiveness measures for the preventive patrol activity. Those departments that in any way monitor the patrolling unit usually seek statistics on the amount of preventive patrol activity, using such activity indicators as number of miles traveled and number of doors and windows checked.

14. Chapman, *Police Patrol*.

Most experiments that have been performed to measure the crime preventive effectiveness of patrol have been marred by poor experimental design and by the irregular way in which crimes are reported. Typically, a change in manning level (usually upward) is attempted to find the marginal effectiveness (in terms of crime reduction) of additional patrolmen. However, even if this effectiveness is significant (and many think a large fraction of crimes are not deterrable by police), studies that attempt to measure it have been inconclusive.[15] The lack of experimental controls is evidenced, for instance, by new orders that often accompany a study and make an officer responsible for each crime occuring in his territory. This inhibits the accurate reporting and categorization of crimes. Usually no control areas are set aside to monitor regular operations during the same period, and any spillover effects from the experimental area to contiguous areas are not analyzed. Irregular crime reporting by citizens, documented by the President's Commission on Law Enforcement and Administration of Justice,[16] typically results in only one of three serious crimes being reported. Due to increased public accessibility to police, an increase of police manpower may change this reporting ratio sufficiently so that measured crime rates increase, even if actual crime rates decrease.

Thus, there is a need for extensive experimental and analytical work to determine to what extent patrol deters and prevents crime. A product of this work would be a number of valid measures of performance of the patrol activity.

The probability of criminal apprehension depends directly on the level of patrolling effort, so as to intercept crimes in progress; on responsiveness, so as to apprehend perpetrators near the crime scene; and on detective follow-up capability. With current limited knowledge, it is not possible to predict how apprehension probability varies with alternative programs. If one focuses on preventive patrol apprehension alone, however, it is possible to construct models predicting frequencies of patrol passings, and these lead to rough estimates of the probability that a patrolling unit will intercept a crime in progress. Such quantification of certain features of preventive patrol should assist future studies in defining critical parameters and suggesting relationships

15. An example of an inconclusive experiment can be found in Samuel G. Chapman, *Police Patrol*, pp. 206–214.
16. President's Commission on Law Enforcement and Administration of Justice, *The Challenge of Crime in a Free Society* (Washington, D.C.: U.S. Government Printing Office, 1967), pp. 20–22.

among them, thereby creating the formal structure needed for controlled experimentation and analyses.

Concerning citizens' subjective opinions, a recent ten-city survey[17] has provided some insights on how citizens perceive police responsiveness to calls, the general level of police protection, and inequities in levels of service provided. Three of the questions asked were as follows: When someone in this neighborhood calls the police for help, do they usually come right away, or do they take quite a while to come? In general, how would you rate the job the police do of protecting people in this neighborhood—*very good*, *good enough*, *not so good*, or *not good at all*? And how would you rate the way police usually treat people in this neighborhood—*very good*, *good enough*, *not so good*, or *not good at all*?

In analyzing the results among the cities, the citizens' perceptions of technical efficiency, as indicated by police responsiveness, seemed to coincide quite closely with the judgments of experienced researchers of U.S. police. The results indicated a high correlation between the perceptions of responsiveness and general protection, thereby corroborating the notion that responsiveness is a useful proxy for more fundamental objectives. Within particular cities, the citizens' replies to all three questions were used to assess perceived inequities of service among various population groups. Work still in progress is aimed at determining the validity of these intracity perceptions.

Marked workload imbalances among police officers, in addition to causing morale problems, can result in a degradation of the quality of performance in the relatively overworked areas. One of a number of internal operating objectives, the reduction of serious imbalances must be considered in any modification of operating procedures. However, the *equalization* of workload is not a primary objective by itself; it bears little relation to the three primary functions of police. In fact, equalization of the quality of performance to the public often requires *unequal* distribution of workload.

As an example, consider the problem of determining how many patrol units to allocate to each of two different commands. For simplicity, assume that the primary measure of performance is the average queue delay at the dispatcher's position caused by patrol unavailabilities in a command. Say we wish to allocate sufficiently many patrol units to each command to keep this average queue delay below some threshold (for example, one minute). Now, if one command has, say, twice the call-for-service volume as the other, an

17. Thomas A. Reppetto, "Survey Methods and the Evaluation of Police Organization" (MIT-Harvard Joint Center for Urban Studies, unpublished mimeograph, 1971).

equal workload criterion would dictate allocating twice as many patrol units to the busier command. Yet, it is a property of queuing systems[18] with several servers (for example, patrol cars) that average delays can be kept below some threshold as the call-for-service rate increases by adding additional servers at a rate *less than proportional* to the call-for-service rate. That is, with greater call-for-service volumes, each server can work an increasingly larger fraction of the time, while the system as a whole maintains acceptable delay properties. Since the patrol force constitutes a spatially distributed queuing system, an effective allocation of patrol personnel is usually not one in which personnel are allocated in direct proportion to anticipated demands for service. Thus, the "busier" command should be allocated less than twice as many units as the other command, resulting in greater workloads for each patrol unit in the busier command. Actual examples are naturally more complicated and usually involve several performance criteria, but the same considerations apply.

1.4. Hazard or Workload Formulas

Many police administrators have used quantitative procedures, in addition to intuitive judgment, when considering the diverse factors involved in allocating patrol personnel. However, the most commonly used procedure substitutes activity indicators for measures of effectiveness, yielding allocations based on number of miles traveled, number of calls for service answered, and number of arrests.

This method, based on *hazard* or *workload* formulas, combines in a subjective way all activity indicators and other factors (for example, number of street miles or number of licensed premises) thought to be relevant to determining the need for patrol services. To illustrate the method, suppose we are to allocate a number of patrol units among I areas of the city. Suppose there are J factors thought to be important in performing this allocation. Let f_{ij} be the amount of factor j associated with area i. For instance, f_{42} may be the total number of street miles in precinct four. The city-wide amount of factor j is

$$F_j = f_{1j} + f_{2j} + \cdots + f_{Ij}.$$

For instance, F_2 may be the total number of street miles in the entire city; and f_{42}/F_2 is the fraction of the city's street miles in precinct four. To arrive

---

18. This property is discussed by A. J. Rolfe, "A Note on Marginal Allocation in Multiple-Server Service Systems" P-4393 (Santa Monica, Calif.: RAND Corporation, 1970).

at a single hazard score (or workload score) for each area, an arbitrary importance weighting w_j is assigned to factor j. It is convenient to normalize the weightings so that they sum to one (or to 100 percent). Then, the hazard score (or workload score) for area i is

$$H_i = w_1 \frac{f_{i1}}{F_1} + w_2 \frac{f_{i2}}{F_2} + \cdots + w_J \frac{f_{iJ}}{F_J}.$$

If this method is used, the number of patrol personnel needed in the area is said to be directly proportional to the hazard score of the area. For instance, if the computed hazard score for precinct four is 0.12, then precinct four would be allocated 12 percent of the total number of patrol units.

The term *hazard formula* is most appropriate when the factors focus on crime hazards, such as licensed premises, parks, and storefronts. The term *workload formula* is more appropriate when the factors focus on activities that consume patrol time. In the former case, use of the method tends to equalize crime hazard among patrol units; in the latter, it tends to equalize workload. But usually both hazard and workload factors are included in the formula. For the sake of brevity, subsequently these formulas are refered to as hazard formulas.

As an example of an implemented hazard formula, the City of Los Angeles has used the following variables and weightings:[19]

$j = $ 1 : selected crimes and attempts	$w_1 = 5/19$
$j = $ 2 : radio calls handled by radio cars	$w_2 = 4/19$
$j = $ 3 : felony arrests	$w_3 = 3/19$
$j = $ 4 : misdemeanor arrests	$w_4 = 1/19$
$j = $ 5 : property loss	$w_5 = 1/19$
$j = $ 6 : injury traffic accidents	$w_6 = 1/19$
$j = $ 7 : vehicles recovered	$w_7 = 1/19$
$j = $ 8 : population	$w_8 = 1/19$
$j = $ 9 : street miles	$w_9 = 1/19$
$j = 10$: population density	$w_{10} = 1/19$

Los Angeles has recently discarded this system and is adopting a commercially available set of computer programs that were derived from queuing models used in St. Louis.

To indicate the diversity in hazard formulas, another large city employs 14 variables, all with equal weightings:[20]

19. J. Kakalik and S. Wildhorn, *Aids to Decision Making in Police Patrol*, R-593 (Santa Monica, Calif.: RAND Corporation, 1971).
20. *Ibid.*

$j = \;\;\; 1$: Part I crimes	$w_1 \;\; = 1/14$
$j = \;\;\; 2$: Part II crimes	$w_2 \;\; = 1/14$
$j = \;\;\; 3$: custody arrests	$w_3 \;\; = 1/14$
$j = \;\;\; 4$: injury accidents	$w_4 \;\; = 1/14$
$j = \;\;\; 5$: ambulance runs	$w_5 \;\; = 1/14$
$j = \;\;\; 6$: fires	$w_6 \;\; = 1/14$
$j = \;\;\; 7$: police "services" rendered	$w_7 \;\; = 1/14$
$j = \;\;\; 8$: population	$w_8 \;\; = 1/14$
$j = \;\;\; 9$: population density	$w_9 \;\; = 1/14$
$j = 10$: area	$w_{10} = 1/14$
$j = 11$: road miles	$w_{11} = 1/14$
$j = 12$: licensed premises	$w_{12} = 1/14$
$j = 13$: store doors	$w_{13} = 1/14$
$j = 14$: schools	$w_{14} = 1/14$

This department also claims to be not satisfied with the hazard system and is currently instituting changes.

The unsatisfactory allocations often derived from a hazard formula are caused by several factors. The inherently linear form of a hazard formula precludes description of the highly nonlinear and complex interactions among system components that are often seen, for example, in police systems. Such a formula also attempts an overly simple deterministic depiction of a system in which many of the variables are probabilistic and often highly interdependent.

As an example, usually one variable in the formula is the number of calls for police service that require the dispatch of a patrol unit to the scene of the call. In practice, the weighting given in this term may be as small as five percent. The insensitivity of the resulting allocations to variations in call-for-service rates has resulted in the formation of large queues of reported calls, with delays often exceeding one hour. The time periods and geographical origins of these queues have been found to be quite predictable. Although the queues could be diminished somewhat by (1) giving the corresponding weighting a larger numerical value or (2) applying the formula over shorter durations (say by the hour rather than by the day or week or year), the general problem persists, because a hazard formula does not relate meaningful measures of system effectiveness to operational policies. That is, a hazard formula, comprising a subjectively weighted sum of quantities, does not provide a police administrator with such policy-relevant information as the response time of the patrol force, or the probability that a patrol car will intercept a crime in progress, or any of a number of other operational quantities. In addition, a police administrator would want to know the effect on each of these variables of a possible alternative strategy or allocation level.

In some instances a hazard formula may actually indicate a need for personnel in areas that already are relatively overallocated. This can arise because factors such as number of arrests and reported crimes depend partially on the number of personnel currently allocated to an area. For instance, crime suspects are more likely to be apprehended in an area that is sufficiently staffed than in one with overworked or saturated resources. The hazard score of the sufficiently staffed area would be artificially inflated by the high arrest rate of that area, thereby "substantiating" the need for additional personnel. The real need for personnel would be in the overworked area, but a hazard formula would not fully reveal this need.

When introduced in the 1930s by O. W. Wilson,[21] hazard formulas provided a major breakthrough in a planning and management area where intuition and command discretion had been the primary determinants of patrol allocation. The procedure was easily hand calculable by someone without specialized training. But recent developments in quantitative modeling and computer programming make reliance on hazard formulas no longer necessary.

The need for new methods in patrol planning and management is exemplified by the inadequacies of hazard formulas. But the need extends beyond the perfunctory "planning" in which hazard formulas have been traditionally used. It encompasses a very wide range of policy questions:

Is a ten percent increase in manpower justified?

What are the trade offs between the activities of responding to calls and performing preventive patrol?

How is an automatic car locator system to be evaluated?

What would be the effects of shifting to one-man cars in parts of the city?

Should the tour structure be changed?

How would helicopter patrol improve responsiveness and patrol effectiveness?

Should dispatching procedures become more formalized?

How should patrol sectors be designed?

If ambulance runs were made the responsibility of police, how would overall performance be altered?

This book begins to build the required structure in which questions such as

21. O. W. Wilson, *Distribution of the Police Patrol Force,* Publication 74 (Chicago, Ill.: Public Administration Service, 1941). Also see O. W. Wilson, *Police Administration,* 2nd ed. (New York: McGraw-Hill Book Company, 1963).

these can be addressed. It does not purport to provide either precise answers to these questions or "canned" procedures to replace currently outdated procedures. Thus, in the spirit of this book, a hazard formula is not merely to be replaced with a more complicated formula or computer program that does not more fundamentally penetrate the planning and management process. Rather, in examining alternatives to current procedures, attention should be given to the classical steps of analysis discussed earlier, from defining the problem and specifying objectives to comparing alternatives and presenting results. The techniques of this book are illustrative of the type of methodology that can be employed in parts of the analysis process. The end result of this process could indeed be a computer program to help in the task of manpower allocation, but the program would be selected with a knowledge of its advantages and limitations and with the full participation of certain planning and management staff within the department. Such participation facilitates innovative use of the adopted methods. And, as modifications become necessary, it assures that the department's staff can detect the need for modifications and perhaps perform them as well.

1.5. Implementation

The need for implementing innovative methods to aid police patrol administrators was discussed by the President's Commission on Law Enforcement and Administration of Justice in 1967:

Although police experts agree that patrol is an essential police activity, the problem of how many policemen, under what orders and using what techniques, should patrol which beats and when, is a complicated highly technical one.[22] . . . The most effective way of deploying and employing a department's patrol force is a subject about which deplorably little is known. Evaluation of differing methods of patrol depends on trying out those methods over long periods of time and calculating the changes in crime rates and solution rates that the changes in patrol techniques have produced. This sort of research has scarcely begun in America, partly because few police departments have the funds or the personnel to devise, develop, and test innovative procedures. The reluctance to abandon traditional methods of operation in favor of untested and therefore potentially unsuccessful ones has also delayed research into new methods.[23]

To help provide the required technical assistance, the Commission recommended establishment in large police departments of operations research

22. President's Commission on Law Enforcement and Administration of Justice, *The Challenge of Crime in a Free Society* (Washington, D.C.: U.S. Government Printing Office, 1967), p. 95.
23. *Ibid.*, pp. 116–117.

groups that would analyze operations, design and evaluate experiments, and provide general technical assistance.

The 1968 Omnibus Crime Control and Safe Streets Act[24] provides federal funds to state planning agencies to develop ". . . a comprehensive statewide plan for the improvement of law enforcement throughout the State." Federal subsidy grants are being provided on the basis of these plans. Thus, police departments in every state are now having to plan and develop improved methods of operation.

Given the impetus of federal programs and increased public attentiveness to police problems, a number of police departments in recent years have started to explore the potential benefits of quantitative aids to decision making, using tools other than hazard formulas. As a result of these studies, one can point to decisions to add more dispatchers to speed response to calls for service (Boston);[25] to experiment with division-wide patrol units to alleviate precinct-level congestion (New York);[26] to replace hazard formula allocations with a scheme based on queuing models (Los Angeles);[27] to reschedule complaint clerks hour by hour to reduce telephone answering delays (New York);[28] to implement a patrol simulation model as a tool for planning and research (Boston).[29] Numerous studies are currently being supported by funds made available under the 1968 Crime Control and Safe Streets Act. These will undoubtedly add to the list of implemented changes resulting directly from quantitative analyses.

Perhaps the best example of a successful implementation is found in the St. Louis Police Department. That department conducted its initial resource allocation experiment in March of 1966 in one police district. Immediately prior to the experiment, call-for-service data were manually tabulated in order to estimate demands by time of day and day of week. Empirical service time distributions were also determined. With this start, the estimated number

24. *Omnibus Crime Control and Safe Streets Act of 1968*, Public Law 90-351, June 19, 1968.
25. R. C. Larson, "Hourly Allocation of Complaint Clerks, Dispatchers, and Radio-Dispatchable Patrol Personnel," in *Law Enforcement Science and Technology II, Proceedings of Second National Symposium on Law Enforcement Science and Technology* (Chicago, Ill.: Illinois Institute of Technology Research Institute, 1968), pp. 247–254.
26. The New York City Rand Institute, *First Annual Report* (New York City Rand Institute, 1970), pp. 26, 27.
27. J. Kakalik and S. Wildhorn, *Aids to Decision Making*.
28. The New York City Rand Institute, *First Annual Report*.
29. J. Williamson, "Computer Simulation of the Boston Police Patrol Forces," available from the Boston Police Department, 1971.

of units required to handle calls for service were assigned to each tour, and remaining units were assigned to crime prevention. A major purpose of the study, besides testing the predictability of demands, was to examine the consequences of the split patrol concept.

The results of the initial experiment led to a grant in June of 1966 from the Office of Law Enforcement Assistance for an 18-month period. The study was divided into three 6-month phases: (1) data collection, (2) test of operational plan, (3) qualitative and quantitative evaluation. The results of this study are reported in *Allocation of Patrol Manpower Resources in the St. Louis Police Department* (vols. 1 and 2).[30]

As a consequence of these and other studies, the department has approved a wide range of recommendations, including the expansion of the resource allocation methodology on a city-wide basis. The implemented procedure involves predicting demand for police services by hour and geographical area and, using these data with a well-known queuing model, estimating the number of patrol cars needed to immediately answer (without dispatching delay) *85 percent* of the predicted incoming calls for service; new estimates are made for each 4-hour time period.

Other recommendations include (1) The use of a variable sector pattern in each district. The number of sectors in each district will vary by time of day and day of week. (2) Stacking (queuing) of radio calls at the patrol car level with only two patrol units in each district designated as units that could receive a stacked call. (Low priority calls are stacked). (3) A restriction of self-initiated requests by patrol officers to be taken off the air (and thus considered "unavailable"). (4) An increased screening of calls to reduce the fraction requiring dispatch and, of those requiring dispatch, to increase the fraction that can be stacked. (5) Consolidation of three districts into one.

The outcome of the St. Louis studies demonstrates the feasibility of a quantitative approach to patrol resource allocation problems. It also indicates that an improved allocation system is not likely to be implemented overnight but rather as the result of continued data collection, experimentation, and evaluation.

The St. Louis studies (as well as others) have also indicated the strong need for new models specifically related to police patrol operations, including response and patrol activities in the field. To a large extent, the administrative and supervisory problems often associated with the patrol force seem to result

30. St. Louis Police Department, 1968.

from a lack of policy-oriented measures of patrol effectiveness and a knowledge of how alternative policies affect these measures. One of our major goals
is to begin to build the required structure that will assist patrol administrators
in future planning of operational procedures and allocation levels.

2

Police Patrol Operations in a Hypothetical City

2.1. Introduction

In the course of developing analytical and simulation models of police patrol and dispatch operations, the question frequently arises, "How would a police department apply these techniques in practice?" The answer to this question will depend strongly on the particular department, the services it performs, its resource constraints, its quantitative capabilities, and its degree of commitment to implement the results. In this chapter a *hypothetical* department (the Simtown Police Department) is examined. The purpose is to illustrate how the point of view, methodology, and insights of quantitative modeling may be successfully utilized in the planning and management process.

For the hypothetical city of Simtown, it is envisioned that the planning and research unit of the police department has been working with a local consulting firm (named Probsolve Associates). This effort started 18 months ago, when the department and Probsolve formed a joint study group to analyze patrol and dispatch operations and to recommend changes in operations. During its first 18 months the group studied a wide variety of alternative dispatch and deployment policies. As a result of its studies, a new dispatch and deployment system is currently being implemented, and plans for future modifications are being formulated.

Some of the hypothetical events of these 18 months are reported in this chapter. As the description indicates, the joint study group was not assigned a narrowly defined task, with fixed deadlines for performance. Rather, the group's assignment is broadly interpreted to be one of continual analysis of operations, evaluation of alternatives, and formulation of recommendations for changes. The group's approach and point of view provide a coherent framework for consideration of priority dispatch structures, car locator systems, new tour assignments, and so forth. It is envisaged that as the group's experience accumulates, its talents will provide an invaluable resource to the department.

With its 23 patrol cars (or *patrol units*), Simtown's resident population is probably between 150,000 and 250,000. There are about 40 actual U.S. cities falling in this population range, such as Worcester, Massachusetts; Jacksonville, Florida; Grand Rapids, Michigan; and Spokane, Washington. Not unlike an actual city of this size, Simtown is divided into 2 divisions, 5 precincts, and 23 sectors (Figure 2.1). A patrol unit is assigned to each sector,

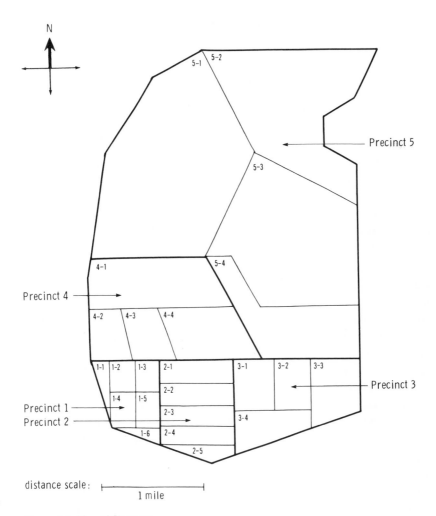

Figure 2.1 Map of Simtown.

and units are restrained to operate within their own precinct. One dispatcher uses a single radio channel to dispatch units in both divisions. Precincts 1, 2, and 3 (comprising Division 1) are downtown precincts, having relatively heavy workloads per square mile. Precinct 4, in the southwestern part of Division 2, is an older residential community. Precinct 5, in the northern and eastern part of Division 2, is a newly annexed and sparsely populated residential community; its workload per square mile is the lightest in the city.

In order to facilitate intuitive understanding of Simtown operations and to keep the discussion to a reasonable length, several simplifying assumptions are used. For instance, it is assumed that each patrol unit patrols its designated sector in a spatially uniform way. This means that if a sector is split into two nonoverlapping territories of equal area, the sector's patrol unit while on patrol is equally likely to be in either territory. It is also assumed that the relative spatial distribution of call-for-service workload does not change by time of day. This means that if sector 2-4 generates twice the workload as sector 2-1 at 10:00 PM, it also generates twice the workload as sector 2-1 at any other time during the day. The tools we have available do not require these assumptions; but in order to make the discussion tractable, it seems reasonable to reach some compromise between the complexities of an actual city and the level of detail required for the illustrative purposes of the model.

2.1.1. History of the Simtown Problem

Before the study group was organized, complaints about Simtown police patrol operations had been received both from citizens and patrol officers. During hours of heavy workload, police response was poor, and citizens who called for police assistance often had to wait an hour or more until the arrival of a police car.

Several incidents involving lengthy police response were widely publicized. In one instance, a liquor store robbery had occurred in sector 2-5 (southern end of Precinct 2) during which the store proprietor triggered a silent robbery alarm. The alarm, when received at the police communication center, resulted in the immediate dispatch of the sector 2-1 unit, the only other unit available in Precinct 2. The responding unit arrived at the store six minutes after the call and found that the robbers had fled. There had been another unit aiding a *lock-out* case[1] on the other side of the block from the robbery, but the dispatcher had not assigned this unit because it was considered *unavailable.*[2]

1. A person who has misplaced or lost his apartment or house key is said to be *locked out*. Police often help such individuals to gain entrance to their homes.
2. In many cities communication with a an *unavailable* unit may not always be possible.

Citizens were also complaining of too little patrol coverage, particularly during high crime hours when it was needed most. Patrol officers complained that too many of their dispatch assignments were outside of their own sectors; especially during hours of heavy workload, they claimed to be figuratively flying about the precinct. As a result any break between assignments was treated as a welcome relief by the men and not as a time to engage actively in crime preventive patrol.

The department was under pressure to examine all alternative methods to improve effectiveness, especially since call-for-service rates were rising at about 20 percent per year, while tight budgetary constraints made additional patrolmen an infeasible alternative. The annual department budget was $5 million, 45 percent of which was consumed by patrolmen's salaries.[3]

2.1.2. Formation of the Study Group

The department decided to seek outside assistance in helping to structure and perhaps solve some of the problems of dispatching and patrol. With the encouragement of the State Planning Agency, set up under the 1968 Omnibus Crime Control and Safe Streets Act, the department and Probsolve Associates jointly wrote a proposal to examine these problems using quantitative methods.

Upon funding of the study, the department and the firm held several lengthy preliminary meetings to discuss overall objectives of the police response system and the patrol force in particular, to outline current known problems of patrol, and to list possible contributions of the study effort. A joint study group was formed, comprising members of both the department and the firm. Members of the group spent several evenings monitoring operations from the communications room and from the rear seats of patrol cars. Many members of the department were interviewed, usually in an informal manner, in an attempt to obtain suggestions for operational improvements.

2.1.3. Descriptions of Operations

Soon a concise and somewhat critical description of dispatch-patrol operations began to emerge as a result of the group's initial efforts. For patrolling units, the police dispatcher had no car position information other than the knowledge that each unit was somewhere in its assigned sector. When dis-

---

The unit's patrol officer(s) may be outside the vehicle and unable to hear a normal radio communication. However, it is technically feasible to provide such communication (for example, a hand radio, or a dispatcher-triggered siren system). See Section 2.5.3.
3. This is a typical figure. Overall, salaries and fringe benefits often account for 95 percent of the total budget. For Simtown, this would leave $250,000 annually to be spent on equipment, technical assistance, and so forth.

patching a unit, it was not feasible to tax the already-congested dispatching radio channel to query units of their locations. In doing a good job with limited information, the dispatcher selected units as if each were near the center of its own sector. This strategy closely resembled a *strict center-of-mass* strategy,[4] which is used in many cities that do not provide the dispatcher with accurate information about car locations.

A unit could be dispatched anywhere within its precinct, with no limit on estimated travel distances. During periods of congestion, back-to-back assignments were not unusual; a unit completing service of one incident would be reassigned directly from the scene to another call anywhere in the precinct. These features of operation are often found in other cities, as well.

For nearly all dispatches, the responding unit could not travel in a straight line "as the crow flies." Instead, the city's regular north-south, east-west street grid required the unit to traverse the total east-west and the total north-south distances between the unit's initial location and the incident's location. This feature of Simtown operation is shared by many midwestern cities and parts of Manhattan but not by older cities with highly irregular street patterns (for example, Boston).

Preventive patrol effort was seriously diminished during periods of congestion. As in many cities, there was no attempt to maintain at least a minimal continuous level of preventive patrol or to have some units specialize in preventive patrol, dispatching them only to certain high priority calls.

There was no formal priority structure and, with very few exceptions, there was usually no attempt made to associate priorities with different classes of calls. When a call arrived from a congested precinct, no attempt was made to assign an available patrol unit from an adjacent uncongested precinct. Calls queued at the precinct level were serviced in order of their arrival (first-come, first-served). With regard to each of these dispatching procedures, Simtown presented an oversimplified picture of operations that are likely to be observed in actual cities. For instance, the ranking of call importance, the likelihood of interprecinct dispatch, and the manner in which queued calls are handled are all likely to depend strongly on individual dispatchers and their perceived role as decision makers. Simtown's initial operations represent one extreme in which the dispatcher plays a minimal role in assigning priorities and requesting out-of-the-ordinary responses.

The preliminary monitoring of operations had indicated that average effec-

4. See the Glossary at the end of the book as well as Section 3.4.1.

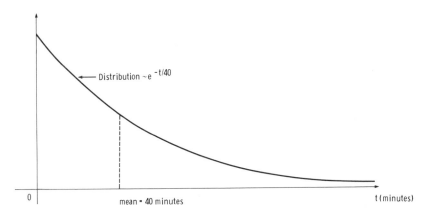

Figure 2.2 Distribution of service time at the scene of an incident.

tive travel speed[5] while responding to incidents was about 10 mph, regardless
of direction of travel. Service time at the scene was distributed as in Figure
2.2, with average service time equaling 40 minutes.[6]

A detailed statistical analysis of calls for service indicated the percentages of
workload generated by each sector. These results are shown in Table 2.1. It
was found that city-wide call-for-service workloads could range from very
light in the early morning hours to near saturation on Friday and Saturday
evenings, but the relative distribution of workload shown in Table 2.1 remained valid under all workload conditions. Since service times in Simtown
do not depend on time or location of the call, the workload distribution
shown in Table 2.1 applies to both the number of calls for service and the
amount of time spent at the scenes of calls for service. In most cities a different distribution would be required to indicate each type of workload; and
in most cities the workload distribution would vary with time of day. For instance, in Manhattan, the Wall Street area "closes up" around 5:00 P.M. on

5. The average *effective* travel speed that must be used in travel time models is usually
less than the average travel speed that one might measure in practice. The average effective travel speed is 1/(average inverse travel speed). See Section 3.1.
6. In most cities a breakdown of incidents by type would indicate that service time distributions depend on type of incident. Depending on the sensitivity of results to these
various distributions, it is desirable to include the important features of their differences
in a simulation model. For actual service time distributions see, for example, N. Heller,
"1967 Service Time Histograms for Police Patrol Activities in St. Louis" (available from
the St. Louis Police Department); or R. C. Larson, "Operational Study of the Police
Response System," Technical Report No. 26 (Cambridge, Massachusetts: M.I.T. Operations Research Center, 1967).

Table 2.1 Sector Workloads and Areas

Sector No.	Precinct No.	Percent of City-Wide Workload*	Area (mile^2)
1-1		4.8	0.065
1-2		5.7	0.075
1-3		4.8	0.075
1-4		6.7	0.0875
1-5		6.2	0.0875
1-6		8.1	0.05
	1	36.2	0.440
2-1		4.3	0.1875
2-2		5.7	0.15
2-3		5.7	0.15
2-4		8.6	0.1125
2-5		3.8	0.1031
	2	28.1	0.703
3-1		5.2	0.20
3-2		4.3	0.175
3-3		3.3	0.294
3-4		8.1	0.225
	3	21.0	0.894
4-1		0.95	0.657
4-2		2.9	0.187
4-3		3.3	0.194
4-4		3.3	0.40
	4	10.5	1.44
5-1		0.48	2.20
5-2		0.71	1.43
5-3		1.2	1.56
5-4		1.9	0.687
	5	4.3	5.88

*Totals may not add due to rounding.

weekdays, while many parts of Greenwich Village do not close up until after midnight.

2.2. Initial Analyses of Operations

Soon deluged with data, the study group felt the need for some quantitative framework to assist in defining critical parameters, suggesting measures of effectiveness, indicating how system characteristics varied with workload, and so forth. To fill this need, the groups decided to employ analytical and simulation models of patrol and dispatch operations.

The group developed a real-time, interactive simulation model within six months. The model consisted of a number of computer programs that could closely replicate actual operation under widely varying loads and different operating policies. (The general structure of this model is discussed in Chapter 6.) Because of the Department's lack of a suitable computer, the actual program was run on a commercially available computer system, with a teletype and display console located at department headquarters. The analytical models (discussed in Chapters 3,4,5,7 and 8) were used in conjunction with the simulation model to help provide interpretations for the simulation results and to suggest alternative policies to simulate.

2.2.1. Three System-Workload Conditions

As the simulation model became operational, simulated system statistics were generated for a wide range of workload conditions. Here we report the group's results obtained for three different workloads, designated as very light, moderate, or heavy.

A *very light* workload represents an idealized situation in which the fraction of time each unit is busy servicing calls, that is, the utilization factor is nearly zero. The study group was aware that this condition is unlikely to be realized in practice, even at traditionally light workload times (for example, rainy Sunday afternoons), but analysis of system operations with a very light load would provide the group with important insights into system operating characteristics.

At *moderate workloads*, the average city-wide time between call arrivals is 6 minutes; on the average the city receives ten calls per hour. In this situation, Precinct 1, with largest call volume, generates an average of 3.6 calls every hour. At the other extreme, Precinct 5 generates only one call every 2.3 hours on the average.

At *heavy workloads*, the average city-wide time between call arrivals is halved to 3 minutes, or a rate of 20 calls per hour. In Precinct 1, for example, the average number of calls generated per hour under heavy workloads is 7.2. Since it takes an average of 2/3 hr to service each call, the average hourly workload in Precinct 1 is 4.84 hr of service time/hour. Since there are six patrol units in Precinct 1, the fraction of time each is busy averages[7] approximately $4.84/6.00 \simeq 0.81$. The corresponding numbers for Precincts 2, 3, 4, and 5, are 0.75, 0.70, 0.35, and 0.14, respectively. Even when city-wide workloads are heavy, Precinct 5 is still relatively unloaded.

Under each of the workload conditions, the simulation model was run with sufficiently many calls for service so that meaningful statistical averages

7. This computation neglects the time spent traveling to and from the scene, which is assumed to be small compared to the time spent at the scene.

would be produced. It was decided that an average of 50 dispatch assignments per unit (requiring 1,150 total calls for service) would provide suitable accuracy.[8]

Summary statistics are shown in Table 2.2 for each precinct for each of the three simulated workload conditions. In the next few sections the group's interpretations of these results are summarized.

2.2.2. Average Travel Times

As can be seen from Table 2.2, the average travel times tend to increase with workload and with sector areas (Table 2.1). The study group found the analytical models of Chapter 3 useful in interpreting these results.

Precinct 2, for instance, can be approximated as five identical rectangular sectors, with dimensions 0.72 mile by 0.19 mile. Under very light load conditions the analytical model[9] predicts the mean travel time to be 1.82 minutes, which is reasonably close to the simulation value 1.77 minutes. The results of Chapter 3 also suggested that by redesigning the sectors in Precinct 2, mean travel time under light load conditions could be reduced approximately 18 percent, to 1.5 minutes. As discussed later (Section 2.8.1), the implications of this result are currently being assessed by the study group.

2.2.3. Dispatch Error Probability

A dispatch is said to be *in error* if at least one available unit is closer to the scene than the one selected by the dispatcher.[10]

Under light load conditions, the dispatch error probability ranges from 0.15 (Precinct 5) to 0.38 (Precinct 2). (See Table 2.2.) These figures further assisted the study group's intuition concerning the dependence of dispatch error on precinct and sector design, number of sectors in a precinct, and spatial distribution of workload. In Precinct 5, for instance, 44.4 percent of the workload is generated in Sector 5-4. This is the smallest sector in the precinct and it has a common boundary with only one other sector in the precinct (see Figure 2.1); thus, it is unlikely that any Precinct 5 car is closer to an incident in Sector 5-4 than is Car 5-4. Moreover, the entire precinct has only four cars, thus limiting the number of cars which might be closer than the sector car.

8. In simulations for which it is important to estimate parameters to two or more significant figures or to perform detailed statistical tests, it would probably be necessary to devote considerable time to determining appropriate sample sizes. The purpose in this chapter is to illustrate gross effects of various policies, and the limited sample of 1,150 incidents is sufficient for this purpose.
9. See Section 3.3, Equation 3.12.
10. The term *error* here does not necessarily imply that the dispatcher is performing poorly with available information. It implies that the dispatcher could make a better decision if additional information were provided him.

Table 2.2 Initial Simulation Statistics

Workload Condition*	Average Travel Time (min)			Dispatch Error† Probability			Average Extra Distance Traveled Given Dispatch Error (mile)			Fraction of Dispatches That Are Intersector Dispatches			Probability that a Call Will Be Queued			Average Waiting Time in Queue (hr)		
	L	M	H	L	M	H	L	M	H	L	M	H	L	M	H	L	M	H
Precinct 1	1.20	1.88	2.49	0.31	0.24	0.13	0.11	0.12	0.12	0.00	0.47	0.73	0.00	0.05	0.62	0.00	0.01	0.38
Precinct 2	1.77	2.34	2.98	0.38	0.32	0.20	0.16	0.19	0.16	0.00	0.33	0.63	0.00	0.05	0.44	0.00	0.01	0.20
Precinct 3	1.92	2.90	3.40	0.25	0.20	0.09	0.16	0.20	0.22	0.00	0.42	0.70	0.00	0.10	0.53	0.00	0.04	0.33
Precinct 4	2.17	2.79	3.23	0.20	0.21	0.18	0.20	0.22	0.20	0.00	0.22	0.41	0.00	0.02	0.03	0.00	0.00	0.01
Precinct 5	4.18	4.75	5.27	0.15	0.22	0.30	0.30	0.50	0.45	0.00	0.05	0.05	0.00	0.00	0.00	0.00	0.00	0.00

*L = light workload; M = moderate workload; H = heavy workload.
†Dispatch error occurs when other than the closest available car is selected by the dispatcher to respond to a call.

Table 2.3 Division 1 Operation: Division-Wide versus Precinct-Wide Dispatching Procedures (under heavy workloads)

	Average Delay in Dispatcher Queue Due to Patrol Saturation (hr)		Probability That Call Will Be Delayed in Queue		Average Travel Time (min)		Dispatch Error Probability		Average Extra Distance Traveled Given Dispatch Error (mile)		Fraction of Dispatches That Are Intersector Dispatches	
	Old*	New	Old	New	Old	New	Old	New	Old	New	Old	New
Precinct 1	0.38	0.10	0.62	0.45	2.49	3.61	0.13	0.13	0.12	0.17	0.73	0.80
Precinct 2	0.20	0.07	0.44	0.42	2.98	3.86	0.20	0.25	0.16	0.22	0.63	0.81
Precinct 3	0.33	0.13	0.53	0.43	3.40	4.88	0.09	0.18	0.22	0.22	0.70	0.79

*Old = precinct-wide dispatching; new = division-wide dispatching.

Precinct 2, with its five elongated sectors, is more likely to have out-of-sector cars closest to an incident. For instance, an incident at the eastern end of Sector 2-3 may be reported when Car 2-3 is at the western end of the sector; then, with reasonably high probability, Car 2-2 or Car 2-4 (or perhaps even Car 2-1 or Car 2-5) would be closer to the scene than Car 2-3. Thus, a dispatcher following a strict center-of-mass dispatching strategy would always assign Car 2-3, resulting in a high chance of error. The values of error probabilities for the other precincts under light load conditions were also interpreted in terms of sector geometry, number of sectors in a precinct, and workload distribution.

The study group noted that the dispatch error probability depends on the administrative decisions that specify dispatch policy and sector configurations. For instance, if a division-wide dispatch policy had been used, all of the error probabilities under light load conditions would be greater than those in Table 2.2, because for each dispatch there would be more cars eligible for assignment and thus more chance for error.

The probability of dispatch error also depends very much on utilization factors. This probability usually reaches its maximum value at a relatively low value of the utilization factor and then decreases to zero as utilization increases to one. (See Section 6.2.2.) The values in Table 2.2 illustrated to the study group how greatly the probabilities can depend on the particular properties of a precinct.

2.2.4. Extra Distance Traveled Given Dispatch Error

Suppose the dispatcher selects other than the closest available car. Say the closest available car would have required one mile travel distance, while the dispatcher-selected car traveled 1.5 miles. Then, the extra distance traveled due to dispatch error is 1.5 − 1.0 = 0.5 mile.

With *very light* workloads the average extra distance traveled, given dispatch error, ranges from 0.11 mile (Precinct 1) to 0.3 mile (Precinct 5). Traveling at an effective speed of 10 mph, these results imply that a perfect resolution car locator system would reduce the average travel time of these dispatches by approximately 40 seconds in Precinct 1 and 108 seconds in Precinct 5. When averaged over *all* dispatches, the travel time saved by car location information is only 12 seconds in Precinct 1 and 16 seconds in Precinct 5.

Under moderate to heavy load conditions, the average travel time saved by car location information is even less. This is caused by two facts: (1) under heavy loads, a sizeable fraction of dispatches are immediate reassignments of a unit at a *known* location (the scene of the last assignment) to a waiting incident, also at a known location; (2) even for those dispatches that are not immediate reassignments, the chance of dispatch error is smaller because of the smaller number of choices available.

Motivated by these results, the study group performed a preliminary cost-effectiveness analysis of a proposed car location system. They concluded that, if the system were to be simply imposed on current operations, its response time reduction benefits were probably not sufficient to warrant its cost (about $1,000 per car purchase price, plus $200 per car per year operating costs). However, the car-locator system did show promise in allowing the patrol force to be deployed in ways previously infeasible. (The study group's efforts in this direction are reported in Section 2.7.2.)

2.2.5. Intersector Dispatching

The amount of intersector dispatching depends directly on utilization factors and distribution of workloads among sectors. Referring to the analytical results of Chapter 8, the group learned that the fraction of dispatches which are intersector dispatches is usually *at least as great as* the *average utilization factor* for a command.[11] This result is modified somewhat at high utilizations when a sizeable fraction of assignments are made from a queue of waiting calls, when the reassignment policy would influence the amount of intersector dispatching.

At simulated *moderate workloads*, the average utilization factors for Simtown's five precincts are 0.40, 0.37, 0.35, 0.16, and 0.07, respectively. From Table 2.2, the corresponding fractions of dispatches that are intersector dispatches are 0.47, 0.33, 0.42, 0.22, and 0.05, respectively. Thus, in one simulation run, Precincts 1, 3, and 4 experienced an amount of intersector dispatching greater than their command-wide average utilization factors. Precincts 2 and 5, due to typical statistical fluctuations about an average, experienced an amount slightly less than their command-wide average utilization factors. City wide, at moderate workloads, a call for service resulted in intersector dispatch 38 percent of the time, whereas the city-wide average utilization factor was 29 percent. The amount of intersector dispatching could be brought closer to 29 percent by smoothing the distribution of workloads.

Under simulated *heavy workloads*, the average utilization factors for the five precincts are 0.81, 0.75, 0.70, 0.35, and 0.14, respectively. The corresponding fractions of dispatches that are intersector dispatches are 0.73, 0.63, 0.70, 0.41, and 0.05, respectively. Thus, within each precinct, the amount of

11. See Section 8.1.

intersector dispatching is usually slightly *less* than the precinct-wide average utilization, principally because a large fraction of assignments are first-come, first-served assignments from queues; the chance that such assignments are intersector assignments is $(N_i - 1)/N_i$, where N_i is the number of units assigned to precinct i.[12] Thus, in Precinct 3, for instance, the fraction of assignments that are intersector assignments approaches $(4 - 1)/4 = 0.75$ as utilization approaches one. City-wide, under heavy workloads, a call-for-service resulted in an intersector dispatch 64 percent of the time, whereas the city-wide average utilization was 58 percent. Thus, city-wide workload imbalance is still sufficiently great at near saturation conditions to cause the amount of intersector dispatching to exceed average utilization levels.

2.2.6. Queue Statistics

Calls arriving from Division 1 during heavy workload conditions are quite likely to incur queuing delays. Fully 62 percent of the calls received from Precinct 1 are delayed in the dispatcher queue, because all cars in the precinct are busy when the call arrives. These calls are delayed an average of 37 minutes. The average delay in the dispatcher queue of all calls from Precinct 1 is 23 minutes. Adding the average travel time (2.49 minutes), the average dispatching and patrol *response* time to calls in Precinct 1 is 25.5 minutes. The corresponding averages for the remaining four precincts are 15, 23, 4, and 4 minutes, respectively.

The study group felt that the lengthy response times in Division 1 could be decreased by instituting innovative dispatch and response policies.

2.3. Analysis of First Proposed Changes

2.3.1. Closest-Car, Closest-Incident Reassignments

The group began to explore systematically alternative modes of system operation. One of the first questions asked was the following: "What would happen if the Simtown Police Department changed its dispatch and reassignment policy from first-come, first-served to closest-car, closest-incident?" Under such a proposed policy, when a car completes service on a previous incident, it is immediately reassigned to the unserved incident judged closest (if there is one) rather than the incident that has been in queue the longest time. Distance estimations to choose the closest car would still be performed on a strict center-of-mass basis.

Simulating the proposed policy under heavy load conditions, the mean travel times were found to be reduced by about 10 percent throughout Di-

12. See Section 8.1.

vision 1. The largest percentage reduction (14 percent) occurred in Precinct 1, where mean travel time was reduced from 2.49 minutes to 2.14 minutes. In Precincts 2 and 3, the mean travel times were reduced 8.5 percent and 9.3 percent, respectively. These modest improvements left unchanged the average delays in the dispatcher queue.[13] Therefore, in order to reduce average queuing delays, any implemented policy would have to incorporate additional changes.

2.3.2. Division-Wide Dispatching

The group next decided to simulate a division-wide dispatching policy. Using this policy, every car in a Division (either 1 or 2) would be eligible for assignment to any incident reported anywhere within that division. No longer would there be a queue of waiting incidents in Precinct 1, for instance, while there were free patrol units nearby in Precinct 2. The new policy would transform five independent multiple server queues (each corresponding to one precinct) into two multiple server queues, each with a larger pool of servers. If adopted, the policy was expected to have greatest effect during hours of heavy call-for-service workload.

Factors Relevant to Division-Wide Dispatching

While working out the details of the proposed policy, the group discovered some pertinent historical facts. The precinct boundaries in Division 1 had been laid out in 1892,[14] when all patrol occurred on foot; one constraint then required the precincts to be sufficiently small so that any point within a precinct could be reached on foot within a reasonable amount of time. Citizens requiring police service usually hailed their local foot patrolman. Those citizens calling headquarters expected lengthy delays, because the only way for headquarters to contact a foot patrolman was by use of the department's call-box system. Calls were sufficiently infrequent so that the need for interprecinct assignments never arose.

In addition to the present precinct boundaries, other remnants of the old system were still visible. The call-box system had been wired to connect each box with only its precinct station house, thus tending to solidify precinct boundaries. Patrolmen's incident reports had always been reviewed by precinct supervisors; and any interprecinct assignments had always required ad-

---

13. In terms of standard queuing theory, implementing a closest-car, closest-incident reassignment policy is equivalent to changing the queue discipline from first-come, first-served to *random*. Although the *average* wait in queue is not affected by the change, the *variance* of the waiting time is *increased*. See Sections 7.8 to 7.9 for further discussion.
14. The areas of Precincts 4 and 5 were annexed later.

ditional, time-consuming paperwork that had to be approved by a supervisor unfamiliar to the patrolmen.

There were other impediments to immediately shifting to an interprecinct dispatching system. Patrolmen usually did not have detailed knowledge of street patterns in other precincts, thus increasing the expected travel time of any interprecinct assignments. Some officers' identity with their own precincts was so strong that they associated a different social status with the patrolmen assigned to each precinct; men in high status precincts disliked going into lower status precincts. Through the years, citizens had been against any change that tended to consolidate precincts, claiming that as taxpayers they had a right to their local police protection.

These and similar conditions had led department planners to believe that breaking down precinct boundaries, even if only to the extent of permitting interprecinct dispatching, would be infeasible. Yet the study team decided to analyze interprecinct dispatching, convinced that sufficiently great operational improvements might overcome the traditionally cited difficulties.

Simulated Operation

The operation of the patrol force was simulated using a division-wide dispatch policy, under the same heavy load conditions discussed in previous sections. From queues of waiting calls, only the call waiting longest in each precinct was considered eligible for immediate dispatch. If there were queues in more than one precinct, the reassigned unit was dispatched to the closest call (using strict center-of-mass distance estimation). In Division 1, the new policy caused marked changes in the following simulation statistics: waiting time in queue, travel time, fraction of assignments that are intersector assignments, probability of dispatch error, and extra distance traveled given dispatch error. The results are shown in Table 2.3. (The policy change had little effect on Precincts 4 and 5.)

As can be seen from Table 2.3, average delays in the dispatcher queue in Division 1 precincts were typically reduced from 20 minutes to 6 minutes. Average travel times, on the other hand, were typically increased by 30 to 40 percent. Average combined dispatching and travel delay was reduced by about 50 percent.

The fraction of assignments that were intersector assignments was increased owing to the larger area to which each car could be dispatched. Fully 80 percent of the assignments in Division 1 were intersector assignments, compared to 69 percent under the former policy.

The probability of dispatch error was increased in each precinct owing to the larger pool of eligible units to assign to calls. Under the new policy, the city-wide probability of dispatch error was 0.20, whereas under the former policy it was 0.16. The most dramatic change occurred in Precinct 3 where the dispatch error probability doubled from 0.09 to 0.18. This can be explained by the large pool of cars from Precinct 2 that become eligible to dispatch to incidents in Precinct 3 under the new policy.

The mean extra distance traveled because of dispatch error (given that error occurs) was increased 33 percent in Division 1, from 0.15 mile to 0.20 mile. Here again possible advantages of a car locator system were found to depend directly on the administrative rules that dictate how the patrol-dispatch system is to function.

2.3.3. Maximum Estimated Travel Distances, Division-Wide Dispatching

Although system queuing delays were reduced with the new division-wide policy, travel times in Division 1 were increased about 39 percent, largely because 80 percent of all assignments were intersector assignments. The study team felt that such a great extent of distant, out-of-sector dispatches could cause problems of morale within the patrol force and problems arising from unfamiliarity with areas distant from assigned patrol areas. In an attempt to improve this situation and, simultaneously, to maintain the advantages of division-wide dispatching, a *maximum estimated travel distance* of 0.75 miles was specified for Division 1 units on preventive patrol. All other characteristics of the division-wide simulation experiment were maintained and the modified experiment was run under identical heavy load conditions.

As a result, *average travel times* in Division 1 were only about 25 percent above those values obtained with no interprecinct dispatching. Intersector assignments remained high, at 78 percent. As expected, average time in the dispatcher queue was slightly greater than that obtained with no maximum travel distance. Averaged over Division 1, the average combined dispatching and travel delay was 10.7 minutes, compared to 9.5 minutes with no limit on estimated travel distance and 21.4 minutes with only precinct-wide dispatching.

Although these changes are not nearly as great as those experienced by first changing from precinct-wide to division-wide dispatching, the study team felt that this analysis helped to clarify the relationship between queuing delays and travel distances away from home sectors. They decided to recommend to the department that any division-wide dispatching policy, if implemented, should include a maximum estimated travel distance away from home sectors.

2.4. Reporting Initial Results

The study team presented a summary of their initial results to the other members of the planning and research unit, the superintendent of patrol and several other ranking officials of the department. The purpose of the briefing, in addition to indicating the potential advantages of a division-wide dispatching policy, was to elicit from interested department personnel their views on the policy questions that should be explored with the simulation and analytical models. It was hoped that others within the department would suggest additional deployment and dispatch strategies and would provide useful feedback on tentative results as they were reported.

After examining the simulation results, the department felt that while a 10 minute average response time under heavy load in Division 1 was acceptable for the great majority of calls, it was definitely unacceptable for very high priority calls, such as officer in trouble, robbery in progress, or seriously injured person. So the department urged the study group to examine alternative means of implementing priority-oriented dispatching procedures.

2.5. Analysis of Formalized Priority Procedures

In an attempt to improve response to high priority calls, the study group examined the types of calls received and decided that the calls could be categorized into three priority levels. Priority 1 calls, comprising 5 percent of all calls, required very rapid response. Siren and lights were used during response to these calls, thereby decreasing any delays due to traffic congestion. A sampling study indicated that average effective speed of response could thereby be increased to 15 mph. Priority 2 calls, comprising 45 percent of all calls, required moderately rapid response. This category included *suspicious person*, *disturbance*, and *noisy group*. Measurements indicated that average effective speed of response to priority 2 calls was 10 mph. Priority 3 calls represented 50 percent of all calls received and did not require rapid response. Included in this category were *parking violation*, *report of past auto theft*, and *lock out*. It was felt that an average response time of even as long as one hour would be adequate to handle these calls. Average effective response speed for these calls was measured to be 8 mph.

2.5.1. Precinct-Wide Dispatching with Priorities

In this first examination of the effects of using different priority levels, it was decided to retain only intraprecinct dispatching (rather than employ division-wide dispatching) in order to be able to compare it to present operations. If the results looked promising, the group could then compare to a division-wide, priority system.

Dispatching Procedures

The first task confronting the group was specification of the dispatcher decision rules to be used when reassigning units to waiting calls. Clearly, the dispatcher should give first preference to higher priority calls, but if a lower priority call was sufficiently closer to the unit than a higher priority call, then the proximity could override the priority difference. After much debate and discussion with dispatchers, the group agreed that a reasonable approximation to a desirable dispatcher reassignment procedure would be as follows: If there are no waiting calls, reassign the unit to preventive patrol in its own sector. If there are any waiting Priority 1 calls, assign the unit to the one judged closest *unless* there is a Priority 2 call judged one-tenth as far as the closest Priority 1 call *or* unless there is a priority 3 call judged one-one hundredth as far as the closest Priority 1 call; if there are any calls in these last two categories, assign the car to the one judged closest. If there are no waiting Priority 1 calls, an analogous procedure for Priority 2 and Priority 3 calls is to be employed.

The group recognized that this overformalization of dispatching procedures precluded some types of occurrences (for example, assigning a unit to an officer in trouble regardless of the closeness of a parking violation). But for the purposes of developing insight and intuition into the general operating characteristics of priority dispatching procedures, they felt that the specified procedure was more than adequate.

Additional procedures involving maximum travel distances in Division 1 would tend to save low priority incidents for the car assigned to the sector of the incident and to reduce the frequency of lengthy journeys away from home sectors: A car on preventive patrol could be dispatched no more than an estimated 1 mile to a Priority 3 incident. A car completing service of a prior incident at the scene of that incident could be dispatched no more than an estimated one-half mile to Priority 2 incidents; there will be no such immediate reassignments for Priority 3 incidents. A car returning to preventive patrol in its own sector could be dispatched no more than an estimated 1 mile to Priority 2 or Priority 3 incidents. There are no maximum distances for Priority 1 incidents. No maximum distances were instituted in Division 2, where intrasector journeys of over 2 miles are possible.

Service times at the scene were assumed to be distributed as in Figure 2.2, independent of priority, but the department had no available data to confirm this assumption. Also the distribution of priorities—Priority 1 : 5 percent, Priority 2 : 45 percent, Priority 3 : 50 percent—was assumed to be identical in all areas of the city. The group decided to run the simulation with these assumptions, thereby quickly providing at least approximate properties of priority dispatching. Simultaneously, the necessary process of data collection was initiated. Should the data indicate a need to modify these assumptions, the group planned to rerun the model to update the initial results.

The system was simulated under the identical heavy load conditions as discussed for nonpriority cases, except that each incident when reported was placed in a priority class according to the distribution (0.05, 0.45, 0.50).[15]

Simulation Results

The new priority policy dramatically reduced response delays to high priority calls in Division 1. Throughout Division 1, the average combined dispatching and travel delay was reduced from 21.2 minutes to 9.8 minutes. To achieve this reduction, the corresponding delay for Priority 3 calls was increased from 21.2 minutes to 30.9 minutes.

The new policy was also accompanied by changes in other statistics. For instance, less important calls tended to be held for the sector car, as intended. In fact, nearly 50 percent of the Priority 3 calls in Division 1 were handled by units within their own sectors. However, only 25 percent of the Priority 1 calls were handled by the sector car. With closest-car, closest-incident dispatching, without priorities, 35 percent of all calls were handled by sector cars.

2.5.2. Division-Wide Dispatching with Priorities

Motivated by the results of the earlier simulation study showing the advantages of division-wide dispatching, even without priorities, the study group next decided to try the same priority policies as described but with division-wide dispatching. The group realized that, as with the earlier division-wide study, certain statistics (for example, travel times and amount of intersector dispatching) would increase; but it was hoped that this would be more than offset by improving availability of cars when needed, thereby improving response to high priority calls.

After running the simulation experiment, it was found that average travel times in Division 1 for Priority 1 incidents increased from 2.2 minutes to

15. Because of the small total number of Priority 1 calls, statistics of Priority 1 operations must be regarded as illustrative. Other runs not reported here have substantiated the general characteristics of the results.

3.5 minutes, because cars more often took longer trips into foreign precincts. However, average queue delay decreased from 9.8 to 1.8 minutes, because cars from foreign precincts were available when needed. This resulted in an average combined dispatching and travel delay of 5.3 minutes (about a 40 percent reduction over any previous policies studied). It was true that 80 percent of the Priority 1 responses were out-of-sector responses, but for such high priority calls, the division-wide, priority policy provided the best operating characteristics of any policy tried up to that time.

2.5.3. Preemptive Priorities

In the Simtown Police Department, it had always been an unquestioned policy to consider any unit servicing an incident to be unavailable for further assignments until completion of service on that incident. This policy was upheld regardless of the type of incident currently being serviced and regardless of the type of incident currently requiring police service. Thus, it was possible to have a unit removing a cat from a tree while a robbery in progress two blocks away would be handled by a distant patrol unit. In fact, it was the publicity of the long delay in the liquor store robbery case (Section 2.1.1) that prompted the police commissioner to ask the study group to assess the consequences of revising this age-old policy.

Historically, the policy had developed as a result of a technological constraint—the inability of dispatchers to communicate with patrolmen busy on previously reported incidents. But this constraint had vanished in recent years, given walkie-talkies, dispatcher-triggered car alarms, and other systems providing continuous communication capability. Many cities other than Simtown had taken advantage of these new capabilities and had instituted dispatching procedures that could interrupt (preempt) a patrol unit servicing a low priority incident to assign it to a high priority incident. Leaving the scene of a partially serviced incident did present possible community relations problems, but most other departments had minimized these problems by providing careful follow-up explanations to complainants experiencing interrupted service.

The study group decided to simulate a precinct-wide, preemptive priority dispatching policy. The preemption was to be implemented as follows: Priority 1 incidents could preempt any patrol unit busy servicing a Priority 3 incident. The interrupted incident would be placed first in the queue of other Priority 3 incidents. Service on interrupted incidents would resume where left off at the time of interruption. Thus, the pool of units which would be eligible to dispatch to a Priority 1 incident would be all units in the precinct of the incident either performing preventive patrol or servicing Priority 3 incidents. The unit judged closest (by a strict center-of-mass strategy) would be assigned. All other parameters of the precinct-wide, priority policy were to remain valid for this proposed policy.

The system was simulated with the heavy workload, thereby making most apparent the effects of preemption. As a result, the average combined dispatching and travel delay in Division 1 was reduced for Priority 1 incidents from 5.3 minutes to 1.4 minutes. Since preemption was allowed, not one Priority 1 incident incurred any delay in the dispatcher queue. Also, average travel time was reduced from 3.5 minutes to 1.4 minutes.

About 65 percent of the dispatch assignments in Division 1 for Priority 1 incidents resulted in preempting a unit servicing a Priority 3 incident. But this represented only a small fraction (about 5 percent) of all Priority 3 incidents serviced.

In addition to response time reduction, another positive result of the preemptive strategy was that 50 percent of the Priority 1 incidents were handled by units within their own sectors, compared to 25 percent without preemption. Thus, when a Priority 1 incident is reported, it is not unusual for the unit assigned to the sector of the incident to be the closest eligible unit, either performing preventive patrol or servicing a Priority 3 incident.

2.6. Current Status of Implementation

A summary of the preemptive priority simulations was promptly presented to interested department personnel. Certain precinct commanders voiced suspicion about overcoming community-relations problems arising from interrupted service. "Consider the community response," one commander argued, "to an interrupted lock-out case in which the complainant is mugged on his doorstep shortly after police leave the scene for a more 'important' call." Another commander pointed out that even a parking violation left unattended could impede the travel of fire apparatus, the resulting delays perhaps causing serious fire damage or even loss of life.

To overcome these objections, the department decided that the dispatcher should ask any patrolman at a Priority 3 incident whether, in his best judgment, he considers interruption unacceptable for that particular incident; if so, the dispatcher would not interrupt service on that call but would seek other units to assign. Basically, this modification reflected the fact that the responding patrol officer has more information about an incident once at the scene than the complaint clerk who takes the initial call report. In a sense, the total number of possible priorities can become much larger once the distinguishing features of an incident are observed at the scene.

With this modification, the department purchased the necessary communications equipment to implement a trial preemptive priority, precinct-wide dispatching strategy in certain parts of Division 1. After the results of this trial are studied, the group expects to revise some of the details of the dispatching procedures but is confident that the concept of preemptive priority dispatching can be implemented within the department.

Also at this time a department committee has been appointed to determine the actions necessary to implement some form of division-wide dispatching. Upon receipt of the committee's report, the study group will begin investigating various forms of division-wide preemptive priority dispatching.

2.7. Other Ongoing Studies
Within the last 3 months the study group has also been exploring other modes of operations that may be incorporated sometime in the future.

2.7.1. Priorities for Preventive Patrol
One preliminary study has focused on the needs for preventive patrol, especially during hours of heavy workload. With a Division 1 utilization factor of 0.75 (at heavy workloads), the effective force on patrol in the division was only $0.25 \times 15 = 3.75$ cars. With current patrol allocations, this number could not be increased without screening out a higher percentage of calls in the communications center, thereby decreasing call-for-service workload of patrol units in the field. The department had always decided against this option, citing that it was department policy to respond (eventually) to every citizen requesting police service. However, the study group did believe that the department would agree to endure greater delays on low priority calls in order to maintain a more continuous patrol coverage and to allow some officers to specialize in patrol. The group wanted to formulate an operating policy that would decrease the chance that all units in a precinct would be simultaneously busy servicing calls, a situation that reduces preventive patrol coverage to zero in the precinct. It was felt that the crime deterrent effect of patrol would be improved with more continuous coverage. In addition, the patrol officer performing this coverage could concentrate on patrol duties, rather than treat patrol periods as rest breaks between dispatch assignments.

As one possible strategy, the Department proposed the following: Reserve 4 units in Division 1 and 2 units in Division 2 for assignment to Priorities 1 and 2 incidents only. The remainder of the time of these units would be spent performing preventive patrol. The remaining 17 units would handle calls of all priorities, as well as engage in preventive patrol. Following the earlier pre-emptive policy, Priority 1 incidents could interrupt any unit performing Priority 3 activity or any unit on preventive patrol. Dispatching was restricted to be precinct wide (not division wide).

Simulating this policy under heavy load conditions, the study group found that the proposed policy yielded the desired effects but perhaps to a lesser degree than hoped for. In Division 1 the utilization factor of the four reserved units dropped from 0.75 to 0.31. Thus, in an 8-hour tour, these units would be assigned to an average of 3.75 incidents, rather than nearly 9 incidents under the former policy. And, over 65 percent of the time of these units could be concentrated on preventive patrol activities.[16]

Other statistics changed in the directions expected. Average travel time in Division 1 for Priority 1 incidents remained low, at 1.5 minutes, and thus average combined dispatching and travel delay for these incidents was 1.5 minutes. The number of intersector dispatches increased slightly, because of the larger utilization factors for the regular patrol units. Also, queuing delays remained about the same for Priority 1 and Priority 2 incidents, but they nearly doubled for Priority 3 incidents; averaged over Division 1, the average wait in the dispatcher queue of Priority 3 incidents was now about one hour.

In the future the group plans another study of this policy, modified to al-low division-wide dispatching in an attempt to decrease queuing delays of Priority 3 calls. In addition, it plans to examine any administrative and morale problems that may arise due to perceived inequities among officers of workload distribution.

2.7.2. Car Locators and Overlapping Patrol Sectors
The Simtown Police Department was aware that with nonoverlapping sectors, when a unit is assigned to an incident, patrol coverage in that unit's sector is reduced to zero. In fact, several recently apprehended burglary suspects had admitted to monitoring[17] the police radio and to hitting their target while the patrol car assigned to the sector of the target was busy servicing a distant call. An overlapping sector plan decreases the probability that patrol coverage will be reduced to zero, but such a plan had been infeasible because of a lack of automatic car locator capability. This capability was needed in order to select the closest car to dispatch to an incident. In the current system, the alloca-

16. This excludes time spent on meals, fuel stops, maintenance, and so forth.
17. To a certain extent, radio scramblers could diminish the amount of radio monitoring.

tion of one car to one sector provides a type of car location information that would be lacking with an overlapping sector plan.

Analytical results in Chapter 7 suggested that travel times in a system with overlapping sectors and perfect car location information should be comparable to travel times in current systems with nonoverlapping sectors and no explicit car location information.[18] Motivated by this result, the study group recently requested the department's permission to set up a program to evaluate and experimentally test an overlapping sector plan. Recently the group was told to go ahead with the program.

The first step was to simulate the proposed plan under varying load conditions to see if the simulated results were promising. If so, the group planned to implement a detailed test on a trial basis in Precincts 1 and 5 to discover effects on crime deterrence, officer morale, and to uncover any inadequacies in the prototype car location system loaned to the department by a local electronics firm.

In the first simulation study, the group decided to allow completely overlapping sectors within each precinct. This was to be carried out in the following manner: Whenever a unit completed service of a call and was returning to preventive patrol, the unit was to select any one of the (former) sectors in its precinct to patrol, with equal likelihood of selecting each one. In effect, the officer in the patrol car would spin a wheel of chance[19] that had equal probability of assigning the unit to each of the precinct's former sectors. Once the area of patrol was determined, the unit would commence patrolling that area in a spatially uniform manner.

In final implementation, this procedure would probably be modified somewhat, but it was felt that this completely overlapping sector strategy would be the most severe test of the concept of overlapping sectors.

The system was simulated under both light and heavy load conditions, assuming precinct-wide dispatching, with no priorities, and perfect car location information. The principle statistic of interest was average travel time.

Under very light loads, the average travel times in Division 1 increased 18 percent. This increase was considered acceptable by the study group, especially since the magnitudes of the Division 1 travel times were relatively low (in the order of one to two minutes). However, the absolute and percentage increases in Precincts 4 and 5 were considered unacceptable. In Precinct 4,

18. See Section 7.7.
19. The second-hand on a wristwatch is a very accessible wheel-of-chance.

average travel time increased from 2.17 to 2.91 minutes; in Precinct 5, it increased from 4.18 to 5.36 minutes. These increases in Division 2 were caused primarily by the fact that workloads were distributed unevenly within the precincts, while the overlapping sector plan distributed patrol units uniformly to each of the former sectors. For instance, former sector 5-4 generated 45 percent of the workload of Precinct 5, yet it received only 25 percent of the patrol coverage under the proposed plan. Even with light loads, approximately 32 percent of the dispatch assignments to incidents in former sector 5-4 found no car within the sector, thus requiring lengthy journeys to reach the scene.[20]

Under heavy loads with first-come, first-served dispatching within precincts, the mean travel times and queuing delays in Division 1 were nearly identical to those of the current system. This fact illustrated to the study group how insensitive system operation is to spatial deployment policy when the system is enduring heavy loads. The Precinct 4 average travel time was found to increase 6.2 percent. In Precinct 5, the average travel time was found to increase from 4.27 to 6.26 minutes (a 47 percent increase). This marked increase was again caused by the large workload in former sector 5-4, which caused lengthy journeys from the northern portion of the Precinct.

Under heavy loads with closest-car, closest-incident dispatching, the average travel times in Division 1 were actually found to be somewhat less than the comparable times in a nonoverlapping sector system. The mean travel time in Precinct 5 was still too large.

In the next set of simulation runs, the study group modified its overlapping sector policies in Precincts 4 and 5. When embarking on preventive patrol, units were to select one of the former sectors, with the likelihood of selection of each sector predetermined by a formula that includes call-for-service workloads of each sector and preventive patrol needs. The resulting mean travel times were found comparable to those of the nonoverlapping sector system.

It has now been decided to continue the program, at least through a trial implementation phase. The continuation will require additional simulation runs, which will incorporate the department's newly implemented preemptive priority dispatching policy. It is anticipated that within 6 months the details of a suggested implementation in Precincts 1 and 5 will be worked out. An additional 2 month implementation period should yield further information

20. Under very light loads, the probability that no car is in former Sector 5-4 at the time an incident is reported is $(3/4)^4 \approx 0.32$.

about imperfect resolution of the car locator system in the downtown area of Precinct 1. Also, it should provide information about an officer's ability to learn all the irregular street patterns of Precinct 5. If the trial implementation phase is judged successful, this information is to be used to develop a modified overlapping sector plan that will first be simulated and then put into practice sometime next year.

2.8. Other Topics on the Agenda
As a result of its interaction with interested departmental personnel and its knowledge of related programs throughout the country, the study group has collected a large number of suggestions for improving patrol operation. Several are briefly described here that the group plans to examine with the aid of simulation and analytical models.

2.8.1. Sector Redesign in Precinct 2
During its first detailed set of simulation runs, the study group noted that the elongated sectors of Precinct 2 could probably be redesigned to decrease average travel time to incidents within the precinct, especially during the hours of light demand. The analytical models had predicted that the average travel time in the precinct during light load conditions would be approximately 1.8 minutes, and this was substantially verified by the simulation run (see Section 2.2.2). Since the total precinct area was 0.703 square miles, the group was also aware that the analytical models predicted that the average travel time (under light loads) could be reduced to $0.667 \sqrt{(0.703)/5}$ mile/$(1/6)$ mile/minute ≈ 1.50 minutes (an 18 percent reduction), provided that the sectors were redesigned to be reasonably compact.[21]

The group very recently simulated Precinct 2 operation with the revised sector boundaries shown in Figure 2.3. Under light loads (center-of-mass dispatching, no priorities), the simulated average travel time was 1.54 minutes, which is quite close to the predicted minimum value. Given a go-ahead by the department, the group will phase into its program this redesign of sectors in Precinct 2.

2.8.2. Family Dispute Units
Recent studies in New York City have indicated the advantages of specially training certain officers to respond to family dispute calls.[22] These calls, usually involving an argument between husband and wife, have proven to be

21. See Section 3.3.
22. M. Bard, *Training Police as Specialists in Family Crisis Intervention* (Washington, D.C.; U.S. Government Printing Office, 1970).

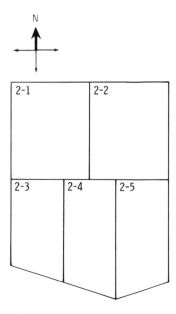

Figure 2.3 Restructuring of sectors in Precinct 2.

quite dangerous for responding officers. In addition, the kind of service required at the scene is usually not of a law enforcement nature but often requires an awareness of the psychology of disputes and methods of counseling to terminate them. The department has decided to train ten officers from Precinct 3 on matters pertaining to family disputes. Then, in two-men teams, the officers will be assigned to one of the Precinct 3 cars that will be designated the family dispute car. Whenever an incident is reported that can be identified as a family dispute, that car, if available, will be sent to the scene. The task of the study group over the next several months is to explore various ways of implementing this procedure to minimize delays to both family dispute calls and other high priority calls. The study group is now proposing several alternative sector structures and dispatching procedures to accomplish this task. The more promising ones will be simulated, and one will finally be chosen for the initial implementation.

2.8.3. Adding Ambulance Calls

Currently the city's emergency ambulance needs are handled by several private companies. These companies have been facing a deteriorating financial situation, with labor and maintenance costs increasing and an increasing number of indigents unable to pay the cost of ambulance service. The companies cannot afford the expense of highly trained drivers, but a recently passed state law requires that all drivers have substantial paramedical training by January 1 of next year. Given this situation, it is highly probable that the private companies will go out of business and that some other means of providing ambulance service will have to be provided. The mayor's office has requested several city agencies, including the police department, to examine the impact upon each agency if it were asked to provide the required ambulance service. The police commissioner has asked the joint study group to perform this task for the police department. The study group is currently laying out several alternative ways in which the department could provide the ambulance service. One which looks promising would require replacing a substantial number of the present cars with modified station wagons, called ambulettes. The officers manning these cars would get the required paramedical training. The study group is now using analytical and simulation techniques to explore alternative ways of revising deployment and dispatching procedures and to determine the number of ambulettes required by place and by time of day. They plan to submit their report to the mayor within 2 months.

2.8.4. Reallocation by Tour
Since the state legislature passed the Three Tour Statute in 1922, the department had been legally constrained to allocate an *equal* number of men to each of the three tours of duty (midnight to 8:00 A.M., 8:00 A.M. to 4:00 P.M., 4:00 P.M. to midnight). In recent years this constraint has been particularly troublesome, because near-saturation loads occurred during predictable periods; but to relieve the congestion, additional men would have to be added to the force around the clock. This was prohibited by budgetary pressures. Examining the situation, the study group sees an opportunity to use the simulation and analytical models in a very important way. Instead of accepting the existing statute as a given constraint, the group plans to examine how the patrol force would function if the law were modified to allow tours with nonequal manning. The study group is convinced that the current total number of men available is sufficient to handle the needs of the city if the tours could be restructured (perhaps even allowing overlapping tours) to reflect the widely varying call-for-service rates and the needs for preventive patrol. The group initially plans to use the queuing model and the allocation algorithm discussed in Chapter 5 to get a rough idea of the number of men required by place and by time of day to achieve a reasonable level of service. Then the response and patrol models will be used to structure thinking about

sector design, workloads, preventive patrol coverage, and so forth. Finally, several detailed simulation tests will be performed to determine the extent of improvement obtained by reallocating the men. If the results are sufficiently promising (and the study group feels they will be), the group plans to make the findings of the study publicly available. Eventually, it is hoped that this may cause a revision in the current law.

3
Travel Time Models

Chapters 3 to 5 focus on the development and interpretation of mathematical models of patrol forces as they currently operate in many cities. In this chapter the concern is with travel time or the time required for a dispatched unit to travel to the scene of an incident. Chapter 4 develops models of preventive patrol operation. The results of Chapters 3 and 4 are directly applicable to the study of response and patrol activities in many cities. One application is illustrated in Chapter 5, where several of the models are used to allocate patrol units to spatially separate commands. In Chapters 6 to 8, where alternative operating procedures are examined, the methods and results of Chapters 3 and 4 are used, as well as results obtained from a simulation model.

Response time is only a proxy measure of police effectiveness, as discussed in Chapter 1, but it is one of the few that (1) is easily measured, (2) is understandable by both citizens and police, (3) is controllable to some extent by policy decisions, and (4) is recognized as an important indicator of police accessibility and responsiveness. The travel time component often consumes over 50 percent of total response time, except during periods of congestion in which queue delays caused by car unavailabilities dominate. Given the acknowledged importance of travel time, it is surprising that many police departments make no attempt to measure it[1] or to obtain quantitative tools to indicate methods for its reduction.

There are several factors that influence travel time, all of which may depend on time of day, day of the week, or season of the year: (1) the total number of calls for police service; (2) the fraction of calls which are screened out prior to dispatch of a patrol unit; (3) the distribution of priority types among calls requiring dispatch, and the dispatcher's procedures for handling calls of various priorities; (4) the total number of radio-dispatchable patrol units (cars, scooters, wagons, foot patrolmen) assigned to each command; (5) the dispatcher's knowledge of car locations and his dispatching strategy, given this knowledge; (6) effective travel speeds achievable by each unit; (7) geometrical configurations of sectors, or more generally, spatial distribution of available patrol units; and (8) impediments to travel such as railroads, parks, rivers, and one-way streets. To some extent all but factors 1 and 8 are partially controllable by policy decision.

1. There are exceptions, including Dallas, Texas.

Traditional police administration texts treat many of these factors and, in some cases, even suggest appropriate criteria of performance. In examining sector geometries, for instance, police planners have traditionally been instructed to design patrol sectors as squares, circles, or as straight lines along particular streets.[2] The straight line, or linear sector, is particularly suited to streets with many store fronts that may require intensive patrol and continual surveillance. The idea behind square or circular sectors is to cover a given area and yet keep at a minimum the possible times required for the patrol unit to travel to the scenes of reported incidents in the sector. O. W. Wilson states that "a square beat permits a maximum quadrilateral area with a minimum distance between any two possible points within it."[3] Embedded in this statement are the ideas of the sector area as a constraint and the minimization of maximum possible travel distance as an objective. Since a specified number of patrol units are typically assigned to a command of given area, it is not unreasonable to treat sector area primarily as a constraint. Some of the models of sector geometry developed here (Sections 3.2 and 3.3) expand on these ideas, including additional performance criteria and taking into account that with mobile patrol units the travel speeds may depend on direction of travel; in such a situation, it may be desirable to design the sector so that the longer dimension corresponds to the direction with higher travel speeds. Also, in other situations it may not be physically possible to implement an optimally designed sector; a planner would want to know the sensitivity of results to alternative sector designs. These and other issues are treated in this presentation of models of sector geometry.

Section 3.4 explains how various dispatching strategies and rates of unavailability influence travel time, particularly when a large fraction of dispatches are cross-sector (or intersector) assignments. The results of this section are revisited in Chapter 7 when it is assumed that the dispatcher is provided with improved car position information to reduce travel times.

Section 3.5 examines the sensitivity of results to travel impediments such as barriers and one-way streets. It also develops results which indicate how street density (as measured in street mileage per square mile) influences travel times.

Section 3.6 poses some questions related to data collection and model validation. In particular, a test for measuring the reasonableness of the right-

2. E. D. Graper, *American Police Administration* (New York: The Macmillan Company, 1921), p. 126.
3. O. W. Wilson, *Police Administration*, 2nd ed. (New York: McGraw-Hill Book Company, 1963), p. 274.

angle, or metropolitan, distance metric is presented, and some effects of data truncations are discussed.

This chapter focuses on factors 5 to 8 mentioned earlier, treating 1 to 4 as given. Certain aspects of factors 1 to 4 are treated later. A summary of definitions for Sections 3.1 to 3.4 is given in Table 3.1. A total summary is given in Section 3.7.

3.1. Travel Times, Distances, and Speeds

Throughout the chapter, travel times are expressed in terms of travel distances and effective travel speeds. If a patrol unit travels d miles in t minutes, its *effective travel speed* v is simply d/t. The effective speed averages out all speed fluctuations due to traffic, making turns, and so forth. It can be interpreted to be that speed which, if constantly maintained over the path of the response journey, would result in the same travel time as that actually experienced by the patrol unit.

To a large extent distances and speeds can be considered separately. For instance, in a particular sector, the spatial distribution of incidents and patrol

Table 3.1 Summary of Definitions for Sections 3.1 to 3.4

D	Distance traveled during a response
V	Effective travel speed during response
T_r	Travel time
$E[\cdot]$	Mathematical expectation
$E\text{-}W$	East–west
$N\text{-}S$	North–south
(X_1, Y_1)	Position coordinates of the patrol unit
(X_2, Y_2)	Position coordinates of the incident
$D_x(D_y)$	$E\text{-}W$ ($N\text{-}S$) travel distance
$T_x(T_y)$	$E\text{-}W$ ($N\text{-}S$) travel time
$v_x(v_y)$	Travel speed $E\text{-}W$ ($N\text{-}S$)
$X_o(Y_o)$	A factor proportional to $E\text{-}W$ ($N\text{-}S$) sector dimensions
A	Sector area ($A = X_o Y_o$)
$f_R(\ )$	Probability density function (pdf) of random variable (r.v.) R
E_{ij}	Event that patrol unit (i,j) is assigned to an incident in sector $(0,0)$ [Figure 3.5]
A_i, B_i	Unions of events E_{ij} (Section 3.4.2)
ρ	Fraction of time units are busy (utilization factor)
A_T	Total area of a command

locations may be the same at, say, 5:00 A.M. and 5:00 P.M. Then, it is likely that the distributions of travel distances to incidents occurring at these times would be similar. This distribution would depend on street patterns and sector geometry. However, responses at 5:00 P.M. might be more likely to incur rush-hour traffic, thus resulting in a smaller effective travel speed then could be obtained at 5:00 A.M.

For the purposes of modeling responses in actual cities, it seems that complicated mathematical models have little to say about effective travel speeds, other than the fact that travel times are quite sensitive to the particular values of travel speeds. Inclusion of travel speeds in an operational model would require a statistical sampling of actual responses at various times and in various parts of the city.[4]

On the other hand, mathematical models can tell us much about travel distances. By focusing on the geometrical configurations of sectors, models can be constructed that yield the average travel distance, for instance, in terms of sector geometries. This approach provides considerable insight into certain aspects of sector design. It also facilitates examination of model sensitivities to certain impediments to travel that can be modeled geometrically.

This is basically the approach followed throughout the chapter. Although the models vary widely in their degree of complexity, each is a rather crude approximation to most actual urban environments. However, the model assumptions (for example, spatial uniformity of demand) are usually no more restrictive than the assumptions usually imposed on, say, queuing systems to arrive at a tractable model. Moreover, it appears that the results of these geometric models are less sensitive to, say, a uniformity of demand assumption than are the results of a queuing model to an assumption of negative exponential service times.

Before developing the response models, it is useful to discuss the relationship linking distance, speed, and time,

$$T_r = \frac{D}{V}$$

where
T_r = travel time,
D = distance traveled during response,
V = effective travel speed during response.

4. See Section 3.6.2 for a discussion of measuring travel speeds, distances, and times.

The average, or expected travel time is

$$E[T_r] = E\left[\frac{D}{V}\right].$$

Since ratios of random variables are dealt with here, the mean of one must not be estimated as the ratio of the means of the other two (that is, $E[T_r] \neq E[D]/E[V]$).

As an example, if D and $1/V$ are uncorrelated,[5]

$$E[T_r] = E[D]E\left[\frac{1}{V}\right].$$

It is a convexity property of mathematical expectations[6] that for any non-negative random variable V,

$$E\left[\frac{1}{V}\right] \geq \frac{1}{E[V]}. \qquad (3.1)$$

Thus, if D and $1/V$ are uncorrelated,

$$E[T_r] = E[D]E\left[\frac{1}{V}\right] \geq \frac{E[D]}{E[V]}.$$

Hence, using $(E[D]/E[V])$ to estimate $E[T_r]$ in such a case results in an optimistically low estimate of average travel time. For instance, if V is a second-order Erlang random variable with mean 20 mph, then

$$\frac{E[D]}{E[V]} = \frac{E[D]}{20},$$

whereas the true expected travel time is a factor of two greater,

$$E[D]E\left[\frac{1}{V}\right] = \frac{E[D]}{10}.$$

In a practical sense these relations imply that a police department cannot infer that a 20 mph average response speed and a 1 mile average travel distance imply a 3 minute average travel time. On the contrary, if the average inverse travel speed is 0.10 hpm and if travel distance and inverse travel speed are uncorrelated, then the average travel time is 6 minutes, not 3 minutes.

Similar arguments suggest that using $E[D]/E[T_r]$ to estimate $E[V]$ can result in a low estimate of mean travel speed. In terms of a specific example, average travel distance divided by average travel time could be 10 mph or less while the actual average travel speed could be 20 mph or more.

In most of our models of patrol travel time, we treat speed as if it were a

5. In practice it is not expected that D and $1/V$ are uncorrelated, but this example illustrates the type of biases one may encounter.
6. M. Loeve, *Probability Theory* (Princeton, N.J.: D. Van Nostrand Company, 1963), p. 159.

deterministic quantity. However, using the above ideas, one sees that it is straightforward to replace a constant speed, say v, with $1/E[1/V]$, provided D and $1/V$ are uncorrelated. If D and $1/V$ are not uncorrelated, then it is usually more difficult to obtain properties of travel time (such as its expected value).

3.2. Mean Travel Times in Single Patrol Sectors

Several models are now developed that relate sector geometries to mean travel times. The results yield certain insights about sector design and model insensitivities.

A regular street grid pattern is assumed in which the minimum travel distance between two points, (x_1,y_1) and (x_2,y_2), is closely approximated by the right-angle, or metropolitan, or Manhattan metric

$$d = |x_1 - x_2| + |y_1 - y_2| = d_x + d_y,$$

where the coordinate axes are defined parallel to street directions. For convenience, we say that the abscissa is directed east-west (E-W) and the ordinate north-south (N-S). We assume that the patrol unit travels a minimum distance path to the incident, traveling at an effective speed v_x E-W (or W-E) and an effective speed v_y N-S (or S-N). Thus the time required for the patrol unit, initially at (x_1,y_1), to travel to the incident, at (x_2,y_2), is

$$t_r = \frac{d_x}{v_x} + \frac{d_y}{v_y} = t_x + t_y.$$

3.2.1. Rectangular Sector

In practice the boundaries of a sector usually coincide with streets. In this first model the assumption is made that the sector boundaries are coincident with only four streets, and thus the sector is rectangular. An illustrative sector and response path are shown in Figure 3.1.

It is also assumed that the positions of the patrol unit and the incident are independent and uniformly distributed over the sector. Given these assumptions, the four random variables (X_1, X_2, Y_1, Y_2) are mutually independent. The random variables X_1, X_2 are uniformly distributed from 0 to X_0, and Y_1, Y_2 are uniformly distributed from 0 to Y_0. It is easy to obtain the probability density functions for the E-W and N-S travel times:

$$f_{T_x}(t) = \frac{2v_x}{X_0^2} [X_0 - v_x t], 0 \leqslant t \leqslant \frac{X_0}{v_x} \tag{3.2}$$

$$f_{T_y}(t) = \frac{2v_y}{Y_0^2} [Y_0 - v_y t], 0 \leqslant t \leqslant \frac{Y_0}{v_y}. \tag{3.3}$$

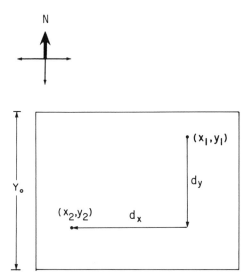

Figure 3.1 Travel distance in a single rectangular patrol sector.

Since $T_r = T_x + T_y$ and T_x, T_y are independent, $f_{T_r}(\cdot)$ is found simply from the convolution of Equations 3.2 and 3.3.

The mean travel time is

$$E[T_r] = C_1 \left[\frac{X_0}{v_x} + \frac{Y_0}{v_y} \right], \tag{3.4}$$

where $C_1 = 1/3 \approx 0.333$.

3.2.2. Diamond-Shaped Sector

Next consider a diamond-shaped sector with area $X_0 Y_0$ (Figure 3.2). Again assume that the positions of the patrol unit and the incident are independent and uniformly distributed over the sector. By straightforward probability arguments, one can show that the expected travel time in this sector is

$$E[T_r] = C_2 \left[\frac{X_0}{v_x} + \frac{Y_0}{v_y} \right], \tag{3.5}$$

where $C_2 = 7\sqrt{2}/30 \approx 0.330$.

3.2.3. Elliptical Sector

In practice elliptical sectors are usually infeasible, because there is no way to pack densely the elliptically shaped objects. Still, it is instructive to obtain the mean travel time for such a sector, because one may feel intuitively that

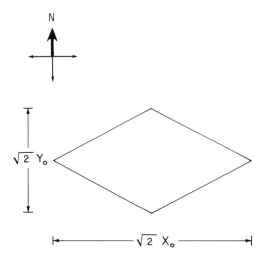

Figure 3.2 Diamond-shaped sector.

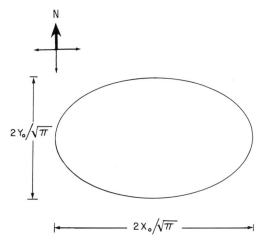

Figure 3.3 Elliptical sector.

in the case $v_x = v_y$ a circle would be the most compact sector and thus would yield the minimum possible mean travel time.

Consider an elliptical sector of area $X_0 Y_0 = A$, as illustrated in Figure 3.3. For this model also it is assumed that the positions of the patrol unit and the incident are independent and uniformly distributed over the sector.

Although the mean travel time could be obtained by direct (and tedious) methods, we use an alternative approach. First consider the Euclidean distance between two points distributed uniformly and independently over a circle of area A. It can be shown by use of Crofton's theorem on mean values[7] that the expected Euclidean distance is

$$E[D_E] = \frac{128}{45\pi} \sqrt{\frac{A}{\pi}} \, .$$

This intermediate result may be valuable in evaluating helicopter patrols, assuming the responding helicopter travels the shortest path "as the crow flies" between two points. Now consider the right-angle distance D between the two points. We can write

$$D = \frac{|X_1 - X_2| + |Y_1 - Y_2|}{\sqrt{(X_1 - X_2)^2 + (Y_1 - Y_2)^2}} \sqrt{(X_1 - X_2)^2 + (Y_1 - Y_2)^2} \, ,$$

or

$$D = R \cdot D_E \, ,$$

where R is the ratio of the right-angle and the Euclidean distance. Thus,

$$E[D] = E[R \cdot D_E] \, .$$

But this expectation can be evaluated directly, because one can show that for a circle R and D_E are independent. And, in Section 3.6.1. we show that

$$E[R] = \frac{4}{\pi} \, .$$

Thus,

$$E[D] = E[R]E[D_E]$$
$$= \frac{4}{\pi} \frac{128}{45\pi} \sqrt{\frac{A}{\pi}} \, .$$

To obtain the mean travel time in an ellipse, we use a scaling property of probability density functions. If random variable U has probability density function $f_U(u)$ and mean $E[U]$, then a random variable having a probability density function $f(w) = 1/a \, f_U(w/a)$ has a mean equal to $a \cdot E[U]$ $(a > 0)$. We now transform a circle of radius $\sqrt{A/\pi}$ to an ellipse with semiaxes of length $X_0/\sqrt{\pi}$ and $Y_0/\sqrt{\pi}$, corresponding to E-W and N-S directions, respectively. Invoking the scaling property, we find the mean right-angle travel time,

7. M. G. Kendall and P. A. P. Moran, *Geometrical Probability* (London: Charles Griffin & Company, 1963), p. 41.

$$E[T_r] = C_3 \left[\frac{X_0}{v_x} + \frac{Y_0}{v_y} \right],$$ (3.6)

where

$$C_3 = \frac{2}{\pi} \cdot \frac{128}{45\pi} \sqrt{\frac{1}{\pi}} \approx 0.325.$$

A somewhat surprising property of the results in this section is the near equality of C_1, C_2, and C_3. For comparable sectors, the mean travel times in elliptical and in rectangular sectors differ by less than 3 percent.

3.3. Optimal Sector Design

The $C_i (i = 1,2,3)$ allow comparisons of expected travel times among different classes of geometric shapes. We are also interested in comparing alternative designs within each class. For this purpose it is useful to write the expected travel time for each of the three above models as

$$E[T_r] = C \left[\frac{X_0}{v_x} + \frac{Y_0}{v_y} \right],$$ (3.7)

where C is a constant whose value depends on geometry and X_0 and Y_0 are directly proportional to E-W and N-S dimensions, respectively, where $X_0 Y_0 = A$. (For convenience we refer to X_0 and Y_0 as the sector length and width, respectively, recognizing that proportionality constants are required to compute the dimensions of nonrectangular sectors.)

Now the question can be asked, "Given that a sector is to have a particular geometric shape, how should its dimensions be selected?" Important factors are E-W and N-S travel speeds and total sector area. First, one would want to design the sector so that the larger dimension corresponds to the direction with greater travel speeds. Second, typically a fixed number of patrol units will be allotted to a command of fixed area, and each unit will be assigned to patrol a sector in which workload considerations dictate the approximate area of the sector. One reasonable statement of the problem of optimal sector design is "Minimize the average travel time $E[T_r]$ subject to the constraint that the sector have a specified area A." Or, more closely in line with O. W. Wilson's criteria, another reasonable statement is, "Minimize the maximum possible travel time within the sector, subject to a sector area constraint."

To minimize $E[T_r]$ subject to $X_0 Y_0 = A$, we substitute $Y_0 = A/X_0$ into Equation 3.7 and take the derivative with respect to X_0, thereby obtaining the optimal[8] sector length

8. It is easily verified that the second derivative is positive, and thus a minimum is obtained.

$$X_0^* = \sqrt{\frac{v_x}{v_y} A} \,, \tag{3.8}$$

Thus, the optimal sector width is

$$Y_0^* = \sqrt{\frac{v_y}{v_x} A} \,. \tag{3.9}$$

These results imply that the sector should be designed so that the average time required to travel E-W equals the average time required to travel N-S.

Although the details are not presented here, the sector dimensions shown in Equations 3.8 and 3.9 also minimize maximum possible travel time within a sector, subject to an area constraint. And the minimum maximal travel times are

$$\min[\max t_r] = k_i \sqrt{\frac{A}{v_x v_y}} \,,$$

where $k_1 = 2$ for rectangles, $k_2 = \sqrt{2} \approx 1.414$ for diamonds, and $k_3 = 2\sqrt{2/\pi} \approx 1.596$ for ellipses. Thus, for either statement of the sector design problem, the traditional rule-of-thumb design—square or circular sectors—is optimal only when N-S and E-W speeds are equal.

Returning to average travel times, the minimal average travel time (subject to the area constraint) is

$$E[T_r^*] = 2C \sqrt{\frac{A}{v_x v_y}} \,. \tag{3.10}$$

As a numerical example, suppose N-S speed is fixed at 20 mph and E-W speed is fixed at 5 mph (a situation which might describe parts of Manhattan). Then, for minimal average travel time, the N-S sector dimension should be four times the E-W dimension. In this case, such a sector design can be expected to reduce average travel time by approximately 20 percent over that obtained by square or circular sectors of equivalent area.

On the other hand, if the sector dimensions are near the optimum and if the area constraint is maintained, it is important to note that the mean travel time is not very sensitive to the exact sector dimensions. For instance, say we select sector dimensions so that the average E-W travel time is twice the average N-S travel time, that is,

$$\frac{X_0}{v_x} = \frac{2Y_0}{v_y} \,,$$

$$X_0 Y_0 = A \,.$$

Then, the average travel time is increased only about 6 percent. This insensitivity results from the fact that if X_0 and Y_0 are near their respective optimal values and if $X_0 Y_0 = A$, then

$$\frac{X_0}{v_x} + \frac{Y_0}{v_y} \approx 2\sqrt{\frac{A}{v_x v_y}} + \frac{[(X_0/v_x) - (Y_0/v_y)]^2}{4Y_0/v_y}$$

$$- \frac{1}{8} \frac{[(X_0/v_x) - (Y_0/v_y)]^3}{(Y_0/v_y)^2} + \cdots \qquad (Y_0/v_y \leqslant X_0/v_x)$$

If the higher order terms are small,

$$\frac{X_0}{v_x} + \frac{Y_0}{v_y} \approx 2\sqrt{\frac{A}{v_x v_y}},$$

so that

$$E[T_r] \approx 2C\sqrt{\frac{A}{v_x v_y}}. \tag{3.11}$$

That is, if X_0 and Y_0 are near their optimal values, the average travel time is directly proportional to the square root of the area, as might be expected intuitively.

This insensitivity and the near equality of $C_1, C_2,$ and C_3 suggest that for an arbitrary sector, average travel time can be approximated

$$E[T_r] \approx \frac{2}{3}\sqrt{\frac{A}{v_x v_x}}, \tag{3.12}$$

provided that the average E-W travel time does not differ too greatly from the average N-S travel time. In fact, for most examples the author has worked out, Equation 3.12 is a remarkably good approximation, even if positions of patrol and incidents are not uniformly distributed. Equation 3.12 appears unsatisfactory only when patrol and/or incidents are concentrated around a small number of points. At one extreme, if the patrol unit is stationed at the center of a square sector whose sides are parallel to directions of travel, the mean travel distance to uniformly distributed incidents would be reduced from 2/3 sector length to 1/2 sector length. At another extreme, if the patrol unit is stationed at a corner of the same sector, the mean travel distance is increased from 2/3 sector length to 1 sector length. But in most actual sectors, effective preventive patrol requires that the patrol unit tour many regions in the sector, not just one or two points. Likewise, incidents are rarely concentrated at just one or two points. Thus, the above results should provide useful guidelines to administrators designing sectors in complex urban environments. Any sector for which Equation 3.12 is not an adequate approximation can be separately analyzed to find mean travel time and other statistics.

Bottoms, Nilsson, and Olson[9] have applied these results to the design of patrol sectors in the Chicago Police Department. Using the models, they have constructed a new sector plan of the city using essentially rectangular sectors designed so that the average intrasector travel time never exceeds approximately three minutes.

The discussion of optimal sector design in this section has focused only on intrasector responses. The problem of optimal sector design is reconsidered in Chapter 8, in which various forms of cooperation among nearby sectors are shown to modify the results obtained here.

3.4. Models Allowing Intersector Dispatching

When an incident is reported from a sector whose patrol unit is busy on a previous assignment, an available unit nearby in another sector is usually assigned. Since a patrol unit typically spends 50 percent or more of its time servicing calls, the need for intersector assignments arises often. Depending on the dispatcher's ability to select an appropriate out-of-sector unit, the travel times of such assignments can be much larger than those associated with intrasector assignments. In large part, the dispatcher's effectiveness depends on the following: (1) his knowledge of the current status of all nearby units (for instance, are all patrol-initiated activities which remove a unit from dispatchable status reported to the dispatcher?); (2) the command role played by the dispatcher (for instance, can an available unit selected by the dispatcher ever refuse an assignment?); and (3) the dispatcher's knowledge of the position of the incident, the positions of nearby units, and street topologies and impediments to travel.

In this section simple models are developed that allow only two states for each unit: available and unavailable. It is assumed that the unit selected by the dispatcher always responds. It is also assumed that the dispatcher does not know the positions of available patrol units, other than the fact each is somewhere in its assigned patrol sector.[10] The focus is on two issues: (1)

9. A. Bottoms, E. Nilsson, and D. Olson, *Third Quarterly Progress Report* (Chicago: Chicago Police Department Operations Research Task Force, 1968).
10. The author has observed instances when even this assumption is not always a valid one. Apparently, a unit will leave its sector occasionally when the patrolman decides that full-time preventive patrol in the sector is not warranted. See R. C. Larson, *Measuring the Response Patterns of New York City Police Patrol Cars*, R-673-NYC/HUD (New York City Rand Institute, 1971).

quantifying alternative dispatching strategies that influence travel time behavior of the system; and (2) examining how travel times increase as the unavailability rates increase.

Chapter 7 examines some of these same issues, where it is assumed that the dispatcher has some more precise type of patrol unit position information.

3.4.1. Dispatching Strategies

Travel time characteristics of the dispatch-patrol system are closely related to the dispatcher's ability to identify and dispatch the most appropriate available unit. For instance, assuming right-angle responses, if the dispatcher knew the exact coordinates (x_j,y_j) of each unit $(j = 1,2,\ldots,J)$ and the exact coordinates (x,y) of the incident, one strategy would be to assign that available unit with minimum total travel time, that is

$$\min\left\{\frac{|x_j - x|}{v_x} + \frac{|y_j - y|}{v_y}\right\}, \quad j \in \text{set of available units.} \tag{3.13}$$

Although this strategy results in the minimal travel time to the current incident, in general, it does not yield minimal average travel time, when the average includes future incidents as well. Particularly when workloads are nonuniformly distributed, one can argue that incurring a slight cost in travel time to the current incident by dispatching, say, the second closest unit may leave the collection of available units in a better state to anticipate future incidents. This idea is rigorously developed in a fire operations context for the case of two cooperating fixed-location fire units by Carter, Chaiken, and Ignall.[11] Their numerical examples suggest that the most significant advantage of selecting other than the closest unit when incidents are nonuniformly distributed is to balance the workloads among units; the travel time reductions achieved by shifting from a closest-unit policy are typically in the order of only 1 or 2 percent. Since it appears very difficult to obtain optimal dispatch strategies for models with more than two units and since nearly minimal travel time is achieved by dispatching the closest unit, closest-unit dispatching is treated here as if it were always the best possible. In implementation, one should recognize that slight modifications to closest-unit dispatching may further improve response behavior by up to 1 or 2 percent.

In most current police department operations, it is not feasible to implement a closest-unit dispatch policy. Not only does the dispatcher not know the positions of the available units (other than the fact that each is somewhere within its sector), he often does not know, or at least take into con-

11. G. Carter, J. Chaiken and E. Ignall, *Response Areas for Two Emergency Units*, R-532-NYC/HUD (New York City Rand Institute, 1971).

sideration, the position of the incident. This idea can best be illustrated by considering two examples with linear concatenated sectors.

On the x-axis, assume sector i covers the interval from $x = i/2$ to $x = (i/2) + 1$ for i even and from $x = -(i + 1)/2$ to $x = -(i - 1)/2$ for i odd, as illustrated in Figure 3.4. Assume further that the position of each available unit is selected from a uniform distribution over the length of the unit's sector.[12] Now, suppose that an incident is reported from $x = 0.25$ (in sector 0). Regardless of his knowledge of the incident's precise position within sector 0, the dispatcher would first attempt to assign unit 0, if available.

Now, how does the dispatcher act if unit 0 is unavailable?

Incident's Position Used

As a first example, assume that the dispatcher knows the incident's position and uses this information if unit 0 is unavailable. Then, if unit 0 is unavailable, the dispatcher tries to assign unit 1 next, which would result in an average travel distance of 0.75 sector length. If unit 1 also is unavailable, unit 2 is tried next, resulting in an average travel distance of 1.25 sector lengths. This searching procedure is continued until the first available unit is found. In essence, the dispatcher is estimating the location of each available unit to be in the center of its patrol sector and is seeking to find that unit with minimum estimated travel distance.

Given some additional assumptions about the distribution of incident positions and about unavailability probabilities, it is not difficult to obtain the average travel distance behavior of this system. For this example, it is further assumed that (1) incident positions are uniformly distributed over the x-axis, independent of patrol positions or other incident positions; and (2) each unit is unavailable with probability ρ, independent of the status of the other units.

Figure 3.4 Infinite array of linear concatenated sectors.

12. This arrangement of sectors could correspond to motorized freeway patrols, for instance, or it could correspond to foot patrols along a street of storefronts.

Simulation studies[13] have shown that this independence assumption is a very good approximation for low to moderate values of ρ, but is inadequate for values of ρ near one. At high values, there is a tendency for unavailable units to "clump" together, thereby invalidating the independence assumption. For this example and for our other analytical models, we will assume independence, recognizing its approximate nature for high values of ρ.

Given the uniform distribution of incidents, we can without loss of generality select the labeling of sectors so that the incident's position is in the left-hand side of sector 0, in the interval $[0,1/2]$. The conditional distribution of the incident's position is uniform over $[0,1/2]$. Now, let state S_i correspond to units $0, 1, \ldots, i - 1$ unavailable and unit i available. Clearly,

$$P\{S_i\} = (1 - \rho)\rho^i \qquad i = 0, 1, 2, \ldots \qquad (3.14a)$$

$$E[D|S_i] = \begin{cases} \frac{1}{3} & i = 0 \\ \frac{1}{4}[2i + 1] & i = 1, 2, \ldots \end{cases} \qquad (3.14b)$$

and,

$$E[D] = \sum_{i=0}^{\infty} E[D|S_i]\, P\{S_i\}. \qquad (3.15)$$

Performing the calculations, we find the mean travel distance for the first example involving linear sectors,

$$E[D] = \frac{1}{3} - \frac{1}{12}\rho + \frac{\rho/2}{1 - \rho}. \qquad (3.16)$$

This function behaves as we expect: It is monotone increasing with ρ, and it blows up as ρ approaches one. Keeping only linear terms in ρ, we find for small ρ,

$$E[D] \approx \frac{1}{3} + \frac{5}{12}\rho. \qquad (3.17)$$

This completes the first example.

The dispatching strategy of this example can be described more precisely as follows: Let $f_{X_j, Y_j}(\cdot,\cdot)$ be the joint probability density function of the coordinates of unit j while patrolling. The dispatcher's estimated position coordinates (x_j^0, y_j^0) of the unit are obtained by a center-of-mass criterion,

13. Simulation studies (see, for example, Chapter 6) have shown that this assumption introduces almost no error into the travel time model for low to moderate values of ρ. However, for high values of ρ (say 0.7 or greater), this assumption brings about slight underestimation of travel time. The elimination of this independence assumption should be an interesting area for future research.

$$x_j^0 = \int_{-\infty}^{\infty} \int_{-\infty}^{\infty} x f_{X_j, Y_j}(x,y)\, dy dx \qquad (3.18a)$$

$$y_j^0 = \int_{-\infty}^{\infty} \int_{-\infty}^{\infty} y f_{X_j, Y_j}(x,y)\, dy dx. \qquad (3.18b)$$

Given an incident reported from (x,y), the dispatcher's strategy is to assign that available unit with minimum estimated travel time, that is,

$$\min \left\{ \frac{|x_j^0 - x|}{v_x} + \frac{|y_j^0 - y|}{v_y} \right\}, \quad j \in \text{set of available units.} \qquad (3.19)$$

Such a strategy is called a modified center-of-mass (MCM) dispatching strategy.

Incident's Position Ignored

Now, what happens if the dispatcher does not consider the exact position of the incident? To illustrate, consider a second example using linear concatenated sectors (Figure 3.4). Again, say the incident is located at $x = 0.25$, but the dispatcher either knows only the sector of the incident or, if he knows its location, he does not use this information. Then, if unit 0 is unavailable, the dispatcher would be indifferent between selecting unit 1 or unit 2, if both were available. It is reasonable to assume that he would be equally likely to choose unit 1 or unit 2 in this case. Thus, the dispatcher is acting as if the available units and the incident are at the center of their respective sectors.

We call the generalization of this strategy a strict center-of-mass (SCM) strategy. More formally, if the incident originates from sector k and if $f_{X,Y}(x,y|k)$ is the conditional joint probability density function for the incident coordinates (X, Y), given the incident occurs in sector k, then the dispatcher acts as if the incident is located at the center-of-mass coordinates of incidents in sector k,

$$E[X|k] = \int_{-\infty}^{\infty} \int_{-\infty}^{\infty} x f_{X,Y}(x,y|k)\, dy dx \qquad (3.20a)$$

$$E[Y|k] = \int_{-\infty}^{\infty} \int_{-\infty}^{\infty} y f_{X,Y}(x,y|k)\, dy dx. \qquad (3.20b)$$

Given an incident reported from sector k, the dispatcher's strategy is to assign that available unit with minimum estimated center-of-mass travel time, that is,

$$\min \left\{ \frac{|x_j^0 - E[X|k]\,|}{v_x} + \frac{|y_j^0 - E[Y|k]\,|}{v_y} \right\}, \quad j \in \text{set of available units.} \quad (3.21)$$

Should this procedure result in a tie (that is, more than one unit with minimal estimated travel time), the tie is broken by random choice. The SCM strategy not only closely approximates current manual dispatching operations, but it has been formally implemented in several semi-automated dispatching systems.[14]

Completing the analysis of an SCM strategy applied to linear concatenated sectors we again assume incidents are uniformly independently distributed over the x-axis, and we focus on an incident occurring in sector 0 at a location uniformly selected over $[0,1]$. For this case let the state S_0 correspond to *unit 0 available* and let the state $S_i (i = 1,2, \ldots)$ correspond to *at least one of the units (2i - 1) or 2i is available and all units 0, 1, . . . , (2i - 2) are unavailable*. Again assuming each unit is unavailable with probability ρ, independent of the status of other units, we obtain

$$P\{S_i\} = \begin{cases} 1 - \rho & i = 0 \\ (1 - \rho^2)\rho^{2i-1} & i = 1, 2, \ldots \end{cases} \quad (3.22)$$

Also, the conditional mean travel distances are easily found,

$$E[D|S_i] = \begin{cases} \frac{1}{3} & i = 0 \\ i & i = 1, 2, \ldots \end{cases} \quad (3.23)$$

Computing the unconditional mean travel distance, we find for an SCM policy and linear sectors

$$E[D] = \frac{1}{3}(1 - \rho) + \frac{\rho}{1 - \rho^2}. \quad (3.24)$$

This function also increases monotonically with ρ and blows up as ρ approaches one. Taking linear terms in ρ, we find for small ρ,

$$E[D] \simeq \tfrac{1}{3} + \tfrac{2}{3}\rho, \quad (3.25)$$

indicating an increase over that obtained with an MCM strategy (see Equation 3.17).

To further compare the two strategies, it is useful to define $\epsilon(\rho) \equiv$ expected value of the difference between travel distances obtained with an SCM policy and an MCM policy, respectively, given a utilization rate of ρ.

We compute $\epsilon(\rho)$ simply by subtracting Equation 3.16 from 3.24, resulting

14. See Section 1.1.

in

$$\epsilon(\rho) = \rho \frac{(1 - \rho)}{4(1 + \rho)} .$$
(3.26)

This function, which illustrates the comparative advantage of an MCM policy over an SCM policy, has the following properties: (1) It is equal to 0 at $\rho = 0$ and $\rho = 1$, indicating no difference between the two strategies, and (2) it is unimodal, reaching a maximum value at $\rho = \sqrt{2} - 1$, at which point $\epsilon(\sqrt{2} - 1) \approx 0.043$. Using expected travel distance as a criterion of worth, we see that MCM is about 6.2 percent better than SCM at $\rho = \sqrt{2} - 1$.

The unimodality of $\epsilon(\rho)$ can be explained as follows: As ρ increases from 0, it is more likely that the dispatcher will have to select an out-of-sector unit, and the advantages of MCM begin to become apparent. However, the only time MCM results in lower mean travel distance than SCM is when both units $(2i - 1)$ and $2i (i = 1,2, \ldots)$ are available and all previous units are unavailable; the likelihood of two such paired units being simultaneously available goes to zero rapidly as ρ increases to one. Thus, the difference in expected travel distances must reach a maximum and then drop back to zero as ρ becomes large.

3.4.2. An Infinitely Large Two-Dimensional Command

Some of the above ideas can now be applied to the two-dimensional analog of the linear sector example. We will find a need to modify slightly the concept of SCM and MCM dispatching strategies.

Consider an infinitely large command comprising a regular lattice of square sectors, as depicted in Figure 3.5. One patrol unit is assigned to each sector and its position while patrolling is selected from a uniform distribution over the area of the sector. Incidents are uniformly, independently distributed over the entire command. We deal directly with travel distance, assuming $v_x = v_y$. According to Figure 3.4, a sector centered at $x = j, y = \ell$ (j, ℓ integers) is called sector (j, ℓ), with corresponding patrol unit (j, ℓ). The focus is on an incident occurring in sector $(0,0)$, whose position is selected from a uniform distribution, independently of the positions of the patrol units. We wish to find how various travel distance properties for this system depend on utilization rates and alternative dispatching strategies.

The following event terminology is useful: E_{ij} = event that patrol unit (i,j) is the unit selected by the dispatcher to respond to the incident in sector $(0,0)$. Given E_{ij}, the travel distance to the incident is

$$(D|E_{ij}) = |X_i - X| + |Y_j - Y|,$$

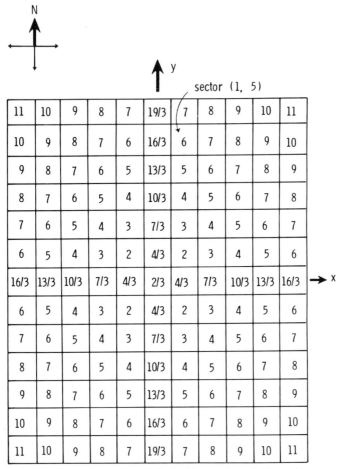

Incident occurs in sector (0,0) in the center of the grid. Using a strict center-of-mass dispatching strategy, the mean travel distance (in sector lengths) from each sector to the scene of the incident is given in each respective sector.

Figure 3.5 A command composed of an infinite grid of square patrol sectors.

where X_i and Y_j are independent random variables uniformly distributed in the intervals $[i - 1/2, i + 1/2]$ and $[j - 1/2, j + 1/2]$, respectively.

Incident's Position Ignored

Now, first consider the case in which the dispatching strategy is SCM, that is, the position of the incident in sector $(0,0)$ is not used by the dispatcher in formulating a dispatching strategy. Then the dispatching decision is made independently of the values assumed by the random variables X, Y, X_i, Y_j. Thus, these four random variables are conditionally independent, given E_{ij}. We find it convenient to group together sectors that are equivalent distances from sector $(0,0)$, defining the events

$$A_i = E_{i0} \cup E_{(-i)0} \cup E_{0i} \cup E_{0(-i)} \qquad i = 1, 2, \ldots$$

$$B_i = \bigcup_{|j|+|\ell|=i} E_{j\ell} \qquad \begin{array}{l} i = 2, 3, \ldots \\ j, \ell \neq 0 \end{array}$$

With the above definitions, there are three required conditional probability density functions for travel distances, all obtained by straightforward arguments (all three functions are plotted in Figure 3.6):

$$f_D\,(\ell|E_{00}) = \begin{cases} 4\ell - 4\ell^2 + \frac{2}{3}\ell^3 & 0 \leqslant \ell \leqslant 1 \\ \frac{16}{3} - 8\ell + 4\ell^2 - \frac{2}{3}\ell^3 & 1 \leqslant \ell \leqslant 2 \\ 0 & \text{otherwise;} \end{cases} \qquad (3.27)$$

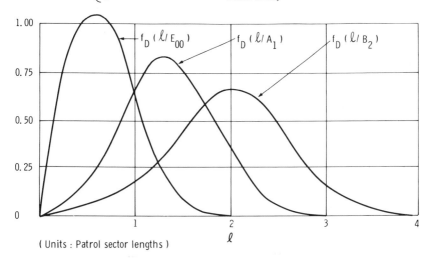

(Units : Patrol sector lengths)

Figure 3.6 Three derived probability density functions.

$$f_D\ (\ell - (i - 1)|A_i) = \begin{cases} \ell^2 - \frac{1}{3}\ell^3 & i - 1 \leqslant \ell \leqslant i \\ \frac{2}{3}\ell^3 - 4\ell^2 + 7\ell - 3 & i < \ell \leqslant i + 1 \\ -\frac{1}{3}\ell^3 + 3\ell^2 - 9\ell + 9 & i + 1 < \ell \leqslant i + 2 \\ 0 & \text{otherwise;} \end{cases} \quad (3.28)$$

$$f_D\ (\ell - (i - 2)|B_i) = \begin{cases} \frac{1}{6}\ell^3 & i - 2 \leqslant \ell \leqslant i - 1 \\ \frac{1}{6}(-3\ell^3 + 12\ell^2 - 12\ell + 4) & i - 1 < \ell \leqslant i \\ \frac{1}{6}(3\ell^3 - 24\ell^2 + 60\ell - 44) & i < \ell \leqslant i + 1 \\ \frac{1}{6}(-\ell^3 + 12\ell^2 - 48\ell + 64) & i + 1 < \ell \leqslant i + 2 \\ 0 & \text{otherwise.} \end{cases} \quad (3.29)$$

The conditional means are

$E[D|E_{00}] = 2/3$

$E[D|A_i] = i + 1/3 \quad i = 1, 2, \ldots$ (3.30)

$E[D|B_i] = i \quad i = 2, 3, \ldots$

(These are shown in the appropriate sectors in Figure 3.5.)

Now, as an SCM strategy has previously been defined, the dispatcher would be indifferent between, say, event A_2 and event B_2. In both cases the estimated center-of-mass travel distance is 2 sector lengths, although the actual mean travel distance associated with A_2 is 7/3 sector lengths. Few dispatchers (including automated ones) that the author has seen take this into account. Yet, it is useful to clarify what is the best decision the dispatcher could make without knowing either the patrol positions or the incident position. This best strategy can be called an *expected strict center-of-mass strategy* $(\overline{\text{SCM}})$; it results when the selection procedure is

$$\min \left\{ \frac{E[|X_j - X|]}{v_x} + \frac{E[|Y_j - Y|]}{v_y} \right\} , \quad j \in \text{set of available units.} \quad (3.31)$$

An $\overline{\text{SCM}}$ dispatching strategy applied to the infinitely large command in Figure 3.5 would result in the following dispatching algorithm:

1. If available, dispatch patrol unit $(0,0)$; STOP. The average travel distance is 2/3 sector length.

2. If unit $(0,0)$ is not available, $i = 1$.

3. If available, dispatch any one of patrol units $(\pm i, 0)$ or $(0, \pm i)$; STOP. The average travel distance is $|i| + 1/3$ sector lengths.

4. If available, dispatch any one of patrol units $(\pm k, \pm \ell)$ such that $|k| + |\ell| =$

$i + 1, 1 \leqslant |k|, |\ell| \leqslant i$; STOP. The average travel distance is $|k| + |\ell| = i + 1$ sector lengths.

5. Increase i by 1. Return to Step 3.

On the other hand, a regular SCM strategy applied to this command would not distinguish steps 3 and 4.

For either strict center-of-mass strategy we would like to obtain the probability density function for the travel distance, not conditioned on which units are available. This is done explicitly for $\overline{\text{SCM}}$; the development for SCM is directly parallel. As for the one-dimensional case, we make the approximating assumption that each patrol unit is unavailable with probability ρ, *independent* of the states of other patrol units. Then, the probability of each event A_k or B_k is obtained by making sector units unavailable from the center outward, in order of increasing estimated travel distance. For sector $(0,0)$,

$$P\{E_{00}\} = 1 - \rho. \tag{3.32a}$$

If unit $(0,0)$ is unavailable, we extend outward from the center and find for $\overline{\text{SCM}}$ dispatching that

$$
\begin{aligned}
P\{A_k\} &= \rho^{[2k(k+1)-3]} (1 - \rho^4), \quad k = 1, 2, \ldots \\
P\{B_k\} &= \rho^{[2k(k-1)+1]} (1 - \rho^{4[k-1]}), \quad k = 2, 3, \ldots
\end{aligned}
\tag{3.32b}
$$

The desired unconditional probability density function for the travel distance is obtained by substituting the above results into the general form of the unconditional probability density function,

$$f_D(\ell) = f_D(\ell | E_{00}) P\{E_{00}\} + \sum_{k=1}^{\infty} f_D(\ell | A_k) P\{A_k\}$$

$$+ \sum_{k=2}^{\infty} f_D(\ell | B_k) P\{B_k\}. \tag{3.33}$$

This function was programmed on a digital computer and is plotted as a function of ℓ and ρ in Figure 3.7. Examining the figure, we observe the distribution of travel distance to become more skewed to the right as ρ becomes larger. This behavior is expected: As ρ increases, the busy probability of the sector unit and the contiguous units increases, thereby increasing the chance that a unit from a distant sector will be assigned.

The mean travel distance is plotted as a function of ρ in Figure 3.8. Note that the mean travel distance is nearly a linear function of ρ for $\rho \leqslant 0.7$. The

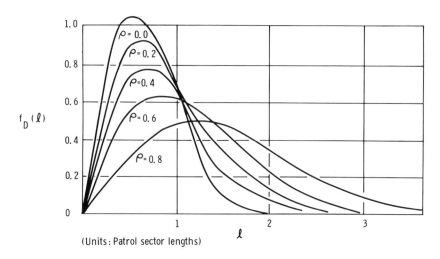

Figure 3.7 Unconditional probability density function of the response distance random variable D.

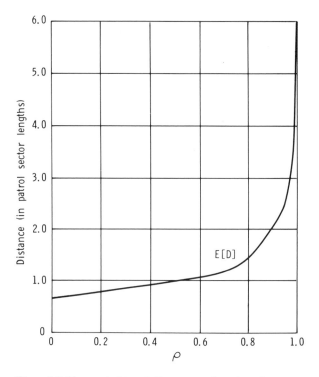

Figure 3.8 Mean patrol travel distance as a function of ρ.

validity of this approximation for $\rho \leqslant 0.7$ is affirmed by examining the first few terms in the series expression

$$E[D] = \tfrac{2}{3}(1 - \rho) + \tfrac{4}{3}\rho(1 - \rho^4) + \tfrac{7}{3}\rho^9[1 - \rho^4] + \cdots + 2\rho^5[1 - \rho^4] + \cdots$$

(3.34)

Taking only linear terms in ρ, we obtain

$$E[D] \approx \tfrac{2}{3}(1 - \rho) + \tfrac{4}{3}\rho = \tfrac{2}{3}(1 + \rho).$$

(3.35)

Essentially, inherent in this approximation is the assumption that either the sector unit associated with the incident or at least one unit in the four contiguous sectors is always available for dispatch. This observation also implies that SCM dispatching is nearly as good as $\overline{\text{SCM}}$ dispatching for this particular two-dimensional command.[15] Thus, although it is straightforward to derive analogous results of SCM dispatching, it is unnecessary for the purposes here.

Incident's Position Used

How is travel time reduced if the dispatcher makes use of the exact position of the incident? To take a simple example, assume an incident is reported from sector $(0,0)$ at $x = 1/2, y = 0$ (on the boundary with sector $(1,0)$). Then, if unit $(0,0)$ is unavailable, the dispatcher should next try to assign unit $(1,0)$, resulting in an average travel distance of $3/4$ sector length. If he does not consider the incident's position and instead selects randomly from any one of the four sectors with a common boundary with sector $(0,0)$, the average travel distance would be $11/8$ sector lengths, an increase of approximately 83 percent over the minimum possible. Of course, an incident on a sector boundary provides the most dramatic travel distance reductions, and other incidents located at interior points do not generally show such large improvements.

Now, given an incident reported from some point (x,y), a dispatcher using this position information would most likely employ the MCM strategy defined in Equation 3.19. However, paralleling the case of SCM dispatching, there is a more general procedure to follow:

$$\min \left\{ \frac{E[|X_j - x|]}{v_x} + \frac{E[|Y_j - y|]}{v_y} \right\}, \qquad j \in \text{set of available units.} \quad (3.36)$$

---

15. In order for $\overline{\text{SCM}}$ dispatching to yield a better decision than SCM dispatching for this command, at least all the units $(0,0)$, $(1,0)$, $(0,1)$, $(-1,0)$, and $(0,-1)$ must be unavailable; in that case a dispatcher following an SCM strategy would be indifferent between unit $(2,0)$, say, and unit $(1,1)$, possibly yielding an extra mean travel distance of $1/3$ sector length. In actual commands without such a regular sector pattern, the differences between the two strategies are likely to be more substantial.

This is called an *expected modified center-of-mass strategy* ($\overline{\text{MCM}}$). In the above example, a dispatcher using an $\overline{\text{MCM}}$ strategy would correctly compute that the expected travel distance between the incident and unit (1,0) is 3/4 sector lengths, whereas use of an MCM strategy would result in an estimate of 1/2 sector length. In practical situations such miscalculations could result in preferences for units different from those obtained with an $\overline{\text{MCM}}$ strategy, possibly resulting in mean travel distances larger than necessary.

However, more striking differences are obtained when comparing MCM or $\overline{\text{MCM}}$ strategies to SCM or $\overline{\text{SCM}}$ strategies. For convenience, definitions of the four center-of-mass strategies are summarized in Table 3.2. Although detailed MCM or $\overline{\text{MCM}}$ response models are not developed here, some simple numerical results indicate the approximate magnitude of the differences.

Table 3.2 Summary of Center-of-Mass Dispatching Strategies

Strategy	Distance Estimation Procedure
1. Strict center-of-mass (SCM)	$\min \left\{ \dfrac{\mid x_j^0 - E[X\mid k] \mid}{v_x} + \dfrac{\mid y_j^0 - E[Y\mid k]\mid}{v_y} \right\}$ $j \in$ set of available units
2. Modified center-of-mass (MCM)	$\min \left\{ \dfrac{\mid x_j^0 - x \mid}{v_x} + \dfrac{\mid y_j^0 - y\mid}{v_y} \right\}$ $j \in$ set of available units
3. Expected strict center-of-mass ($\overline{\text{SCM}}$)	$\min \left\{ \dfrac{E[\mid X_j - X\mid]}{v_x} + \dfrac{E[\mid Y_j - Y\mid]}{v_y} \right\}$ $j \in$ set of available units
4. Expected modified center-of-mass ($\overline{\text{MCM}}$)	$\min \left\{ \dfrac{E[\mid X_j - x\mid]}{v_x} + \dfrac{E[\mid Y_j - y\mid]}{v_y} \right\}$ $j \in$ set of available units

Definitions:
(X_j, Y_j) Random variables indicating position coordinates of patrol unit j

(X, Y) Random variables indicating position coordinates of the incident (conditioned only on the sector of the incident)

(x_j^0, y_j^0) Center-of-mass coordinates of patrol unit j (Equations 3.18)

$(E[X\mid k], E[Y\mid k])$ Center-of-mass coordinates of incidents in sector k (Equations 3.20)

(x, y) Exact position of the incident

Without loss of generality we can assume that the incident in sector (0,0) is located in the east-northeast segment of the sector: $0 \leqslant y \leqslant x \leqslant 1/2$ (Figure 3.5). Each of the four dispatching strategies dictates that unit (0,0) should be dispatched, if available, resulting in an average travel distance of 2/3 sector lengths. If unit (0,0) is not available, both SCM and $\overline{\text{SCM}}$ dictate dispatch of any of the units (1,0), (0,1), (–1,0), (0,–1), yielding an average travel distance of 4/3 sector lengths. On the other hand, assuming unit (0,0) not available, both MCM and $\overline{\text{MCM}}$ require the dispatcher to try unit (1,0) first, resulting in an average travel distance of 23/24 sector length, a 37.5 percent reduction over that obtained with SCM or $\overline{\text{SCM}}$. If unit (1,0) is not available, the dispatcher should next try unit (0,1), resulting in an average travel distance of 29/24 sector length, a 12.5 percent reduction over SCM or $\overline{\text{SCM}}$. Computing the first few terms in a series expression for $E[D]$, we obtain for either MCM or $\overline{\text{MCM}}$ dispatching

$$E[D] \approx 0.667 + 0.292\,\rho + 0.250\,\rho^2 + \cdots \tag{3.37}$$

Computation of additional coefficients in this series becomes quite tedious; for each power of ρ one must further subdivide the region $0 \leqslant y \leqslant x \leqslant 1/2$, and the value of the coefficient is dependent on whether MCM or $\overline{\text{MCM}}$ dispatching is utilized.

Compared to SCM or $\overline{\text{SCM}}$ dispatching, the average amount of travel distance *reduction* possible by employing MCM or $\overline{\text{MCM}}$ dispatching is a unimodal function of ρ (the utilization factor), starting at 0 at $\rho = 0$ and returning to 0 at $\rho = 1$; the maximum appears to be near $\rho = 0.5$. At that value, the average reduction is about 0.1 sector length, or about a 10 percent reduction compared to SCM or $\overline{\text{SCM}}$ dispatching. Although such a reduction may not appear large, automatic car location systems with perfect resolution often do not decrease average travel distance of an SCM dispatching system by more than 10 to 20 percent (see Chapter 7).

3.4.3. A Command of Finite Area

We would like to use the above results to approximate the mean travel time in a finite-area command, at least for sufficiently low utilization rates. At high utilizations we have to consider the possibility of queues forming, and this is treated in Chapter 7.

The command, of total area A_T, is assumed to be divided into N rectangular sectors, each of nearly equal area and designed to minimize mean intrasector travel time (allowing $v_x \neq v_y$, in general). It is assumed that the probability that any particular patrol unit is unavailable for dispatch is equal to ρ.

Finally, it is assumed that the probability of a queue forming is sufficiently small so that we can ignore the different travel time behavior of any dispatches from queues.

Because of the finiteness of the command, there are boundary effects that reduce the number of contiguous sectors a dispatcher can interrogate for a nearby out-of-sector available unit, especially when the incident is in an outlying sector whose patrol unit is unavailable.

For $\overline{\text{SCM}}$ dispatching this has the effect of introducing terms of order ρ^2, ρ^3, and ρ^4 into Equation 3.34, thereby reducing the range of validity of the linear approximation Equation 3.35. Still, one can settle for the linear approximation, realizing that in some commands having few sectors the approximation may slightly underestimate mean travel distance; in practice, the error terms could be added to yield greater accuracy. Using Equation 3.35 with a scaling property, we obtain for either SCM or $\overline{\text{SCM}}$ dispatching

$$E[T_r] \approx \frac{2}{3} \sqrt{\frac{A_T}{N v_x v_y}} (1 + \rho) \quad \text{for } \rho \leqslant 0.7. \tag{3.38}$$

Recognizing that this result is based on several assumptions and approximations, we must apply it with care. However, it does provide a useful approximation to the average SCM or $\overline{\text{SCM}}$ travel time in a command of area A_T with N sectors (each of approximately equal area and workload) and travel speeds v_x and v_y. Incorporated in the result are what is expected to be the first-order interrelationships among these parameters: Mean travel time increases as the square root of the sector area, linearly with utilization ρ ($\rho \lesssim 0.7$) and inversely with travel speed.

Similar approximate results could be obtained for MCM or $\overline{\text{MCM}}$ dispatching, and in general, these results would be more sensitive to boundary effects.

A summary of the assumptions and results of the travel time models in Sections 3.2 to 3.4 is given in Table 3.3 and 3.4.

3.5. Sensitivities to Model Assumptions

In actual urban environments a responding patrol unit may encounter travel impediments such as barriers (for example, rivers or railroad tracks) and one-way streets. The purpose in this section is to explore the sensitivity of model results to several of these complications.[16] In turn, (1) barriers,

16. Some of the results in this section were initially reported in R. C. Larson, *Response of Emergency Units: The Effects of Barriers, Discrete Streets, and One-Way Streets*, R-674-HUD (New York City Rand Institute, 1971).

Table 3.3 Summary of Assumptions of Two-Dimensional Travel Time Models

A. Single Sector

Travel distance between two points (x_1,y_1) and (x_2,y_2) is

$d = |x_1 - x_2| + |y_1 - y_2|$.

Travel speed east–west is v_x; travel speed north–south is v_y.

The positions of the patrol unit and the incident are independent and uniformly distributed over the area of the sector.

The sector geometry can be rectangular, diamond-shaped, or elliptical.

B. Many Sectors (the following additional assumptions are employed)

All sectors are rectangular and designed to minimize mean travel time for intrasector assignments, subject to an area constraint.

One of several center-of-mass dispatching strategies is used.

The utilization rate of each patrol unit is approximated to be independent of the state (busy or patrolling) of every other patrol unit. The utilization rates of all units are equal.

C. Approximation to a Finite Command (the following additional assumption is employed)

The probability that a queue of waiting call reports will form is very small.

Table 3.4 Summary of Results of Two-Dimensional Travel Time Models

A. Single Sector

The mean travel time for an intrasector assignment as a function of sector size and geometry (Sections 3.2.1, 3.2.2, 3.2.3).

For an area-constrained sector, the sector dimensions that (1) minimize mean intrasector travel time and (2) minimize maximum possible intrasector travel time (Section 3.3).

B. Many Sectors

A comparison of four types of dispatching strategies, each of which attempts to select and assign the closest available unit without accurate patrol unit position information.

An approximate form of the unconditional pdf for travel time in a command with many sectors (Equation 3.33), assuming expected strict center-of-mass dispatching.

C. Finite Command

An approximate formula for mean travel time in a finite command with sufficiently small utilization rate (Equation 3.38), assuming strict center-of-mass dispatching.

(2) discrete street grids, and (3) one-way street grids shall be considered. By examining simple models that include these complications, we can get some idea of how each impedes response. A summary of definitions is given in Table 3.5.

Table 3.5 Summary of Definitions for Section 3.5

D	Distance traveled assuming no impediments to travel
D_e	Extra distance traveled
(X_1, Y_1)	Position coordinates of the patrol unit
(X_2, Y_2)	Position coordinates of the incident
b	E–W location of barrier
a	Height of barrier
$\{A_i\}$	A set of mutually exclusive, collectively exhaustive events
$n(m)$	E–W (N–S) number of blocks in rectangular discrete grid sector
$\lfloor x \rfloor$	Largest integer less than or equal to x

3.5.1. Barriers

First the model of a rectangular patrol sector discussed in Section 3.2.1 is reexamined. The purpose is to discover how a barrier that impedes travel increases average travel time. For convenience, we deal directly with travel distance, which is assumed to be right angle.

We again assume that the patrol position (X_1, Y_1) and incident position (X_2, Y_2) are uniformly distributed over the sector and are mutually independent. For this case it is already known (Equation 3.4) that

$$E[D] = \tfrac{1}{3}[X_0 + Y_0]. \tag{3.39}$$

Now assume we erect a negligibly thick barrier of height $y = a$ at $x = b$ (Figure 3.9) $(0 \leqslant a \leqslant Y_0, 0 \leqslant b \leqslant X_0)$. The travel distance for this case can be written as the sum of "old" travel distance and a *perturbation* distance, $D' = D + D_e$,

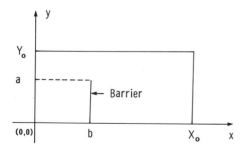

Figure 3.9 Rectangular patrol sector with one partial barrier.

where

D_e = extra distance traveled due to the barrier.

The expected travel distance is

$$E[D'] = E[D] + E[D_e].$$ (3.40)

Since $E[D]$ is known, we need only compute $E[D_e]$. For this purpose we write

$$E[D_e] = \sum_i E[D_e|A_i] \, P[A_i],$$ (3.41)

where the events A_i are mutually exclusive and collectively exhaustive. In particular, consider the events

$A_1 : D_e > 0$

$A_2 : D_e = 0.$

Event A_1 requires that the patrol unit and the incident be on opposite sides of the barrier:[17]

$Y_1 < a$

$Y_2 < a$

$\min [X_1, X_2] \leqslant b$

$\max [X_1, X_2] > b.$

When coordinate positions are uniformly distributed and independent, we easily compute

$$P[A_1] = 2 \left[\frac{b}{X_0} \frac{a}{Y_0} \right] \left[\frac{X_0 - b}{X_0} \frac{a}{Y_0} \right].$$ (3.42)

Conditioned on event A_1, we can write

$(D_e|A_1) = 2 \min [Z_1, Z_2],$

where

$Z_1 = a - (Y_1|A_1)$

$Z_2 = a - (Y_2|A_1).$

Thus, Z_1 and Z_2 are uniformly independently distributed on $[0,a]$. By standard methods, we find

$$E[D_e|A_1] = \tfrac{2}{3} a.$$ (3.43)

17. Points $(x = b, y < a)$ are grouped arbitrarily with all points to the left of the barrier.

Thus, using Equations 3.39 to 3.43, we have the desired result,

$$E[D'] = \frac{1}{3}(X_0 + Y_0) + \frac{4a^2}{3X_0^2 \, Y_0^2} \, b(X_0 - b)a. \tag{3.44}$$

As an example, suppose we have a unit-area square sector with a barrier originating at a boundary half-way point,

$X_0 = Y_0 = 1$

$b = 1/2.$

Then,

$$E[D'] = \frac{2}{3}\left[1 + \frac{a^3}{2}\right]. \tag{3.45}$$

This function is plotted for $0 \leqslant a \leqslant 1$ in Figure 3.10. Note that a barrier of height $a = 1/2$, say, yields a mean travel distance of 0.708, which is only about 6.3 percent greater than the mean travel distance with no barrier (0.677).

We can use Equation 3.44 to find the average travel distance for the case in which a barrier extends completely from $y = 0$ to $y = Y_0$ with one crossing point at $y = a$ (for example, a river at $x = b$ with a bridge at $y = a$). The

Expected total
travel distance

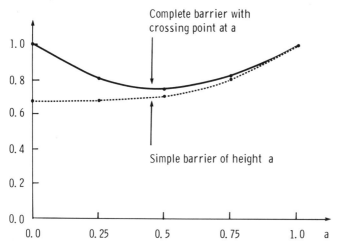

Figure 3.10 Expected total travel distance for a square patrol sector of unit area: two types of barriers.

travel distance for this case can be written

$$D'' = D' + D'_e,$$

where

D'_e = extra distance traveled compared to the distance D'.

By symmetry with the case of one simple barrier,

$$P[D'_e > 0] = 2\left[\frac{b(Y_0 - a)}{X_0 Y_0}\right]\left[\frac{(X_0 - b)(Y_0 - a)}{X_0 Y_0}\right]$$

$$E[D'_e | D'_e > 0] = \tfrac{2}{3}(Y_0 - a).$$

Thus,

$$E[D''] = \frac{1}{3}(X_0 + Y_0) + \frac{4b(X_0 - b)}{3X_0^2 Y_0^2}\,[a^3 + (Y_0 - a)^3]. \tag{3.46}$$

This function is also plotted in Figure 3.10 for the example

$$X_0 = Y_0 = 1, \quad b = 1/2.$$

An interesting and important property of these results is the relative insensitivity of average travel distance to moderately large barriers.

The same methods can be used to examine certain questions of equity of service. As computed earlier, the mean travel distance is averaged over all points in the sector, whereas only those points below $y = a$ experience any degradation in service compared to a situation with no barrier. Points near $y = 0$ experience the most significant degradation. For instance, a point located to the left of a simple barrier at a height y experiences the following mean extra travel distance:

$$E[D_e | y] = \frac{X_0 - b}{X_0 Y_0}(a^2 - y^2), \quad 0 \leqslant y \leqslant a. \tag{3.47}$$

One may also wish to examine the effects of barriers using additional performance measures such as maximum possible extra travel distance and conditional expected extra travel distance, given that the extra distance is positive.

These methods are directly applicable to several operational problems. For instance, they can be used to study the effect of designing sectors around barriers. If the sector boundaries can be made to coincide with the barriers, then the barriers have no effect on intrasector travel distance. If this is attempted, however, care must be taken to consider the amount of intersector dispatches and to assess the effects of the barrier(s) for these responses. If a boundary must be within a sector, the methods can be used to study the effect of alternative sector geometries. In general, the sector design that best achieves some criterion such as minimal average travel time will be modified by the presence of the barrier.

3.5.2. Grid of Streets

We now examine the case in which patrol units and incidents are confined to an n by m grid of equally spaced two-way streets forming square blocks of unit area, as illustrated in Figure 3.11. Assume that the positions of the patrol unit (X_1, Y_1) and the incident (X_2, Y_2) are independent and uniformly distributed over the streets of the grid. In addition, assume that the travel distance D between (X_1, Y_1) and (X_2, Y_2) is a shortest path that remains on the streets of the grid. We wish to obtain an expression for $E[D]$ and compare it to the continuous model of Section 3.2.1.

In the development we allow n and m to assume any nonnegative integer values excluding the trivial case $n = m = 0$. Although n and m are called the

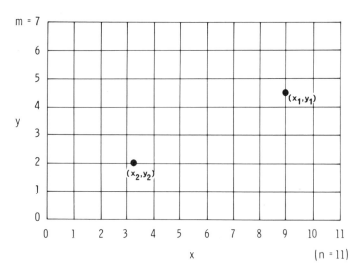

Figure 3.11 Discrete grid representing rectangular patrol sector.

sector dimensions note that because blocks are defined to have unit area, n and m are dimensionless integers.

We write

$$E[D] = \sum_{i=1}^{4} E[D|A_i]P[A_i], \tag{3.48}$$

where the A_i and their probabilities are

A_1: patrol unit and incident both on east-west (E-W) streets

$$P[A_1] = \frac{n^2(m+1)^2}{[(n+1)m + (m+1)n]^2};$$

A_2: patrol unit on E-W street, incident on north-south (N-S) street

$$P[A_2] = \frac{n(m+1)m(n+1)}{[(n+1)m + (m+1)n]^2};$$

A_3: patrol unit and incident both on N-S streets

$$P[A_3] = \frac{m^2(n+1)^2}{[(n+1)m + (m+1)n]^2};$$

A_4: patrol unit on N-S street, incident on E-W street

$$P[A_4] = \frac{n(m+1)m(n+1)}{[(n+1)m + (m+1)n]^2}.$$

Consider event A_1. We can write

$$E[D|A_1] = E[D_x|A_1] + E[D_y|A_1], \tag{3.49}$$

where

D_x = total E-W travel distance,
D_y = total N-S travel distance.

If the patrol unit did not have to follow N-S streets but could travel N-S anywhere, then because X_1 and X_2 are uniformly, independently distributed over $[0,n]$, the mean E-W travel distance would be

$$E[(|X_1 - X_2|)|A_1] = \frac{1}{3}n. \tag{3.50}$$

But if $Y_1 \neq Y_2$ and if X_1 and X_2 both fall in the same set of N-S blocks (that is, if $\lfloor X_1 \rfloor = \lfloor X_2 \rfloor$), then

$$D_x = |X_1 - X_2| + 2\min[V, 1 - W],$$

where

$$V = \min[U_1, U_2]$$
$$W = \max[U_1, U_2]$$

and U_1 and U_2 are uniformly, independently distributed over $[0,1]$. The probability of both X_1 and X_2 falling in the same set of N–S blocks is $\dfrac{1}{n} \cdot \dfrac{m}{m+1}$. Thus we can write

$$E[D_x|A_1] = E[(|X_1 - X_2|)|A_1] + E[2\min(V, 1 - W)]\left[\frac{1}{n}\frac{m}{m+1}\right]. \tag{3.51}$$

By standard methods, we compute the expected value of the perturbation term,

$$E[2\min(V, 1 - W)] = 1/3. \tag{3.52}$$

Using Equations 3.50 to 3.52, we obtain

$$E[D_x|A_1] = \frac{1}{3}\left[n + \frac{m}{n(m+1)}\right]. \tag{3.53}$$

We must now find $E[D_y|A_1]$. Unlike the E–W distance, we can write the N–S distance as the absolute value of the difference of the respective coordinates,

$$(D_y|A_1) = [(|Y_1 - Y_2|)|A_1]. \tag{3.54}$$

For any pair (i, j) $(i = 0, 1, \ldots, m; j = 0, 1, \ldots, m)$,

$$P[Y_1 = i, Y_2 = j] = \frac{1}{(m+1)^2}. \tag{3.55}$$

Using Equations 3.54 and 3.55, we can show that

$$P[D_y = 0|A_1] = \frac{1}{m+1}$$

$$P[D_y = k|A_1] = \frac{2(m - k + 1)}{(m+1)^2} \qquad k = 1, 2, \ldots, m. \tag{3.56}$$

We can now compute

$$E[D_y|A_1] = \sum_{k=0}^{m} kP[D_y = k|A_1].$$

Using Equation 3.56 and the facts that

$$\sum_{i=0}^{m} i = \frac{m(m+1)}{2}$$

and

$$\sum_{i=0}^{m} i^2 = \frac{m(m+1)(2m+1)}{6},$$

we have

$$E[D_y | A_1] = \frac{m(m+2)}{3(m+1)}. \tag{3.57}$$

Combining Equations 3.53 and 3.57, we have the desired conditional expected travel distance,

$$E[D|A_1] = \frac{1}{3}\left[n + m + \frac{m(n+1)}{n(m+1)}\right]. \tag{3.58}$$

Consider event A_3. By symmetry we see this is the same as event A_1 with x and y interchanged. Thus, $E[D|A_3]$ is found by interchanging n and m in Equation 3.58.

Consider event A_2. We have

$$(D|A_2) = [(|X_1 - X_2|)|A_2] + [(|Y_1 - Y_2|)|A_2].$$

For the E-W distance we can write

$$E[(|X_1 - X_2|)|A_2] = \sum_{i=0}^{m} E[(|X_1 - X_2|)|X_2 = i, A_2]\, P[X_2 = i|A_2] \tag{3.59}$$

$$= 2\sum_{i=0}^{n} E[X_1 - X_2 | X_2 = i, X_1 \geqslant X_2, A_2]\, P[X_1 \geqslant X_2 | X_2 = i, A_2]\, P[X_2 = i|A_2].$$

Since X_1 is uniformly distributed on $[0,n]$,

$$E[X_1 - X_2 | X_2 = i, X_1 \geqslant X_2, A_2] = \frac{n-i}{2}; \tag{3.60}$$

$$P[X_1 \geqslant X_2 | X_2 = i, A_2] = \frac{n-i}{n}. \tag{3.61}$$

Since X_2 is uniformly distributed on the integers $0, 1, \ldots, n$,

$$P[X_2 = i|A_2] = \frac{1}{n+1} \qquad i = 0,1,\ldots,n. \tag{3.62}$$

Using Equations 3.60 to 3.62 in Equation 3.59, we obtain

$$E[(|X_1 - X_2|)|A_2] = 2 \sum_{i=0}^{n} \frac{(n-i)^2}{2n(n+1)}$$

or

$$E[(|X_1 - X_2|)|A_2] = \frac{2n+1}{6}. \tag{3.63}$$

Similarly, we obtain

$$E[(|Y_1 - Y_2|)|A_2] = \frac{2m+1}{6}. \tag{3.64}$$

Combining these results, we have

$$E[D|A_2] = \frac{1}{3}(n+m+1). \tag{3.65}$$

Consider event A_4. By symmetry we see this is the same as event A_2 with x and y interchanged. Thus

$$E[D|A_4] = E[D|A_2]. \tag{3.66}$$

Finally, the desired result $E[D]$ is found by substituting the earlier results in Equation 3.48 yielding

$$E[D] = \frac{1}{3}(n+m) + \frac{4n(m+1)m(n+1)}{3[(n+1)m + (m+1)n]^2}. \tag{3.67}$$

For practical problems one wishes to know how closely the continuous formulation (Section 3.2.1) approximates the more exact grid formulation. In fact, one can easily show that

$$\frac{1}{3}(n+m) \leqslant E[D] \leqslant \frac{1}{3}(n+m+1), \tag{3.68}$$

where the left-hand inequality becomes an equality when n or m is zero and the right-hand inequality becomes an equality when $n = m$. Thus, *the continuous approximation is never in error by more than 1/3 block length.*

The percent by which the continuous formulation underestimates the average travel distance is shown for square sectors in Table 3.6 for $n = 1$, $2, \ldots, 10$. While the error for one-block sectors is considerable (33.3 percent), the continuous approximation is quite good (less than 10 percent error) for sectors of dimension five blocks or more.

In police circles there appears to be a continuing debate as to whether sec-

Table 3.6 Comparison of Mean Travel Distances Computed from Continuous and Discrete-Grid Models (square sectors)

n = Sector Dimension (block lengths)	Percent by Which Continuous Formulation Underestimates Mean Travel Distance = $\dfrac{1}{2n+1} \times 100\%$
1	33.3
2	20.0
3	14.3
4	11.1
5	9.1
6	7.7
7	6.7
8	5.9
9	5.3
10	4.8

tor area or sector street mileage is more important in determining travel time characteristics of a sector. Increased street density, as measured in street miles per square mile, has been thought to decrease average travel distance, but the nature of this relationship has remained unexplored because of the lack of a model. Applying the grid model to this question, assume one has a square grid sector of area one square mile in which the spacing between adjacent parallel streets is $1/n$ mile. The street density is $2(n + 1)$ street miles per square mile. The mean travel distance is

$$E[D] = \frac{2}{3} + \frac{1}{3n} \text{ mile.}$$

The relationship between $E[D]$ and street density is plotted in Figure 3.12. Note, for instance, that if the street density is 10 street miles/mile^2, the mean travel distance (0.75) differs from that obtained by the continuous formulation (0.667) by about 12.5 percent. One may conclude that, given the model assumptions, street density can be an important factor in determining mean travel distance, particularly in regions with relatively small street densities. For regions with moderately large street densities, sector area is a much more important factor. (See Section 3.3).

For grid sectors the question of optimal sector design is more difficult than for sectors that can assume noninteger dimensions. With the continuous model (Section 3.3), it is assumed that the sector area must equal a prespecified constraint value A; sector dimensions were then found that mini-

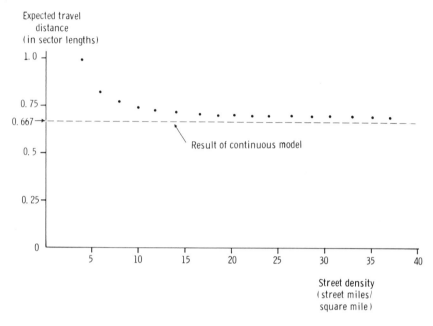

Figure 3.12 Expected travel distance versus street density.

mize mean travel distance (or travel time), subject to the area constraint. As a result of the optimization, it was found that average travel time is quite insensitive to exact sector design, provided the area constraint is maintained and provided the design is reasonably close to the optimal design.

We now wish to explore optimal sector design of grid sectors. As a reasonable area constraint, we require

$$nm \geqslant A. \tag{3.69}$$

The problem is to find values of n and m that minimize $E[D]$, subject to Equation 3.69. It is not difficult to show that the optimal n and m are found by the following algorithm:

Step 1: Set $i = \lceil \sqrt{A} \rceil$, where $\lceil x \rceil \equiv$ smallest integer greater than or equal to x.
Step 2: Set $j = i - 1$ if $i(i - 1) \geqslant A$; otherwise set $j = i$.
Step 3: Set $k = i + 1, l = j - 1$.
Step 4: If $kl \geqslant A$, set $i = k, j = l$; return to Step 3. Otherwise STOP; the optimal sector dimensions are $n = i$, $m = j$.

As an example, suppose $A = 53$ (blocks). Then we are to find that rectangular sector which contains at least 53 blocks and which has minimum possible average travel distance. The steps are as follows:

Step 1: $i = \lceil \sqrt{A} \rceil = 8$.
Step 2: $j = i - 1 = 7$, because $i(i - 1) \geqslant A$.
Step 3: $k = 9, l = 6$.
Step 4: Since $(9) \cdot (6) \geqslant 53, i = 9, j = 6$.
Step 3': $k = 10, l = 5$.
Step 4': Since $(10)(5) < 53$, STOP. The optimal sector dimensions are $n = 9$, $m = 6$.

The average travel distance of the optimal sector is $E[D] \simeq 5.33314$ (block lengths). The average travel distance for a sector with dimensions $n = 8$, $m = 7$ is $E[D] \simeq 5.33331$. Thus, for all practical purposes the two designs are equivalent in achieving minimal average travel distance. By inequality Equation 3.68, we note that the maximum reduction in $E[D]$ that can occur in Steps 3 and 4 is $1/3$ block length. In fact, for most situations, the insensitivity about the optimum is even more pronounced than the inequality suggests. Acknowledging the idealized nature of the grid model and the stated sector design problem, it is still useful to know that such insensitivities reveal a range of design options when other important design considerations (for example, demographic characteristics of a sector) may suggest that one design is preferred to others.

3.5.3 One-Way Streets

As a final examination of model sensitivities, we study the problem of one-way streets. Assuming one-way constraints, it is not difficult to imagine situations in which a relatively nearby patrol unit may have to travel a rather roundabout route to reach the scene of an incident. A question of interest is, "How do one-way travel constraints increase travel distances or travel times?"

In an attempt to answer this question, the results of a model detailed elsewhere are summarized. We assume that patrol units and incidents are confined to a discrete grid of equidistant one-way streets, the direction of travel alternating from street to street (Figure 3.13). As in the previous section, we assume that the positions of the patrol unit (X_1, Y_1) and the incident (X_2, Y_2) are independent and uniformly distributed over the grid. It is also assumed that the travel distance D' from (X_1, Y_1) to (X_2, Y_2) is a shortest path that remains on the streets of the grid and obeys the one-way constraints.

Analysis of this model reveals the following facts for large sectors:

1. If the incident is in front of the patrol unit (that is, if the patrol unit does not effectively have to make a U-turn), the average extra distance traveled due to one-way constraints is 1 block length;

2. If the incident is behind the patrol unit and if the next cross street allows the unit to turn in the direction of the incident, the average extra distance traveled caused by one-way constraints is 2 block lengths;

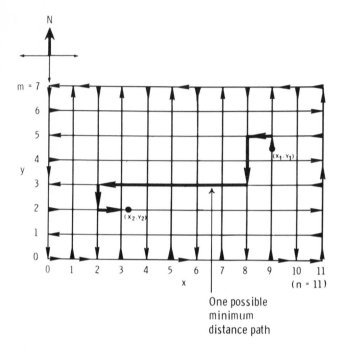

Figure 3.13 Discrete grid representing rectangular sector with one-way streets.

3. If the incident is behind the patrol unit and if the next cross street does not allow the unit to turn in the direction of the incident, the average extra distance traveled due to one-way constraints is 4 block lengths; 25 percent of these responses incur an average of 6 extra block lengths.

If we assume a response speed of 12 mph and a block length of 0.1 mile, those responses requiring an average of 6 extra block lengths incur an increase of 3 minutes in average travel time.

3.6. Some Issues Related to Data Collection

When applying models of response time in an actual city, one usually designs data collecting procedures to derive numerical estimates of model parameters and to test the validity of certain model assumptions. The general topic of parameter estimation and model validation is a far reaching one and there is not space here to treat many of the issues involved.[18] However, in view of the importance of the right-angle distance metric assumption in many of the

18. Some of the results in this section were initially reported in R. C. Larson, *Measuring the Response Patterns of New York City Police Patrol Cars*, R-673-NYC/HUD (New York City Rand Institute, 1971).

models, a procedure is proposed that can be used to test the reasonableness of that assumption. To carry out the procedure, it is necessary for the officers of each patrol unit to record the unit's position and odometer mileage at time of dispatch and at the scene of the incident. This procedure is discussed in Section 3.6.1.

Some effects are also discussed of data truncations that are likely to arise in a data collecting effort. For instance, "How does one estimate average mileage traveled if the data are truncated to the nearest mile or tenth of a mile?" This and related questions are discussed in Section 3.6.2. A summary of definitions is given in Table 3.7.

3.6.1. Test of the Right-Angle Distance Metric

If the positions of the patrol unit and the incident are (x_1, y_1) and (x_2, y_2), respectively, and if the coordinate axes are defined parallel to directions of travel, then the right-angle distance metric requires that the travel distance be

$$d = |x_1 - x_2| + |y_1 - y_2|.$$

In an experiment in which we record the initial and final response coordinates, there is no guarantee that travel directions will be parallel to any prespecified set of coordinate axes. In fact, since street directions change from one area to another, the right-angle travel distance could assume any value between

$$\sqrt{(x_1 - x_2)^2 + (y_1 - y_2)^2} \text{ and } \sqrt{2} \sqrt{(x_1 - x_2)^2 + (y_1 - y_2)^2}.$$

One way to test the reasonableness of the right-angle distance metric is to measure the Euclidean travel distance for each response, to compute the ratio

Table 3.7 Summary of Definitions for Section 3.6

Ψ	Angle at which the directions of travel are rotated ($0 \leqslant \Psi \leqslant \pi/2$)
R	Ratio of the right-angle and the Euclidean distances
$F_R(\ )$	Cumulative distribution function of R
σ_R^2	Variance of R
θ	A random variable distributed over $[0,1]$
K	Recorded (quantized) mileage for a journey (K is an integer)
α	An additive time constant
J	Recorded (quantized) time (J is an integer)
S_c	K/J

of the recorded travel distance to the measured Euclidean distance, to plot the empirically found cumulative distribution of this ratio, and to compare this to the theoretical distribution. This is particularly convenient because the theoretical distribution, given the validity of the right-angle metric and given an isotropy assumption, does not depend on the origin and rotation of the particular coordinate system used.

Consider two points (x_1, y_1) and (x_2, y_2) defined relative to any fixed coordinate system. Let $\Psi (0 \leqslant \Psi \leqslant \pi/2)$ be the angle at which the directions of travel are rotated with respect to the straight line connecting the two points. Given Ψ, the right-angle travel distance between (x_1, y_1) and (x_2, y_2) is (Figure 3.14)

$$d = [\cos \Psi + \sin \Psi] \sqrt{(x_1 - x_2)^2 + (y_1 - y_2)^2}.$$

Thus, given Ψ, the ratio of the right-angle and the Euclidean distances is

$$(R \mid \Psi) = \cos \Psi + \sin \Psi = \sqrt{2} \cos \left(\Psi - \frac{\pi}{4} \right).$$

The cumulative distribution function of R is

$$F_R(\nu) = P[R \leqslant \nu]$$

$$= P \left[\sqrt{2} \cos \left(\Psi - \frac{\pi}{4} \right) \leqslant \nu \right]. \tag{3.70}$$

Now, if we make the isotropy assumption that Ψ is uniformly distributed over the interval $[0, \pi/2]$

$$F_R(\nu) = 2 \int_{\cos^{-1}(\nu/\sqrt{2}) + \pi/4}^{\pi/2} \frac{2}{\pi} \, d\mu,$$

or

$$F_R(\nu) = 1 - \frac{4}{\pi} \cos^{-1} \left(\frac{\nu}{\sqrt{2}} \right), \quad 1 \leqslant \nu \leqslant \sqrt{2}. \tag{3.71}$$

This function is plotted in Figure 3.15. The probability density function is

$$f_R(\nu) = \frac{d}{d\nu} F_R(\nu) = \frac{4}{\pi} \frac{1}{\sqrt{2 - \nu^2}}, \quad 1 \leqslant \nu \leqslant \sqrt{2}. \tag{3.72}$$

The median is $\sqrt{2} \cos (\pi/8) \approx 1.306$. The mean and variance are

$$E[R] = \frac{4}{\pi} \approx 1.273 \tag{3.73}$$

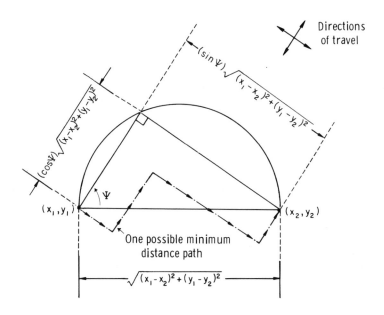

Ψ = Angle of rotation of street grid, relative to the straight line connecting (x_1, y_1) and (x_2, y_2).

$(R \mid \Psi)$ = Conditional ratio of right angle and Euclidean travel distances, given Ψ

= $\cos \Psi + \sin \Psi$

Figure 3.14 Relationship between right angle and Euclidean travel distances, given a rotated street grid.

$$\sigma_R{}^2 = 1 + \frac{2}{\pi} - \frac{16}{\pi^2} \approx 0.0155. \tag{3.74}$$

Thus on the average, the patrol unit travels about 1.273 times the Euclidean distance (given the model assumptions). A reasonable test of the right-angle distance metric would be to compare the empirical distribution of ratios of recorded travel distances and Euclidean distances to $F_R(\ )$ and to compare the empirically found average R to 1.273.

It is reasonable to question the isotropy assumption because most sector designs are such that Ψ will not be uniformly distributed between 0 and $\pi/2$.

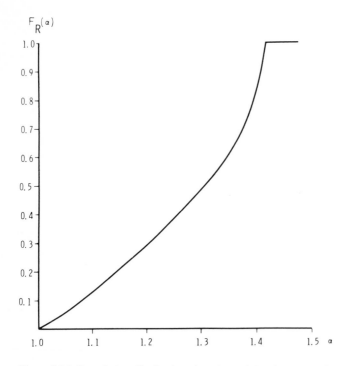

Figure 3.15 Cumulative distribution function of R, the ratio of the right-angle and Euclidean travel distances.

For instance we would expect a square sector whose sides are parallel to travel directions to yield an $E[R]$ greater than $4/\pi$, because "diagonal" responses appear more likely. To find $E[R]$ for a square sector, assuming the positions of the incident and the patrol unit are uniformly and independently distributed, we write

$$R = \frac{1 + R_{yx}}{\sqrt{1 + R_{yx}^2}},$$

where R_{yx} is the ratio of the N–S and E–W travel distances,

$$R_{yx} = \frac{D_y}{D_x}.$$

(See Section 3.2.1.) Since

$$f_{D_x,D_y}(x,y) = 4(1 - x)(1 - y) \qquad 0 \leqslant x \leqslant 1, 0 \leqslant y \leqslant 1,$$

it is easy to derive the pdf for R_{yx}. The result is

$$f_{R_{yx}}(r) = \begin{cases} \dfrac{2}{3} - \dfrac{1}{3}r & 0 \leqslant r \leqslant 1 \\[2mm] \dfrac{2}{3r^2} - \dfrac{1}{3r^3} & 1 \leqslant r < \infty. \end{cases} \tag{3.75}$$

Now the desired result is found by computing

$$E[R] = \int_0^\infty \frac{1+r}{\sqrt{1+r^2}} f_{R_{yx}}(r) \, dr.$$

Then we obtain

$$E[R] = \frac{1}{3}[5 \log(1+\sqrt{2}) + \sqrt{2} - 2]$$

$$\approx 1.274. \tag{3.76}$$

Thus, in this square sector, the patrol car travels an average of 1.274 times the Euclidean distance. This confirms the intuition that square sectors yield a greater $E[R]$, but the result is closer to $4/\pi$ than we might have previously expected.

For a square sector rotated at a $45°$ angle to the directions of travel, intuition might lead one to think that $E[R]$ would be less than $4/\pi$. To investigate this conjecture it is useful to observe that

$$|x_1 - x_2| + |y_1 - y_2| = \sqrt{2} \max[|x_1' - x_2'|, |y_1' - y_2'|],$$

where the primed variables are defined relative to a coordinate system rotated at $45°$ with respect to the original coordinate system. Then,

$$E[R] = \sqrt{2} \int_0^1 \int_0^1 \frac{\max[x,y]}{\sqrt{x^2+y^2}} 4(1-x)(1-y) \, dx \, dy,$$

yielding

$$E[R] = \frac{1}{3}[4\sqrt{2} \log(1+\sqrt{2}) + 2\sqrt{2} - 4]$$

$$\approx 1.271. \tag{3.77}$$

Again, intuition is correct but again the result is closer to $4/\pi$ than might otherwise have been expected.

Therefore, we may conclude that it is still reasonable to compare an empirically found average R to 1.27 to test the right-angle distance hypothesis. However, certain sector designs may modify the isotropy assumption so that the distribution $F_R(\ )$ given in Equation 3.71 may not be entirely valid.

3.6.2. Some Effects of Data Truncation

Many of the data entries in an actual experiment will be truncated,[19] either to the nearest minute or to the nearest mile or tenth of a mile. In this section we discuss some of the quantitative effects of such truncations.

Travel Distances

Assume that recorded travel distances are quantized, where the unit of quantization is 1 mile.[20] Then for a journey of length D, the recorded travel distance equals the sum of D and the accumulated odometer mileage at the moment of dispatch since the last odometer reading change, the sum truncated to the largest integer in the sum. This recorded travel distance can either underestimate or overestimate the actual travel distance by as much as 1 mile. Such errors are particularly troublesome when we consider that many responses are in the 0.25 to 2.0 mile range. A 0.9 mile journey could be recorded as a zero-mileage journey; or, a 1.05 mile journey could be recorded as a two-mile journey. A question of interest is, "How can we extract meaningful inferences from these data?"

Let

D = actual travel distance,
θ = a random variable distributed over the interval $[0,1]$.

If θ represents the accumulated odometer mileage at the moment of dispatch since the last odometer reading change, then the recorded mileage for the journey K can be written

$$K = \lfloor D + \theta \rfloor, \tag{3.78}$$

where

$\lfloor X \rfloor$ = greatest integer less than or equal to X.

It is convenient to think of θ as a random "phase angle." The sets of (D,θ) pairs that give rise to different values of K are shown in Figure 3.16.

From physical considerations, the following assumptions seem reasonable:
1. The random variables D and θ are independent;
2. Here θ is uniformly distributed over the interval $[0,1]$.

Given these assumptions, if the cumulative probability distribution of D is known, say $F_D(\ )$, then the probability distribution for K is readily com-

---

19. As the discussion will show, these truncations are not simple "roundings" of a number to an integer but involve an additive "phase angle" before rounding.
20. With a simple redefinition of a unit of distance, this discussion is applicable to other levels of quantization (for example, tenth-of-a-mile quantizations).

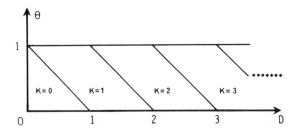

D = Travel distance
θ = Random phase angle
K = ⌊D + θ⌋

Figure 3.16 Sets of (D, θ) pairs that generate different values of K.

puted:

$$P[K = k] = \int_0^1 d\theta \, [F_D(k + 1 - \theta) - F_D(k - \theta)], \qquad k = 0,1,2,\ldots \qquad (3.79)$$

Regardless of the functional form of $F_D(\ )$, one can show that

$$E[K] = E[D] \qquad (3.80)$$

$$E[K^n] \geqslant E[D^n] \qquad n = 2,3,\ldots \qquad (3.81)$$

Thus, (1) here K is an unbiased estimator of $E[D]$; (2) the variance of K (that is, $E[K^2] - E^2[K]$) is greater than or equal to the variance of D. To obtain Equation 3.80 and 3.81, it is convenient to write

$$E[D^n] = \sum_{k=0}^{\infty} \int_0^1 (k + u)^n f_D\,(k + u)\,du, \qquad n = 1, 2, \ldots. \qquad (3.82)$$

Similarly,

$$E[K^n] = \sum_{k=0}^{\infty} \int_0^1 E[\lfloor D + \theta \rfloor^n | D = k + u]\, f_D(k + u)\, du, \qquad n = 1, 2, \ldots. \qquad (3.83)$$

But, if $D = k + u$,

$$\lfloor D + \theta \rfloor^n = \begin{cases} k^n & \text{with probability } 1 - u, \\ (k + 1)^n & \text{with probability } u. \end{cases}$$

Thus,

$$E\left[\lfloor D + \theta \rfloor^n \mid D = k + u\right] = k^n(1 - u) + (k + 1)^n u. \tag{3.84}$$

For $n = 1$, we see that the integrands of Equations 3.82 and 3.83 are identical and thus Equation 3.80 is shown to be true. For $n = 2, 3, \ldots$, it is clear that Equation 3.81 will hold if

$$(k + u)^n \leqslant k^n(1 - u) + (k + 1)^n u, \qquad k = 0, 1, 2, \ldots \tag{3.85}$$
$$0 \leqslant u \leqslant 1.$$

But Equation 3.85 is easily shown to be true by expanding both sides and comparing term by term.[21]

In the context of a data gathering experiment, several observations about Equations 3.80 and 3.81 are relevant. First, for the statistical average of the recorded mileages to be an unbiased estimator of the *true* average travel distance, it is necessary that *zero-mileage* journeys be recorded and used in the statistical tabulations. Second, since the results do not depend on the level of quantization, it is appropriate to estimate $E[D]$ by averaging together responses quantized to the nearest mile as well as those quantized to the nearest tenth of a mile. Third, since in all likelihood the variance of any estimator using K will be greater than the variance of the corresponding estimator using D, sample sizes will have to be larger, in general, than they would have to be if one had direct samples from $F_D(\ )$.

Recorded Times

Truncations similar to those of the previous sections occur when durations of activities are computed. Assume an activity commences at time T_1 and terminates at time T_2. The exact duration of the activity is $T_2 - T_1 \equiv T$.

Now assume that the times are recorded by some mechanism that records time x as $\lfloor x + \alpha \rfloor$, for some fixed α. For instance, a time-stamp clock is usually set to record a time m minutes, s seconds, as m minutes (that is, $\alpha = 0$). For a person who rounds to the nearest minute, $\alpha = 0.5$. As long as α is fixed, its exact value is not important.[22] Using this mechanism, the recorded duration of the activity is $\lfloor T_2 + \alpha \rfloor - \lfloor T_1 + \alpha \rfloor$.

The *random phase* assumption for the case of time truncations implies that $T_1 - \lfloor T_1 \rfloor$ is uniformly distributed over $[0,1]$ and is independent of $T_2 - T_1$. Both of these assumptions are very reasonable for call-processing activities in the police response system. Given these assumptions, the discussion of the

21. The inequality 3.85 is strict everywhere except at the endpoints, $u = 0$ and $u = 1$. Thus, Equation 3.81 is a strict inequality as long as D has some nonzero probability of assuming a noninteger value, a very reasonable assumption in practice.
22. In fact, the value of α may be unknown.

previous section applies directly once we identify the correspondence:[23]

$D : T_2 - T_1 = T$

$\theta : T_1 + \alpha - \lfloor T_1 + \alpha \rfloor \equiv \phi$

$K : \lfloor T_2 + \alpha \rfloor - \lfloor T_1 + \alpha \rfloor \equiv J.$

Of particular importance in experimental work, J is an unbiased estimator of $E[T]$, but its variance, in general, is larger than that of T.

Computed Speeds

Both distance and time truncations of the type discussed here come into play when computing response speeds, making statistical inference of actual speeds a very difficult problem. For instance, a journey whose recorded time is zero minutes yields an infinite measured response speed; a journey whose recorded distance is zero miles yields a response speed of zero. In this final section the general directions of the statistical biases are investigated.

For a journey of length D and duration T, the effective travel speed is

$$S \equiv \frac{D}{T}.$$

The average effective speed is

$$E[S] = E\left[\frac{D}{T}\right].$$

In practice, the computed travel speed S_c is obtained by taking the ratio of two truncated variables, that is,

$$S_c \equiv \frac{K}{J},$$

where

K = truncated travel distance,

J = truncated travel time.

We wish to show that S_c is biased estimator of $E[S]$, the bias tending to overestimate actual effective travel speeds, that is,

$$E[S_c] \geqslant E[S]. \tag{3.86}$$

To obtain this result, it is convenient to write

---

23. The analogue of Equation 3.78 is $J = \lfloor T + \phi \rfloor$. It is obtained by writing

$J = \lfloor T_2 + \alpha \rfloor - \lfloor T_1 + \alpha \rfloor = \lfloor T_2 + \alpha - (\lfloor T_1 + \alpha \rfloor) \rfloor$
$\quad = \lfloor T_2 + \alpha + \phi - T_1 - \alpha \rfloor = \lfloor T_2 - T_1 + \phi \rfloor = \lfloor T + \phi \rfloor.$

$$E[S] \equiv \sum_{k=0}^{\infty} \sum_{j=0}^{\infty} \int_0^1 \int_0^1 Q_1(k,j,u,v) f_{D,T}(k+u, j+v) \, du \, dv, \tag{3.87}$$

where

$f_{D,T}(.,.)$ = joint probability density function of D and T,

$$Q_1(k,j,u,v) = \frac{(k+u)}{(j+v)}.$$

Now the expected truncated travel speed can be written

$$E[S_c] = \sum_{k=0}^{\infty} \sum_{j=0}^{\infty} \int_0^1 \int_0^1 E[S_c(\theta,\phi) \, | D = k+u, T = j+v] f_{D,T}(k+u, j+v) \, du \, dv$$

$$\tag{3.88}$$

where $E[S_c(\theta,\phi)|D = k + u, T = j + v]$ = conditional expected truncated travel speed, given $D = k + u$ and $T = j + v$, the expectation taken with respect to the phase angles θ and ϕ.

From physical considerations, it is reasonable to assume that θ and ϕ are statistically independent of D and T and of each other. Given this assumption, one can write[24]

$$E[S_c(\theta,\phi)|D = k+u, T = j+v] = \int_0^1 \int_0^1 \frac{\lfloor k+u+\theta \rfloor}{\lfloor j+v+\phi \rfloor} \, d\theta \, d\phi$$

$$= [k(1-u) + (k+1)u] \left[\frac{1}{j}(1-v) + \frac{1}{j+1} v \right]$$

$$\equiv Q_2(k,j,u,v). \tag{3.89}$$

Comparing Equations 3.89 and 3.88 with 3.87, we note that Equation 3.86 will be true if

$$Q_2(k,j,u,v) \geqslant Q_1(k,j,u,v) \quad \begin{aligned} &k = 0, 1, \ldots, \\ &j = 0, 1, \ldots, \\ &0 \leqslant u \leqslant 1, \\ &0 \leqslant v \leqslant 1. \end{aligned} \tag{3.90}$$

But Equation 3.90 is readily verified by direct computation, and thus Equation 3.86 must be true.

Without further assumptions, it is not possible to obtain an upper bound

24. For the case $j = 0$, one can set $(1/j) = +\infty$.

for $E[S_c]$. In fact, if J has a nonzero probability of assuming the value zero, $E[S_c] = +\infty$.

A similar argument shows that measured inverse travel speeds are biased estimators of actual mean inverse travel speeds, again the bias tending toward overestimation, that is,

$$E\left[\frac{1}{S_c}\right] \geqslant E\left[\frac{1}{S}\right]. \tag{3.91}$$

Thus, in estimating typical values of travel speeds and inverse travel speeds, statistics such as medians should be more helpful than means. In fact, means can be in error by very large amounts.

3.7. Summary

Our tour of travel time models in this chapter has focused on single-sector designs, intersector dispatching strategies and associated travel times, impediments to travel, and data collection. Using analytical models, we have sought to gain physical insights into operating properties of the response process that are not readily obtainable from other means, for instance emperical tables of travel times.

First (in Section 3.1) we discussed the interrelationships among travel times, distances, and effective travel speeds. The effective travel speed is equal to the trip mileage divided by the travel time and thus averages out all speed fluctuations due to traffic, making turns, and so forth. Since inverse effective travel speed is the critical variable in determining travel times, a large average effective travel speed does not necessarily imply a small average travel time. As an illustration, actual average effective travel speeds could be 20 mph or more while the average travel time and average travel distance could appear to yield an effective travel speed of 10 mph or less. Stated another way, average travel distance divided by average travel time could be 10 mph or less, while the actual average travel speed could be 20 mph or more. This arises because one response with very small travel speed effects the travel time average much more than several responses with relatively large speeds. For the case of uncorrelated distances and inverse speeds, this property is summarized by an inequality Equation 3.1 which, if not recognized, could result in an underestimate of mean travel times or mean effective travel speeds.

Section 3.2 focused on the effects of sector geometry upon mean intrasector travel times. For each of three models it is assumed that the positions of the patrol unit and the incident are independent and uniformly distributed and that travel distance is right-angle, indicating an urban street grid. For comparable sectors, elliptical sectors were found to have the lowest mean travel time, followed by diamond-shaped sectors and rectangular sectors. However, the mean travel times in comparable elliptical and rectangular sectors differ by less than 3 percent. These results indicate a general insensitivity of mean travel time to the particular class of geometric shape of the sector, provided the shape is not too irregular.

Given that a sector is to have a particular general shape (for example, rectangular), we were also interested in the problem of selecting its dimensions (Section 3.3). For each of the three sector geometries of Section 3.2, sector dimensions were found that minimize average intrasector travel time, subject to the constraint that the sector have a specified area. The minimal achievable mean travel time is nearly equal (less than 3 percent difference) for all three sector shapes and is achieved by designing the sector so that average E–W travel time equals average N–S travel time. These same sector dimensions also minimize the maximum possible travel time in the sector. For comparable sectors, the minimum maximal travel time is lowest for diamond-shaped sectors, is 13.0 percent greater for elliptical sectors, and is 41.4 percent greater for rectangular sectors. Traditional police administration texts have recommended circular or square sectors as a rule-of-thumb for minimizing intrasector travel times. Our derived sector dimensions indicate that for either criterion—average intrasector travel time or maximum possible intrasector travel time—square or circular sectors are optimal only when effective east-west and north-south speeds are equal.

Further examination of the models revealed a general insensitivity to exact sector dimensions, however. For area-constrained sectors in which average east-west and north-south travel times do not differ too greatly, say by a factor of 2 or more, the total average intrasector travel time is quite close to the minimum possible. This insensitivity led to a formula (Equation 3.12) for average intrasector travel time (in terms of sector area and travel speeds) that should provide a useful approximation in complex urban environments. This result suggests that for well-designed sectors in which effective east-west and north-south speeds are equal, average intrasector travel distance is approximately equal to two-thirds the square root of the sector area.

This approximate result also provides insight into a trade off between travel time and preventive patrol coverage. If the patrol unit were not initially positioned at a *random* point in its sector caused by preventive patrol duties but rather were placed near the sector center, the factor of two-thirds in the formula could be reduced to one-half. This implies that most patrol administrators are willing to incur an average intrasector travel distance (or time) 25 percent greater than the minimum possible in order to provide patrol coverage for the entire sector.

The general nature of the relationship between travel time and sector area also has broader policy implications. Incremental changes in the total number of patrol units, which would modify sector areas, will have small effects on average intrasector travel distance (or time), which varies only as the square root of the sector area. For instance, a 10 percent increase in the total number of patrol units would result in only a 5 percent decrease in average intrasector travel time. In order to achieve a 50 percent decrease in average intrasector travel time, it would be necessary to quadruple the total number of patrol units.

Next models were examined allowing intersector dispatching (Section 3.4). Given that an intersector dispatch must be made, the dispatcher's ability to identify and select the most appropriate out-of-sector car is critical in maintaining reasonably small travel times. The focus in Section 3.4 was on dispatching strategies that minimize estimated travel time, assuming that the dispatcher has no information regarding the position of available patrol units other than the fact that each is patrolling somewhere in its respective sector. Four such strategies were identified, two in which the dispatcher takes account of the exact position of the incident and two in which he does not. The latter two are strict center-of-mass stragegies (SCM and $\overline{\text{SCM}}$) and the former are modified center-of-mass strategies (MCM and $\overline{\text{MCM}}$). Their definitions are summarized in Table 3.2. The SCM strategy is probably the model that most closely approximates most current dispatching operations, either manual or automated. Yet, each of the other three provides better estimates of travel times and each is implementable without an expensive automatic car locator system.

To illustrate the difference between SCM and MCM strategies, we first examined linear concatenated sectors. Such sectors could correspond to motorized freeway patrols or to foot patrols along a street of storefronts. The following assumptions were made:

Each available patrol unit is positioned randomly in its own sector according to a uniform distribution;

Each patrol unit is unavailable with probability ρ, independent of the status of other patrol units;

Incidents are uniformly distributed over the entire region of patrol, independent of the positions of patrol units or other incidents;

The dispatcher selects that unit he believes to be closest to the incident, using either a strict center-of-mass or a modified center-of-mass strategy.[25]

The mean travel distance as a function of ρ was found for each type of dispatching strategy (Equations 3.16 and 3.24). The MCM offered the greatest average improvement over SCM at $\rho \approx 0.414$, at which point the average travel distance experienced with MCM is about 6.4 percent less than that experienced with SCM. For the case in which the sector unit is busy and the two units in contiguous sectors are free, the MCM reduces mean travel distance from 1 sector length to 3/4 sector length, a 25 percent reduction.

The two-dimensional analog (Figure 3.5) of the straight line sector configuration provided illustrations of the differences among all four dispatching strategies. The dramatic differences occur when comparing MCM or $\overline{\text{MCM}}$ strategies to SCM or $\overline{\text{SCM}}$ strategies. The average travel time for particular dispatches can be decreased 40 percent or more by shifting from an SCM or $\overline{\text{SCM}}$ strategy to an MCM or $\overline{\text{MCM}}$ strategy. Averaged over all dispatches, MCM or $\overline{\text{MCM}}$ can decrease average travel times by as much as 10 percent, compared to those obtained with SCM or $\overline{\text{SCM}}$. Thus, whenever possible, the dispatcher should be aware of the exact position of the incident and use this information when selecting an out-of-sector unit.

For modeling current SCM strategies, a formula (Equation 3.38) was proposed that should serve as a useful approximation for computing mean travel time in cities which employ an SCM strategy. This formula is used in the resource allocation algorithm in Chapter 5.

The effects of barriers and street grids (both one-way and two-way) on travel time were studied in Section 3.5. Barriers of two types were studied: partial and complete barriers. The first extends part way into a sector, possibly corresponding to a park or cemetary. The second cuts through the entire sector, with one crossing point, possibly corresponding to a river with one bridge in the sector. Expressions 3.44 and 3.46 for mean travel distance were found for both types, assuming a rectangular sector with uniformly and independently distributed incidents and patrol. Equation 3.44 revealed a general insensitivity of the mean travel distance to small- and moderate-sized barriers (Figure 3.9). Even complete barriers affect mean travel distance by a smaller amount than we might have expected intuitively. However, the pres-

25. For linear concatenated sectors, there is no difference between SCM and $\overline{\text{SCM}}$ strategies or between MCM and $\overline{\text{MCM}}$ strategies.

ence of a barrier degrades the level of service differently in different parts of a sector, causing possible marked increases in mean travel distance in certain areas.

Next the case was examined in which patrol units and incidents are confined to a rectangular grid of equidistant two-way streets (Figure 3.11). Incident and patrol positions were assumed to be independent and uniformly distributed over the grid. The travel distance between the patrol unit's initial position and the incident position was assumed to be a shortest path that remains on the streets of the grid. Examination of this model revealed that the mean travel distance computed from the continuous model (Section 3.2.1) is never in error by more than 1/3 block length.

The effects of street density (that is, street miles per square mile) on travel distance and the problem of optimal sector design were also examined with the two-way street grid model. Street density was found to be a much less critical factor in determining mean travel time than sector area. (Figure 3.12). For the sector design problem, a procedure was given which finds the grid dimensions (n and m) that minimize mean travel distance, subject to the constraint that the sector have an area at least equal to A (that is, $nm \geqslant A$). Insensitivities to exact sector dimensions were found to parallel those found for the continuous model.

For one-way streets, the question was asked, "How is mean travel distance increased when a responding unit is constrained to travel one-way streets?" As in the previous section, it was assumed that the positions of the patrol unit and the incident are independent and uniformly distributed over a grid. It was also assumed that the travel distance from the patrol unit's initial position to the incident is a shortest path that remains on the streets of the grid and that obeys the one-way constraints. Quoting results derived elsewhere, it was found that for large grids the average extra distance traveled due to one-way streets is 2 block lengths. Slightly over 6 percent of all responses require an additional average travel distance of 6 block lengths. If response speed is 12 mph and a block length is 0.1 mile, the one-way constraints cause travel time to be increased an average of 3 minutes in these cases.

In Section 3.6 several issues were examined pertaining to data collection and model validation. Given the importance of the right-angle distance metric in many of the travel time models, a procedure was devised to test the reasonableness of that metric. Implementation of the test requires that the passenger officer record the patrol unit's position and odometer reading at time of dispatch and at time of arrival at the scene. The test centers about the random variable R, the ratio of the right-angle and Euclidean distances between two points. The value of R depends on the angle at which the mutually perpendicular directions of travel are rotated with respect to a straight line connecting the two points. The mean value of R was found to be remarkably insensitive to alternative sector designs that one may think would markedly affect it. The models suggest that the average value of R should be quite close to 1.27. This means that, on the average, a unit responding in an urban environment travels about 1.27 times the straight line distance, as the crow flies. This prediction should not be difficult to test in practice.

We finally examined the effects of data truncations that are likely to occur in measuring travel times and travel distances. The recorded travel distance is the sum of the actual travel distance and the accumulated odometer mileage since the last change in mileage reading, the sum truncated to the largest integer in the sum. Such crude roundings can cause large errors since many responses are in the 0.25 to 2.0 mile range. However, given some physically reasonable assumptions, we showed that the truncated travel distance is an unbiased estimator of the true average travel distance (Equation 3.80). This result holds regardless of the level of quantization (for example, mile or tenth of a mile), as long as zero-mileage journeys are used in the statistical tabulations. The variance of the truncated distance is usually greater than the variance of the true distance. Next we demonstrated that directly analogous results apply to time truncations that are likely to characterize data of the police response system. Finally we showed that effective travel speeds computed by dividing the truncated travel distance by the truncated travel time are biased estimators of average effective travel speed, the bias tending toward overestimation (Equation 3.86). A similar statement (Equation 3.91) applies to effective inverse speeds computed in this manner. Thus, such statistics as medians are more appropriate for estimating typical values of effective travel speeds and effective inverse travel speeds.

4

Models of Preventive Patrol

Preventive patrol, as discussed in Chapter 1, is the second major activity of
radio-dispatched patrol units. And frequently the amount of time spent on
preventive patrol exceeds the amount of time spent answering calls for service. Thus, cost considerations alone make preventive patrol an important
activity. But more fundamentally, such patrol is supposed to prevent crime
by removing crime hazards and to deter crime by posing the threat of apprehension. Thus, preventive patrol is supposed to play a key role in affecting
overall levels of crime.

Given the theoretical importance of patrol, it is somewhat surprising that
no widely accepted methods are employed for determining the need for
patrol. Hazard formulas, as discussed in Section 1.4, include such factors as
number of arrests, number of licensed premises, and number of reported
crimes; but such indicators of workload do not provide information relating
crime and patrol strengths to measures of performance. Moreover, such indicators can wrongly indicate a need for additional personnel in high arrest
rate areas where actual needs may be in low arrest rate areas with overworked
personnel.

Apparently many cities determine the level of preventive patrol effort after
the fact, treating time on patrol as the time left over after other duties are
performed. This can have the perverse effect of providing most patrol during
least busy hours and least patrol during busiest hours. This property is shown
in Figures 4.1 and 4.2,[1] which depict typical 24-hour profiles of radio-
dispatched patrol cars in New York City in 1969 in Precincts 103 and 105.
From Figure 4.1, for instance, 73 hours of preventive patrol was provided
in Precinct 105 from midnight to 8:00 A.M. on February 18, 75 hours from
8:00 A.M. to 4:00 P.M., and 57 hours from 4:00 P.M. to midnight. Fully
54 percent of the day's *radio run* (call-for-service) activity occurred during
the 4:00 P.M. to midnight tour, whereas only 28 percent of the day's preventive patrol effort occurred during this period. The midnight to 8:00 A.M.
tour incurred only 12.5 percent of the radio run activity but received 36 percent of the preventive patrol effort. While the desired nature of the relationship between call-for-service activity and preventive patrol activity is not

1. R. C. Larson, "Measuring the Response Patterns of New York City Police Patrol Cars,"
R-673-NYC/HUD (New York City Rand Institute, 1971), pp. 32, 34.

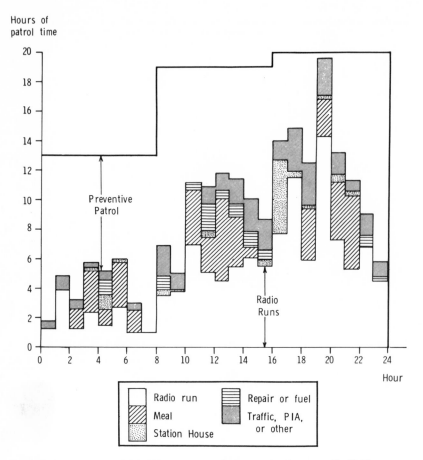

Figure 4.1 Twenty-four-hour activity profile, Precinct 105, February 18, 1969.

known, it would be very surprising if more preventive patrol is consistently required when fewer calls for service are received.[2]

In an experiment recently performed in St. Louis, the patrol force was split into a responsive force and a preventive force.[3] The responsive force serviced

2. Patrolling officers during early morning hours provide eyes for a sleeping citizenry, which would indicate a need for at least a minimal amount of patrol during these hours to detect crimes and other unusual events. But it is doubtful if the imbalances in preventive patrol strength that are often observed over a 24-hour period can be justified solely on these grounds. Evidence of the boredom of excessive early morning patrol is provided by recently published reports of patrolmen sleeping in their cars during these hours. (*The New York Times*, August 3, 1969, p. 68; Sept. 1, 1971, pp. 1, 44.)

3. *Allocation of Patrol Manpower Resources in the St. Louis Police Department*, vols. 1 and 2, report of St. Louis Police Department, 1968.

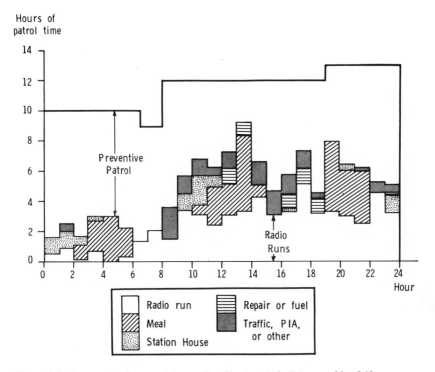

Hours of
patrol time

Figure 4.2 Twenty-four-hour activity profile, Precinct 103, February 28, 1969.

calls from the public while the preventive force concentrated on crime preventive patrol. The advantage of the partitioning, said the proponents, is that
when both responsive and preventive tasks are performed by the same patrol
unit, the officer has a tendency to consider the responsive tasks his job, while
time spent patrolling as time between jobs. On the other hand, with a partitioning members of the preventive force would consider crime prevention
their prime responsibility. In carrying out the experiment, the number of
units needed on the responsive force was determined from call-for-service
data and a model of patrol operations, thereby satisfying a performance criterion for responsive activities. But whatever remaining units were available for
assignment were assigned to the preventive force. There was no attempt to
define performance criteria for preventive patrol activities and to address the
trade offs between responsive and preventive activities. Thus, this St. Louis
experiment is a specific example in which the level of preventive patrol is
determined by the resources remaining after allocating for calls for service.

   In addition to determining the required levels of patrol, there are important questions regarding the methods of patrol. For radio-dispatched units, the randomness of patrol has received much recent attention. Historically, patrol started in a most nonrandom manner in many departments, where fixed-position police call boxes were used to monitor a foot patrolman's progress through his beat. In these departments, the patrolling officer was to traverse a given route, calling in from designated call boxes at preassigned times. But such predictable patrol patterns pose little deterrent threat of apprehension to potential criminals. The current prevalence of motorized patrol has reduced the number of such foot beats, but the need for unpredictability remains in all types of patrol.

Stressing the need for unpredictable patrol patterns, R. D. Smith[4] introduced the term *random patrol* into police literature in 1960. Blumstein and Larson (1967) developed a simple analytical model for spatially uniform random patrol in order to estimate the probability that police would pass and detect a crime in progress.[5] Elliot (1969) quoted one of Koopman's search theory results and attempted also to compute probabilities of space-time coincidence of crime and random patrol.[6] Bottoms, Nilsson, and Olson (1968) have applied some of these ideas to operational problems in the Chicago Police Department.[7]

Even given this recent interest, there is still a great need for further experimental and analytical work aimed at determining the relationships between crime and patrol and at providing patrol administrators with improved methods for planning and managing preventive patrol activities. The work in this chapter is just an initial attempt to provide some of the necessary analytical results.

First, it is assumed that various parts of the city are to receive differing levels of preventive patrol attention, or coverage. The patrolling unit is assumed to traverse the streets in an unpredictable manner but on the average

4. R. D. Smith, *Random Patrol* (Washington, D.C.: Field Service Division of the International Association of Chiefs of Police, 1960).
5. A. Blumstein and R. C. Larson, "A Systems Approach to the Study of Crime and Criminal Justice," in *Operations Research for Public Systems*, P. M. Morse and L. W. Bacon, eds. (Cambridge, Mass.: The M.I.T. Press, 1967), pp. 159–180.
6. J. Elliot, "Random Patrol," in *Law Enforcement Science and Technology II, Proceedings of the Second National Symposium on Law Enforcement Science and Technology* S. Cohn, ed. (Chicago, Ill.: Illinois Institute of Technology Research Institute, 1969), pp. 557–560.
7. A. Bottoms, E. Nilsson, and D. Olson, *Quarterly Progress Reports* (Chicago: Police Department Operations Research Task Force, 1968).

passing each point as frequently as indicated by the level of coverage for that point. These assumptions lead to a model for predicting the average patrol frequency at each point, or equivalently, the average time between patrol passings. Incorporated in this result is the fraction of time busy on other activities, thereby explicitly indicating the trade off between patrol intensity and time spent responding to calls for service. The model can be used to predict the probability that a unit will pass (and perhaps detect) an incident of specified duration. If the incident is a crime, this serves as an estimate of the crime-intercept probability.

After examining various other features of the model, the problem of determining the required patrol coverages is addressed. The question of interest is, "Given the recent pattern of crimes and given a limited amount of preventive patrol, how should the patrol effort be allocated along streets to best achieve some objective?" Applying some of Koopman's search theory ideas to this problem, one finds that the allocation that maximizes apprehension probability depends in a rather complicated way upon recent crime rates, again indicating the inadequacy of a linear hazard formula. But the method illustrated needs much more refinement, including experimental test, before implementation by police.

A summary of required further work, both analytical and experimental, is given in Section 4.3. A summary of definitions is given in Table 4.1.

4.1. Patrol Frequency Model
First a model is developed that predicts the average frequency of patrols in terms of the following quantities:
Speed of patrol
Street miles in a sector
Fraction of time spent patrolling
A patrol coverage function.

Initially a patrol sector is considered in which no calls for service are generated. That is, the only function of the patrol unit is to patrol the D miles of streets in the sector. Although the D street miles crisscross in a complicated pattern, imagine placing the individual street segments end-to-end on a one-dimensional scale (say the x-axis) in such a way that any point on a street in the sector corresponds uniquely to some point x, where $0 \leqslant x \leqslant D$. Then, we assume that analysis of crime trends and patrol effectiveness has helped us to specify a patrol coverage function $e(x)$ such that

Table 4.1 Summary of Definitions for Chapter 4

D	Number of street miles in a patrol sector
$e(\cdot)$	Patrol coverage function ($0 \leqslant e(\cdot) \leqslant 1$)
L	Average effective street mileage per sector sweep
$\nu(x)$	Average patrol frequency at a point x
$t(x)$	Average time between patrol passings at x
ρ	Fraction of time a unit is performing activities other than patrol
$P(x, \ell)$	Probability that point x is passed on a patrol of length ℓ
T_c	Sector coverage time, or time to traverse all street segments in a sector at least once
$p(x)$	Probability density function for the location of a crime
P	Probability of patrol passing a crime
Φ	A measure of the total amount of patrol available

$0 \leqslant e(x) \leqslant 1$ ($0 \leqslant x \leqslant D$). The function $e(x)$ is intended to show the relative amount of patrol attention given to various points within the sector. A point x_1 for which $e(x_1) = 1$ is a point that would receive, on the average, the maximum possible patrol coverage. A less important point x_2 for which $e(x_2) = 0.25$, for instance, would receive on the average one-fourth the coverage of the point x_1. That is, on the average, point x_2 would be passed by the patrol unit one-fourth as often as point x_1.

We now wish to derive certain simple properties of the patrol passing process. To do this, one must make some assumptions about the manner in which actual patrol occurs or should occur in a sector. Since so few studies of preventive patrol have been reported, the feasibility of any set of assumptions would have to be checked in actual operating conditions. We will assume that the patrolling unit selects a nondeterministic patrol path which, on the average, yields the relative amounts of patrol coverage required by the coverage function $e(\cdot)$. To achieve the required randomness, we imagine that the patrol sector is divided into n street segments (possibly corresponding to the segments between adjacent intersections) and that the coverage function $e(\cdot)$ is constant for all x ($0 \leqslant x \leqslant D$) corresponding to one segment. Since a segment may be traversed in either of two directions of travel, it is helpful to consider separately the two ways of passing a point (that is, from the left and from the right). After a segment is traversed in a particular direction, another segment and direction of traversal are selected by a Markov trial, the outcome of which depends only on the segment just traversed and direction of traversal.[8] Clearly, the topology of streets would greatly limit the number of possible outcomes of any particular trial. Yet, on the average, this method of patrol could produce the required patrol coverages specified by $e(\cdot)$.[9]

4.1.1. Average Effective Street Mileage per Sector Sweep

Now we wish to consider the integral

$$L = \int_0^D e(x)\,dx. \tag{4.1}$$

Since $e(x)$ is a piecewise-constant function, the integral is always well defined. Here L is the average effective street mileage per sector sweep. By this terminology it is meant that L is the average distance traveled between passings of any point x for which $e(x) = 1$, that is, a point of maximum patrol coverage. This is seen as follows: Assume the patrolling process is in the steady state and select an arbitrary segment of the patrol path of infinitesimal length $\delta\ell$. A point x_0 is said to be *passed* by the segment if the segment overlaps x_0. Since the process is in the steady state, the probability that the segment overlaps x_0 is proportional to $e(x_0)\delta\ell$. Clearly, the normalizing factor is L^{-1}, therefore the desired overlap probability is $[e(x_0)\delta\ell]/L$. Since successive street segments and directions of traversal are assumed to be selected according to a Markov chain, one can assume that passings of the point x_0 from a particular direction form a renewal process. (Note that distance in this model plays the role usually associated with time in a renewal process.) Since the total passings of x_0 are found by summing the passings in each of two directions, the total patrol passing process at x_0 is the pooled output of two renewal processes. We now use the well-known renewal theory result that

8. To avoid lengthy discussion of special cases of questionable practical significance, it is assumed that the Markov chain is aperiodic and irreducible. For an introduction to Markov chain analysis, see, for example, Emanuel Parzen, *Stochastic Processes* (San Francisco: Holden-Day Publishers, 1962), Chapter 6.

9. One could postulate coverage functions that are infeasible in the sense that the topology of streets prohibits a patrolling car from achieving the desired relative patrol coverages. For example, one might specify that a particular one-way street segment should be heavily patrolled and that all connecting segments should not receive any patrol. Although the question of feasibility is an interesting one, we will deal only with feasible coverage functions. Recently, the topic of feasible coverages has been discussed by M. Rosenshine, "Contributions to a Theory of Patrol Scheduling," *Operational Research Quarterly* 21 (1970), pp. 99–106.

the mean time between renewals is equal to the inverse of the steady-state rate of occurrence of renewals, even if the renewals constitute the pooled output of several simple renewal processes.[10] Since the steady-state rate of renewals at x_0 is $e(x_0)/L$, the average distance traveled between renewals is $L/e(x_0)$; thus the average distance traveled between passings of any point x such that $e(x) = 1$ is equal to L, as asserted.[11]

4.1.2. Patrol Frequency

The distance L can be transformed into time by assuming a patrol speed s (in mph). Then, the earlier results imply that the patrol-passage rate at x is

$$v(x) = \frac{se(x)}{L} \text{ (patrols per hour)}. \tag{4.2}$$

The mean time between passings is the reciprocal,

$$t(x) = \frac{L}{se(x)}. \tag{4.3}$$

In addition, in a short time period $\tau [\tau \ll t(x)]$, the probability that the patrol unit will pass the point x is approximately $\tau se(x)/L$.

If all sectors in a city were designed to have equal L, then all points of equal patrol importance would receive equal patrol intensity. The parameter L thus appears to be a better indicator of the street mile patrol workload in a sector than is the total street mileage D.

It is assumed to this point that the patrol unit has no-call-answering duties. In actual operation, a patrol unit typically spends 50 percent or more of its time answering calls and performing other nonpatrol activities. If it is assumed that a fraction ρ of a patrol unit's time is spent performing activities other than patrol, then the average patrol frequency at point x in the sector is reduced to[12]

---

10. D. R. Cox, *Renewal Theory* (New York: John Wiley & Sons, 1962).
11. This result can also be obtained by modeling the patrol passing process as transitions in a two-state semi-Markov process where the current state corresponds to the direction of travel of the last passing. For an introduction to semi-Markov processes, see for example, R. A. Howard, "Systems Analysis of Semi-Markov Processes," *IEEE Transactions on Military Electronics*, MIL-8 (1964), pp. 114–124 or S. M. Ross, *Applied Probability Models with Optimization Applications* (San Francisco: Holden-Day Publishers, 1970).
12. Consider a long time interval T. A fraction ρ of the period T is spent answering calls and a fraction $1 - \rho$ is spent performing patrol. When performing patrol, the patrol rate is the usual $se(x_0)/L$. Thus the expected number of patrol passings in time T is

$$T \frac{se(x_0)}{L} (1 - \rho)$$

$$v(x) = \frac{se(x)}{L}(1 - \rho).$$
(4.4)

This result indicates directly how increased call-for-service activity, as reflected by a larger ρ, diminishes preventive patrol intensity.

Assuming reasonable parameter values in applying this result to several cities, the average patrol frequency is computed to vary widely from about 0.05 patrols per hour (usually in residential areas) to over 6 patrols per hour (most often in densely populated core areas).

4.1.3. Distribution of Distance Traveled between Passings

Given the Markov trial assumption, the distance traveled between passings of a point x_0 is associated with the recurrence time in a semi-Markov process. A state of the process corresponds to a particular segment and direction of traversal. The occupancy time of a state is equal to the length (in miles) of the corresponding segment. In a particular application, it may be useful to apply semi-Markov methods to derive the distribution of distance traveled between passings.[13]

A much cruder approximation to the distribution of recurrence time can be obtained by following a method of Koopman.[14] Imagine that the patrol car performs a patrol of length ℓ miles. Divide the patrol path into n segments such that $\ell/n \ll 1$. In the steady state, the probability that a particular segment of length (ℓ/n) overlaps with a point x_0 is $(\ell/n)[e(x_0)/L]$. If the patrol is long enough and if the patrol is random, that is, selected according to $e(\cdot)$, the positions of the vast majority of the n segments are independent of the position of any particular segment. Then the probability that at least one segment overlaps with x_0, $P_n(x_0, \ell)$, is

$$P_n(x_0, \ell) = 1 - \left(1 - \frac{\ell e(x_0)}{nL}\right)^n.$$

We now let n become increasingly large (that is, we divide the patrol path into smaller segments) and obtain

$$P(x_0, \ell) = \lim_{n \to \infty} P_n(x_0, \ell) = 1 - e^{-\ell e(x_0)/L}.$$
(4.5)

---

or, on the average, there are

$$\frac{se(x_0)}{L}(1 - \rho)$$

patrol passings per unit time.

13. See Howard, "Systems Analysis" and Ross, *Applied Probability*.
14. B. Koopman, "The Theory of Search, Parts I, II, and III," *Operations Research* 4 and 5 (1956-1957), pp. 324-346, 503-531, and 613-626.

If we assume a patrol speed s and length of patrol t, then

$$P(x_0, st) = 1 - e^{-ste(x_0)/L}$$

$$= 1 - e^{-\nu(x_0)t}. \tag{4.6}$$

4.1.4. Sector Coverage Time

It is important to note that with random patrol, $t(x)$ (as defined in Equation 4.3) is not equal to the average time to patrol all the street miles in a patrol sector, but rather the average time between passings of a point x. Between these passings, certain other points may be passed several times and other points may not be passed at all.

For instance, a 10-mile sector with $e(x) = 1$ for $0 \leqslant x \leqslant 5$ and $e(x) = 1/2$ for $5 < x \leqslant 10$ has $L = 7.5$ miles. Traveling at 10 mph, the average time between passings of a maximum coverage point is 45 minutes. With deliberate routing the minimum time required to traverse all streets in the sector can be as small as 60 minutes. But with random patrol the average time to traverse all streets in the sector at least once could be much greater than 60 minutes.

The time required to patrol every point in a sector at least once is called the *sector coverage time* T_c. In the general case, statistics of T_c are found by examining the time required for the semi-Markov patrol model to occupy at least once any set of states containing all street segments. However, the computations are tedious and no general formula appears to be available.

4.1.5. Unknown Coverage Function

In applications one may not know $e(x)$. This can arise because no attempt has been made to determine what $e(x)$ should be and then forward this information to the patrol unit. In such a situation, actual coverages as determined by the patrol unit can only be estimated by monitoring certain points in the sector and counting the numbers of patrol passings in a given period of time.

Without $e(x)$, given only the total street mileage D and speed of patrol s, one may wish to assign some physical significance to the patrolling time D/s. It is clear that D/s is not the average time between passings of an arbitrary point x_0 unless $e(x) = 1$ for all x, where $0 \leqslant x \leqslant D$. Still, using the coverage function concept, it is possible to obtain an interpretation for D/s.

Assume we select some point X in the sector, with the probability of choosing $x \leqslant X \leqslant x + dx$ proportional to $e(x) dx$. That is, we favor points of higher patrol coverage in direct proportion to $e(x)$. Given $X = x$, the average time between patrol passings is $t(x) = L/se(x)$ where $e(x) > 0$. Now, the average time between patrol passings, not conditioned on a value of X, is

$$\int_0^D t(x) \frac{e(x)}{L} dx = \int_0^D \frac{L}{se(x)} \frac{e(x)}{L} dx = \frac{D}{s}.$$

Thus, D/s is the average time between patrol passings of a point in the sector selected from the pdf $e(x)/L$, where $0 \leqslant x \leqslant D$.

4.2. Allocation of Preventive Patrol Effort

Perhaps the most perplexing problem encountered in the allocation of police patrol forces is the determination of the need for preventive patrol. The purpose of this section is to introduce one possible conceptual framework for the problem.

4.2.1. Koopman's Formulation

Koopman[15] derives the optimal distribution of search effort for a situation similar to that of police preventive patrol.[16] His notation and police patrol terminology are used here.

Assume we know the probability density function $p(x)$, where $p(x) dx$ is probability that a crime which occurs in the sector takes place between x and $x + dx$. We have shown earlier that it is not unreasonable to approximate with an exponential law the probability $P(x, st)$ that a patrol unit passes a point x during a time interval of length t. Thus, if there is a probability $p(x) dx$ that a crime of duration t will take place in the interval $(x, x + dx)$, the probability that it will occur in this interval and be passed is

$$p(x) [1 - e^{-\nu(x)t}] dx,$$

where we have assumed independence of the positions of crime and patrol.[17] The overall probability of patrol passing a crime of duration t is

$$P = \int_{-\infty}^{\infty} p(x) [1 - e^{-\nu(x)t}] dx. \qquad (4.7)$$

Koopman calls $\nu(x)t$ the search density $\phi(x)$.

As a special case of Equation 4.7, if patrol is uniform (that is, if $\nu(x) = \nu$), then

$$P = P^0 \equiv 1 - e^{-\nu t}. \qquad (4.8)$$

15. *Ibid.*
16. Koopman's method has been generalized by J. de Guenin, "Optimum Distribution of Effort: An Extension of the Koopman Basic Theory," *Operations Research* 9 (1961), pp. 1–7.
17. See Section 4.3.1 for a discussion of this assumption.

In this case, intercept probability[18] is independent of the spatial distribution of crimes. The motivation for allocating patrol more heavily in high crime areas is to obtain intercept probabilities greater than P^0.

A measure of the total amount of (patrol) search available is given by the positive constant

$$\Phi \equiv \int_{-\infty}^{\infty} \phi(x)\,dx. \tag{4.9}$$

For the preventive patrol problem,

$\Phi = st$ (miles).

One reasonable statement of the preventive patrol allocation problem is as follows: Find the preventive patrol frequency function $v(x)$ where $v(x) \geqslant 0$, which of all functions satisfying Equation 4.9 maximizes the expression P given in Equation 4.7.

4.2.2. Koopman's Solution
The solution to this problem (obtained by Koopman) is as follows:

Step 1. Graph the natural logarithm of the given pdf $p(x)$ for all x at which $0 < p(x) < +\infty$.

Step 2. Draw a horizontal line H, and keeping it always parallel to the x-axis, move it up or down until the area S above this line H and under curve $y = \log p(x)$ has a value precisely equal to the total available quantity of searching effort Φ. Mark as $A = A_1, A_2$, and so forth the perpendicular projection onto the x-axis of the segments cut off from H by the graph $y = \log p(x)$.

Step 3. The answer: No patrol should be made *outside* the intervals A_1, A_2, and so forth. *Inside* these intervals, the function $v(x)t$ should be equal to the length cut off by H and y from the vertical line drawn for the fixed x in question.

4.2.3. Example
To illustrate these ideas, consider the following simple example:[19]

$s = 5$ mph,

$D = 10$ miles,

$t = 3$ minutes $= 0.05$ hour, and

$p(x) = \dfrac{1}{2(e^5 - 1)}\, e^{x/2}, \quad 0 \leqslant x \leqslant 10.$

18. The terms *passing probability* and *intercept probability* are used interchangeably, recognizing that passing or intercepting a point on a street at which a crime is taking place does not imply detection or apprehension.
19. These parameters are chosen for analytical tractability. It is doubtful, for instance, that an actual patrol sector would be characterized by a crime distribution which is an increasing exponential function of distance.

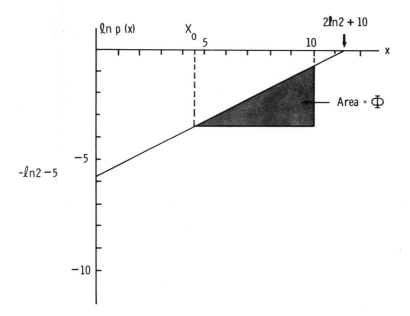

Figure 4.3 Graph of *ln p (x)* versus *x* for the example of preventive patrol allocation.

That is, we have one patrol sector in which the patrolling unit has no call answering duties and we have mapped the street pattern onto the x-axis in such a way that crime density grows exponentially with distance. We write

$$\log p(x) \approx -\log 2 - 5 \log e + \frac{x}{2} \log e$$
$$= -\log 2 - 5 + \frac{x}{2} = y.$$

This function is graphed in Figure 4.3. For this example, the search effort is $st = 0.25$ mile. We must determine x_0 (Figure 4.3) so that the triangular region has an area equal to $\Phi = 0.25$. The appropriate value is $x_0 = 9$. Thus, the method suggests that patrol effort should be allocated only to the worst mile of the 10-mile sector and that, within this mile, effort should be proportional to $x - 9$ where $9 \leqslant x \leqslant 10$. We thus obtain the optimal coverage function

$$e(x) = \begin{cases} x - 9 & 9 \leqslant x \leqslant 10 \\ 0 & \text{otherwise,} \end{cases} \tag{4.10}$$

which is plotted in Figure 4.4. The effective street miles per sector sweep is

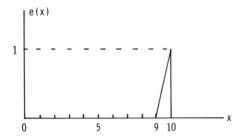

Figure 4.4 Optimal coverage function for the example of preventive patrol allocation.

$$L = \int_0^{10} e(x)\,dx = \frac{1}{2}\text{ mile,}$$

and the patrol frequency (in passes per hour) is

$$v(x) = \begin{cases} 10(x-9) & 9 \leqslant x \leqslant 10 \\ 0 & \text{otherwise.} \end{cases}$$

We can compute the crime intercept probability, given an optimal allocation. We have

$$P = \int_{-\infty}^{\infty} p(x)\left[1 - e^{-v(x)t}\right] dx$$

$$= \int_9^{10} \frac{1}{2(e^5-1)} e^{x/2} \left[1 - e^{-10(x-9)(0.05)}\right] dx$$

$$\approx 0.09.$$

That is, on the average, 9 out of 100 crimes of duration three minutes will be passed by deploying patrol effort according to $e(x)$, as given in Equation 4.10.

One can compare this probability to that obtained for any other coverage function. For instance, assume that patrol effort is allocated uniformly over the entire sector (that is, that $e(x) = 1, 0 \leqslant x \leqslant 10$). Then

$$P = P^0$$

$$= 1 - e^{-vt}$$

$$\approx 0.025.$$

That is, with uniform random patrol, intercept probability is only 0.025 compared to 0.09 for optimal random patrol.

Table 4.2 Summary of Results of Chapter 4

1. The average distance traveled between passings of a point of maximum patrol coverage (Equation 4.1).

2. The average frequency of patrol passings of a unit with call-answering duties (Equation 4.4).

3. The probability of space-time coincidence of a patrol unit and an independently located incident of known duration (Equations 4.6 and 4.7).

4. An illustrative method for the allocation of preventive patrol effort (Section 4.2).

The probability that any particular crime will occur in the interval [9.75,10] is approximately 0.118. One could argue that the best strategy for the patrol car would be to patrol the worst quarter mile in a strictly periodic manner, passing each point once every 3 minutes. With such a strategy, any 3-minute crime that occurred in [9.75,10] would be passed with certainty, thus raising the intercept probability to 0.118. However, the assumption of random patrol does not allow for this type of strategy. Such a strategy, if adopted, would almost certainly modify the crime density function $p(x)$, making crime outside of [9.75,10] more likely.[20] If the patrol car patrols [9.75,10] in a *random* manner, obeying the model assumptions, the passing probability is approximately 0.075, or about 17 percent less than that achieved with optimal random patrol.

4.3. Summary and Discussion
The models of this chapter are summarized in Table 4.2. They only roughly approximate the behavior of actual police units on preventive patrol. Here we compare several of the results with what we might expect from actual operation. Also, we discuss needed further work.

4.3.1. Relationship between Positions of Crime and Patrol
If a crime of duration τ occurs at x ($\tau \ll \nu^{-1}(x)$) independently of the position of the patrol unit, then the probability of space-time coincidence of crime and patrol is approximately $\nu(x)\tau$. This quantity could be considered to be a reasonable upper bound on the probability of patrol detecting a crime while in progress. First, space-time coincidence does not guarantee detection; second and more fundamentally, it is likely that a potential criminal would

20. Even random patrol concentrated in one area would be likely to change the spatial distribution of crimes. Thus, one would assume in practice that estimates of $p(x)$ would be updated regularly, reflecting changes in crime patterns due to recent patrol patterns. This in turn would lead to an updated patrol pattern, as reflected in a revised coverage function $e(x)$.

act only after acquiring information regarding the position of the patrol unit, thus violating the independence assumption. For instance, immediately after a car passes we would expect some minimum time (say the time to circle a block) during which the probability of passing is extremely low. This would be a time of unusually low detection probability, and if it were found that a large number of crimes were committed during this time, the assumption of incident and patrol position independence would be invalidated.[21]

The required randomness could be restored in several ways. First, several contiguous patrol sectors could be merged, and each unit would be assigned to patrol all the streets in the larger area. Second, certain patrols could be assigned to follow other patrols at an appropriate distance; then, given that a patrol unit has just passed, the probability that another is closely behind is not reduced to zero.

Adding call-answering duties decreases the randomness of patrol passings. Anyone, including potential criminals, can monitor a patrol unit's activity in some manner (for example, visual observation or listening to the police radio) and determine when a particular car is not patrolling. Then, since units are typically assigned to nonoverlapping sectors, a crime can be committed with near zero probability that the patrol car will pass during the commission of the crime. Randomness would again be restored by merging several adjacent sectors so that with high probability some cars are always patrolling.[22]

The motorized patrolman also behaves in a way that tends to invalidate the assumption of incident and patrol position independence (for those cases in which the incident is a crime). We would expect that, at a given time, the frequency of patrol passings at a particular point would depend on a patrolman's assessed probability that a crime is likely to occur at that point. This judgmental probability is a function of the conditions of the sector at that particular time as well as events (for example, other crimes) that have taken place in the recent past. Thus, we speculate that the potential criminal is trying to evade patrol detection by obtaining patrol status information and that the patrolman is trying to increase the probability of detection (over that achieved by following long-term historical patterns) by guessing the positions of maximum crime likelihood.

Given these conflicting behaviors, Equation 4.7, giving the probability of a patrol passing during an incident, must be used with the greatest of caution.

21. The author has heard footpatrolmen, who have a patrol speed $s \approx 3$ mph, complain that stores are hit in a given block just after they pass that block.
22. This was also discussed in Section 2.7.2.

It gives the probability that a patrol car, which chooses its position from $e(\cdot)$, will pass an incident of specified duration, given that the incident location is independently selected from $p(\cdot)$. If the position of crime and patrol car are not independent, then Equation 4.7 is not the probability of detection of a criminal committing an observable crime of duration t.

4.3.2. The Magnitude of Intercept Probabilities

Employing reasonable parameter values, the intercept probabilities appear remarkably small. For instance, say $\nu = 1$ patrol per hour, and $\tau = \frac{1}{60}$ hour = 1 minute, then the probability of intercepting a crime of duration one minute (possibly a street robbery) could not be expected to exceed $\frac{1}{60}$. Intercept probabilities are even smaller in residential areas where patrols are much less frequent than 1/hr.

There are at least two implications of this result. First, the task of detecting crimes in progress cannot be assigned solely to police patrol. Cooperative citizens, alarm devices, and other detectors are required to increase detection (and apprehension) probability. Second, the crime deterrent aspect of patrol is brought to question. Do infrequent patrols that are sometimes monitorable pose a true threat of detection and apprehension? This question will require further research.

4.3.3. Allocation of Preventive Patrol Effort

The fact that computed intercept probabilities are small does not imply that no effort should be expended in planning allocations of preventive patrol effort. An increase in intercept probability from 0.01 to 0.02, say, could result in a doubling of on-scene apprehensions.

A primary purpose of including Koopman's search-allocation method was to indicate that, given a specified criterion (for example, maximization of intercept probability), the best way to allocate patrol effort is not necessarily to allocate in direct proportion to crime density. This example illustrates the inadequacy of a linear hazard formula. Qualitatively, Koopman's method suggests that patrol effort should grow as the logarithm of the crime density and that certain areas, where the likelihood of crime is particularly low, should not be patrolled at all. Clearly much more refinement of this model is required before it can be implemented by police, but we would expect the qualitative features of Koopman's solution to hold (that is, an allocation of effort that grows slower than linearly with crime density and street segments where no patrol effort should be expended).

4.3.4. Extension and Further Work

The preliminary results of this chapter immediately suggest needed further work, both analytical and experimental. Particularly with reference to the allocation of patrol effort, the following questions arise:

1. To what extent is an optimal patrol coverage function realizable? That is, can a patrol unit actually patrol the streets according to some set of rules that provides the required time and space randomness and that, on the average, gives the coverage specified by the coverage function?

2. How closely does a unit have to approach the optimal coverage in order to achieve satisfactory results? Or, equivalently, what is the sensitivity of the solution about the optimum?

3. To what extent is the crime distribution modified by patrol strategies? The answer to this question should indicate the frequency with which patrol allocations should be revised, reflecting a change in crime distribution.

4. How should each crime type be evaluated to reflect its relative seriousness? In other words, what are the disutilities of the various crime types?[23]

5. What is the conditional probability that a crime will be detected, given that it occurs a certain distance ℓ from the patrol unit and in a particular physical environment (for example, on the street at night)?

6. To what extent should administrative and political constraints be included in a preventive patrol allocation algorithm? Although Koopman's solution suggests that certain regions should not be patrolled, the resulting allocation probably violates constraints on minimal acceptable patrol frequencies throughout a city.

Regarding both the objectives and how to fulfill the objectives, it is clear that preventive patrol activity still requires much further study. Published police theories of preventive patrol,[24] usually subjective in nature, have suggested several (often conflicting) lists of objectives and strategies. One would expect that analytical modeling of certain features of patrol activity would provide needed assistance to patrol administrators. Although many of the models in this chapter incorporate only proxy measures of effectiveness, they should provide assistance in understanding the physical operation of patrol activity and in providing a framework from which to build a more complete theory.

In Chapter 5 are incorporated some of the results of this and preceding chapters in an algorithm for assigning patrol units to precincts (or higher level area commands).

23. For a discussion of the disutilities of crime, see T. Sellin and M. Wolfgang, *The Measurement of Delinquency* (New York: John Wiley & Sons, 1964).
24. See the various selections in S. G. Chapman, *Police Patrol Readings* (Springfield, Ill.: Charles C Thomas, Publisher, 1964).

5

Patrol Allocation Algorithm

Using models of patrol activity, it is possible to develop a policy-oriented algorithm for allocating patrol units, command-by-command, throughout a city. The algorithm discussed in this chapter is proposed as a preferable alternative to widely popular hazard formulas (Section 1.4).

The purpose of the algorithm is to provide police administrators with a useful and rational method to allocate patrol units. It is structured so that police policy, as stated by administrators, can be input directly into the algorithm. Then, the city-wide allocation of patrol units is determined so that policy objectives are achieved in the best possible way.

With the allocation procedure, most of the individual policy objectives are stated in terms of constraints. For instance, it may be decided that the average travel time should not exceed 4 minutes in a particular command. Then, the algorithm supplies the command with enough patrol units so that this objective and all other policy objectives (constraints) are satisfied. The specific list of objectives is supplied by police administrators. In this illustration of the method, the following variables are used to represent the allocation objectives in each command:

1. The time required for an assigned unit to travel to the scene of a reported incident;

2. The frequency of patrols;

3. The number of preventive patrol hours for every outside crime which is reported; and

4. An administrative objective which states a minimum acceptable number of patrol units in each command.

In addition it is assumed that police administrators wish to minimize any delay at the dispatcher's position due to unavailability of patrol units in a command.

With limited police resources, it is possible that a specific set of policy objectives is unobtainable. If so, the algorithm indicates the additional number of patrol units required to meet the stated objectives. To allocate the currently available number of units, the algorithm then requires a more modest set of objectives.

Part of the material in this chapter was presented at the 36th National Meeting of the Operations Research Society of America, "Models of Police Patrol: An Application to New York City," November 1969.

The algorithm is easily programmed on a digital computer and can be executed using a moderate amount of computer time.

As discussed in Chapter 2 about Simtown, we would expect any allocation procedure to be used in an iterative manner, with allocations periodically being revised as a result of implementation experiences, further data analyses, and model revisions. Thus, it is doubtful if any table of manpower levels generated by hand or by computer should be implemented directly without further examination. An allocation algorithm will not replace an administrator's decision making but assist it by providing a consistent framework for considering alternatives. Such an algorithm should have the properties that (1) administrators cannot find significant fault with the objective function and the constraints and (2) computed outputs are physically meaningful and intuitively appealing. Given such a tool, police resources can be allocated on a rational basis that offers clear advantages over sheer intuition or subjective hazard formulas.

The algorithm we propose in this chapter appears to be one reasonable procedure for considering allocations of police patrol forces. The mathematical details are developed in Sections 5.1 to 5.3. An application of the method using data from the New York City Police Department is discussed in Section 5.4. The nontechnical reader may wish to proceed directly to Section 5.4.

5.1. Mathematical Formulation

In this section the problem is mathematically formulated and the solution method is outlined. A summary of definitions is given in Table 5.1.

5.1.1. Mean Delays and Delay Costs

Define $W_{ci}(N_c) \equiv$ average dispatching queue delay incurred by i priority calls originating from command c, given that N_c patrol units are assigned to command c, where $i = 1, \ldots, N_p$ = total number of priority classes, and $c = 1, \ldots, I$ = total number of commands.

Assume that priority class i calls originate from command c in a Poisson manner at an average rate λ_{ci} calls per hour. In order to incorporate the relative importance of delay of a call in a particular priority class, assign a cost C_{ci} to priority class i calls originating from command c; this is a cost per unit of delay incurred in the dispatcher queue. The total city-wide average cost incurred per hour due to delays in the dispatcher queue is

$$\sum_{c=1}^{I} \sum_{i=1}^{N_p} C_{ci} \lambda_{ci} W_{ci}(N_c), \tag{5.1}$$

Table 5.1. Summary of Definitions for Section 5.1

N_p	Total number of priority classes
I	Total number of commands
$W_{ci}(N_c)$	Average dispatching queue delay incurred by i priority calls originating from command c, given that N_c patrol units are assigned to command c.
λ_{ci}	Average rate at which priority i calls originate from command c in a Poisson manner
C_{ci}	Cost per unit of delay incurred in the dispatcher queue by priority i calls from command c
R	Total number of constraints specified for each command
N_{cr}^0	Minimum number of patrol units required at command c in order to satisfy constraint r
N_c^0	Smallest integer such that all constraints related to command c are satisfied
$^cN_k^0$	Cumulative minimal number of allocatable units for the first k commands
$C_c(M)$	Optimal cost function

given that N_c patrol units are assigned to command c. The problem is to assign the $N_c(c = 1,2,\ldots,I)$ in a way that minimizes the average cost of delay and yet does not violate any of the prespecified constraints. This assignment is performed by optimally allocating to commands sequentially, in the usual dynamic programming manner,[1] insuring at each stage (corresponding to a command) that no constraint is violated.

5.1.2. Constraints

We assume that each constraint is a monotone function of the number of patrol units assigned and is separately computable for each command. A monotone nonincreasing (nondecreasing) constraint would specify a maximum (minimum) allowable value of some quantity. For instance, the average patrol travel time is a monotone decreasing function of the number of assigned patrol units, and the corresponding constraint specifies a maximum allowable average value of the patrol travel time. For constraints that have these properties, once a number of units N^0 is found which satisfies a particular constraint, any greater number $N > N^0$ also satisfies the constraint.

Let there be R constraints specified for each stage (command) and let N_{cr}^0 be the minimum number of patrol units required at command c in order to

1. For example, see R. E. Bellman and S. E. Dreyfus, *Applied Dynamic Programming* (Princeton, N.J.: Princeton University Press, 1962).

satisfy constraint $r(r = 1,2, \ldots ,R)$. The vector $[N_{c1}^0, N_{c2}^0, \ldots , N_{cR}^0]$ is called the *patrol unit constraint vector* for command c. Let

$$N_c^0 = \max [N_{c1}^0, N_{c2}^0, \ldots , N_{cR}^0] .$$

That is, N_c^0 is the smallest integer such that all constraints related to command c are satisfied. A constraint r is called a *restrictive constraint* if $N_{cr}^0 = N_c^0$. In general, any number of constraints could be restrictive constraints.

Define the cumulative minimal number of allocatable units for the first k commands,

$$^c N_k^0 \equiv \sum_{j=1}^{k} N_j^0, \quad k = 1, 2, \ldots , I.$$

For instance, $^c N_I^0$ is the minimum of number of units required solely to satisfy constraints throughout all I commands in the city.

5.1.3. Dynamic Programming Formulation

Now one can specify the dynamic programming solution method to the problem.

Define the optimal cost function as $C_c(M) \equiv$ minimal achievable delay cost per hour incurred by calls from commands 1 through c by optimally assigning a total of M units to commands 1 through c. Then $C_c(M)$ and the optimal allocation of units can be determined iteratively from the following recurrence relation:

$$C_c(M) = \min_{N_c' \geqslant N_c \geqslant N_c^0} \left[\sum_{i=1}^{N_p} C_{ci} \lambda_{ci} W_{ci}(N_c) + C_{c-1}(M - N_c) \right] \qquad (5.2)$$

$$c = 1,2, \ldots , I$$
$$M \geqslant {}^c N_c^0$$

where

$$N_c' = M - {}^c N_{c-1}^0 ,$$

$$C_0(M) \equiv 0, \text{ all } M.$$

This equation has the following intuitive interpretation: the minimal average delay cost through the cth command is the minimum of the sum of the cost incurred by command c calls with N_c units assigned and the minimal cost incurred by the remaining $c - 1$ commands with $M - N_c$ units optimally assigned.

An algorithm to "solve" Equation 5.2 iteratively is straightforward to program on a digital computer, particularly if special properties involving the decision variable N_c and the delay function $W_{ci}(N_c)$ are exploited to reduce required computer storage and to speed execution time.

We have thus specified the solution method to the patrol allocation problem. In the next two sections, we discuss the specific equations used in the present formulation.

5.2. Dispatcher Queue Delay Equation

The allocation algorithm presented in Section 5.1 can be used with any dispatching delay equation. To employ an analytically tractable model, we must aggregate much of the fine structure of patrol activity. Such aggregate models are useful for *global* allocation purposes, for instance, in assisting police administrators to determine the approximate number of patrol units to assign to each command in order to maintain reasonably small dispatching delays. One model is suggested here that should be useful for this purpose. In addressing more detailed problems, such as sector geometry, intersector travel time, and repositioning, we must rely on other models, including simulation models.

The model we suggest is a multiserver priority queueing model due to Cobham.[2] Applied to police dispatching, there are five assumptions of the model:

1. A call will be delayed at the dispatcher position only if *all* units in a command are unavailable for dispatch assignment.

2. Commands operate independently; there is no intercommand dispatching.

3. Incident reports arrive at the dispatcher station in a Poisson manner. During a given time period, priority class i incident reports arrive from command c at average rate λ_{ci}; where $i = 1, 2, \ldots, N_p$; and $c = 1, 2, \ldots, I$.

4. The total service time (travel time plus time at the scene of the incident) is a negative exponential random variable with mean $(1/\mu)$, regardless of priority class.

5. From each command, arrivals are dispatched first-come, first-served (FCFS) within each priority class. Priority 1 calls get first preference and priority N_p calls get last preference. There is no preemption.

Assumption 4 is the least satisfactory; the mean service times do appear to depend on the type of call, and a negative exponential distribution is only a very crude fit to actual service time distributions.[3]

Despite the shortcomings of this aggregate model, the delay equation has

2. A. Cobham, "Priority Assignment in Waiting Line Problems," *Operations Research* 2 (1954), pp. 70–76.
3. See, for example, the very valuable data base provided by N. Heller in 1967 *Service Time Histograms for Police Patrol Activities in St. Louis* (available from St. Louis Police Department).

several properties that should be useful for allocation purposes. The first property is the convexity of the mean wait as a function of the number of patrol units assigned; this property implies that the marginal return (in terms of average delay reduction) of each additional patrol unit is less than that of the preceding unit.[4] The second property is that commands with relatively large demand rates can utilize the assigned units a greater fraction of the time than commands with smaller demand rates and can still achieve the same mean delay in queue. This is a general property of multiserver queuing systems that indicates in terms of police operations the advantages of larger commands with relatively high utilization rates and large pools of patrol units. The third property is that there is a first-order distinction given among priority classes. Although the model does not allow differences in service rates among priority classes, it does allow preferential servicing among the classes. It also allows one to assign different costs to the delays in the various priority classes. The definition of the types of police calls that fall into each priority class should provide for an important administrative control of system operation.

For Cobham's model the average delay incurred by a priority i call originating from command c is

$$\overline{W}_{ci}(N_c) = \frac{B_c(N_c)}{\left[1 - \frac{1}{N_c\mu_c}\sum_{k=1}^{i-1}\lambda_{ci}\right]\left[1 - \frac{1}{N_c\mu_c}\sum_{k=1}^{i}\lambda_{ci}\right]} \tag{5.3}$$

$$c = 1, 2, \ldots, I$$

$$i = 1, 2, \ldots, N_p$$

where

$$B_c(N_c) = \frac{(N_c\rho_c)^{N_c}/(N_c\mu_c)}{N_c!(1 - \rho_c)\left[\sum_{k=0}^{N_c-1}\frac{(N_c\rho_c)^k}{k!} + \frac{(N_c\rho_c)^{N_c}}{N_c!(1 - \rho_c)}\right]},$$

$$\rho_c = \frac{\lambda_c}{N_c\mu_c},$$

---

4. This property is discussed by A. J. Rolfe in "A Note on Marginal Allocation in Multiple-Server Service Systems," *RAND* P-4393, June 1970.

$$\lambda_c = \sum_{i=1}^{N_p} \lambda_{ci},$$

$$\frac{1}{N_c \mu} \sum_{i=1}^{N_p} \lambda_{ci} < 1,$$

λ_{ci} = average rate at which priority i calls arrive from command c,

N_c = number of patrol units assigned to command c.

5.3. Constraint Equations

Any number of constraints can be specified independently for each command. In the present application of the algorithm there are 4 types of constraints. They are given as follows:

1. $t_{ci}^0 \equiv$ maximum allowable average travel time from receipt of dispatch order until arrival at the scene, for priority i calls originating from command c.

2. $v_c^0 \equiv$ minimum allowable average patrol frequency for command c.

3. $\tau_c^0 \equiv$ minimum allowable average number of preventive patrol hours for each outside crime in command c.[5]

4. $M_c \equiv$ minimum allowable number of patrol units that must be assigned to command c due to administrative constraints.

5.3.1. Average Travel Time

From Chapter 3, Equation 3.38, we obtain for the average travel time,[6]

$t_{ci}(N_c)$ = average travel time of units responding to priority i calls originating from command c.

$$t_{ci}(N_c) \approx \frac{2}{3v_{ci}} \sqrt{\frac{A_c}{N_c}} \left(1 + \frac{\lambda_c}{N_c \mu_c}\right), \qquad (5.4)$$

where

v_{ci} = effective response speed in command c to priority i calls;

A_c = area (in square miles) of command c;

$$\lambda_c = \sum_{i=1}^{N_p} \lambda_{ci};$$

5. This constraint was suggested by police personnel, who wished to see patrol effort directly related to reported crime occurrence.

6. Here we have set ρ_c equal to $\lambda_c/N_c\mu_c$.

N_c = number of patrol units assigned to command c;
μ_c^{-1} = average total time required for a patrol unit to service a call in
        command c.

Since Equation 5.4 cannot be solved explicitly for N_c, given the con-
straint value t_{ci}^0, we simply iteratively increase N_c by one until $t_{ci}(N_c) \leqslant t_{ci}^0$
for all i, where i = 1, 2, . . . , N_p. This procedure gives us N_{c1}^0, the first entry
in the patrol unit constraint vector for command c.

In the derivation of Equation 5.4, it was assumed that the utilization factor
(fraction of time spent servicing calls) was not greater than about 0.7. If situations arise in which the utilization factor is greater than 0.7, Equation 5.4
will give an underestimate of the mean travel time. (This has not yet been
troublesome in applications, because commands with high utilization factors
are usually small in area and have a high demand rate per unit area. Thus, in
these commands travel time is not a restrictive constraint since travel distances are relatively small.)

5.3.2. Average Patrol Frequency
For constraint 2, the patrol frequency constraint, we use Equation 4.4. As a
first approximation, we can set the patrol coverage function equal to unity
and assume that each patrol sector within a command has an equal number
of patrollable street miles. Or, the alternative approach of assuming an unknown coverage function can be used (Section 4.1.5); in that case the patrol
frequency constraint applies to a point in the command selected from a pdf
proportional to the coverage function. In either case, Equation 4.4 can be
written

$$v_c(N_c) = \frac{s_c}{(D_c/N_c)} \left(1 - \frac{\lambda_c}{N_c \mu_c} \right) \tag{5.5}$$

where

$v_c(N_c)$ = average number of patrol passings per hour of a point[7] in command
        c with N_c units assigned
    s_c = speed of a patrolling vehicle in command c
    D_c = total number of street miles in command c

and the other parameters are defined as before.

We obtain N_{c2}^0, the minimal number of units required to satisfy the patrol
frequency constraint, by choosing the smallest integer N_c such that the fol-

---

7. The point is an arbitrary point if we assume uniform coverage; otherwise the point is
one selected from a pdf proportional to the coverage function.

lowing inequality (obtained from Equation 5.5) is satisfied:

$$N_c \geqslant \frac{v_c^0 L_c}{s_c} + \frac{\lambda_c}{\mu_c}.$$

(5.6)

5.3.3. Average Number of Preventive Patrol Hours for Each Outside Crime

To estimate the average number of preventive patrol hours for each outside crime, an estimate of the frequency of crime occurrence is needed, as well as the amount of time a unit spends on patrol. Aggregating over an 8-hour tour, one obtains

$$\tau_c(N_c) = \frac{8\left(1 - \frac{\lambda_c}{N_c \mu_c}\right)N_c}{K_c},$$

(5.7)

where

$\tau_c(N_c)$ = average number of preventive patrol hours for each outside crime in command c with N_c units assigned.

K_c = average number of outside crimes in command c per 8-hour tour,

and other parameters are defined as before. We obtain N_{c3}^0, the minimal number of units required to satisfy this constraint, by choosing the smallest integer N_c such that the following inequality (obtained from Equation 5.7) is satisfied:

$$N_c \geqslant \frac{K_c \tau_c^0}{8} + \frac{\lambda_c}{\mu_c}.$$

(5.8)

5.3.4. Administrative Minimum

For constraint 4, the administrative constraint, N_{c4}^0 is trivially equal to M_c^0.

5.3.5. Constraint Code

The output of the algorithm indicates which constraint would be the restrictive constraint if the number of patrol units assigned to each command were the minimal number required solely to satisfy constraints. A restrictive constraint is indicated by a single letter code. The code is as follows:

T = travel time constraint

P = patrol frequency constraint

C = patrol hours per outside crime constraint

M = administrative constraint

Q = an internal constraint requiring the utilization factor to be less than 1.

Since the patrol unit constraint vector may have more than one entry with the identical maximum value (that is, more than one constraint may be restrictive), the order of testing the constraints is important if only a single letter code is to be printed. This is, by code, (Q, M, P, T, C). Thus, for instance, if the code letter Q is given with an allocation, the internal constraint requiring the utilization factor to be less than 1 is a restrictive constraint; in addition, any of the other four constraints *may be* restrictive constraints. On the other hand, if the code letter C is given, then the only restrictive constraint is the one specifying the minimal number of patrol hours per outside crime.

5.4. Application to New York City

In this section an application is discussed of the patrol allocation algorithm using data from the New York City Police Department (NYPD). The application we discuss is allocation of the radio motorized patrol (RMP) force to precincts. As mentioned previously, more aggregated geographical commands (such as divisions) could be used if desired.

This computational exercise using the algorithm could have been performed with hypothetical data in a manner similar to our treatment of Simtown (Chapter 2). Instead, data estimates provided by NYPD and the New York City Rand Institute are used here, recognizing that any allocation based on rough estimates is only illustrative of the capabilities of the method. Implementation of the method as a basis for resource allocation would require detailed statistical analysis of demands for service, response speeds, and other data needed for the models. In all likelihood, these parameters would depend on precinct, hour of day, day of week, and time of year.

5.4.1. Data

Values for the following types of data were estimated for each precinct:

Call-for-service demand (λ_c)

Number of outside crimes per tour (K_c)

Patrol car response speed following dispatch (v_c)

Patrol car speed while performing crime preventive patrol (s_c)

Average total time required to service an incident (μ_c^{-1})

Precinct area (A_c)

Precinct street mileage (D_c)

Call-for-service demand was estimated from an 8-week sample of radio-run (dispatch) data gathered in August–September, 1968. Unfortunately, there

was no separation by priority class (that is, $N_p = 1$). Separate estimates were
made for each precinct for each of 12 tours during the week:

Tours 1, 2, 3, 4: Midnight–8:00 A.M. tour on weekdays, Friday, Saturday,
Sunday, respectively.

Tours 5, 6, 7, 8: 8:00 A.M.–4:00 P.M. tour on weekdays, Friday, Saturday,
Sunday, respectively.

Tours 9, 10, 11, 12: 4:00 P.M.–midnight tour on weekdays, Friday, Saturday, Sunday, respectively.

(Here "weekdays" are Mondays, Tuesdays, Wednesdays, and Thursdays.)
The limited sample size prevented any finer breakdown (say by the hour of
day).

The numbers of outside crimes per tour were estimated from August–September 1968 data and from city-wide data on occurrence times of felonies.

Effective response speed following a dispatch was set at 10 mph for each
precinct and for each tour. The speed of a patrolling unit was estimated from
mileage data usually collected for auto maintenance purposes; this speed
was estimated to be 6.5 mph.

The average total time required to service an incident was set equal to 40
minutes for each precinct and for each tour.

Precinct area and street mileage were taken from NYPD statistics.

5.4.2. Current Allocation Levels

During the 8-week study period, the number of RMP units that were placed
on duty on each tour were recorded for each precinct. The average number
on duty for a given tour in the week (tour 1,2, . . . , 12) was then computed
to facilitate comparison of actual allocations with those derived from the allocation algorithm.

5.4.3. The Saturday Evening Tour: 4:00 P.M.–Midnight

During the summer months, the demands on the police patrol force are
usually greatest in the evening hours, particularly on Friday and Saturday
evenings. Here actual system operation on Saturday evenings (4:00 P.M.–midnight tour) is examined and this operation is compared to that derived from
the allocation algorithm. To facilitate the comparison, the total number of
units allocated city-wide by the algorithm *is set equal* to the *actual number
allocated* city wide.

Actual Saturday Operation

The actual RMP allocation levels in each precinct (during August–September
1968) and models of patrol activity are used to estimate the manner in which

the RMP force operates during the Saturday evening tour. These computations are given for 20 illustrative precincts in Table 5.2. The respective columns, left to right, contain

(1) The precinct designation;

(2a) The actual average number of RMP units allocated to the precinct;

(2b) The closest integer approximation to 2a;

(3) The average number of radio runs per hour throughout the precinct;

(4) The estimated average queue wait at the dispatcher's position incurred by a call received from the precinct, because all precinct cars were busy;

(5) The average travel time (minutes) of the dispatched unit to reach the scene of the reported incident;

(6) The fraction of time that RMPs are busy servicing radio runs;

(7) The average number of times per hour that an RMP passes an *average* point in the precinct;

(8) The average number of hours of preventive patrol per outside crime.

At the top of Table 5.2 we have indicated that there are 609 units allocated city wide and that the (city-wide) average dispatcher queue wait is estimated to be 3.5 minutes.

To illustrate the use of the table, consider Precinct C. The average number of RMP units allocated is 6.1 (column 2a), which is rounded to 6 (column 2b), the nearest integer. The average radio-run frequency during the Saturday evening tour is 3.8 radio runs per hour (column 3). The average dispatcher queue wait, due to car unavailability, is estimated to be 0.57 minute (column 4). The average travel time to the scene of a call is computed to be 2.1 minutes (column 5). The fraction of time spent servicing radio runs is 0.42 (column 6). The average number of patrol passes per hour is 1.09 (column 7); this implies that the average time between patrol passes is about 55 minutes. For each outside crime that occurs during the Saturday evening tour in the precinct, there are approximately 9.3 car hours of crime preventive patrol (column 8).

Examining the table, we note that there are wide variations throughout the city of almost every variable. For instance, throughout the city (including all 77 precincts) the average dispatcher queue delay is negligible (less than 0.01 minute) in 14 precincts but exceeds 5 minutes in 10 precincts.

Utilization factors vary from 0.03 to 0.89. As we would expect, busy precincts, because of the high patrol utilization factors, receive the least amount of crime preventive patrol. For instance, two of the 77 precincts each provide less than 1 hour of crime preventive patrol for each serious out-

Table 5.2 Actual System Operation: Saturday Evening Tour (Average dispatcher queue wait, city-wide, = 3.5 minutes; total RMP units allocated = 609 units)

(1) Precinct	(2) Number of RMP Units (a) Average	(b) Nearest Integer	(3) Average Number of Radio Runs per Hour	(4) Average Dispatcher Queue Wait Due to Car Unavailability (Minutes)	(5) Average Travel Time (Min)	(6) Fraction of Time Busy Servicing Radio Runs	(7) Average Patrol Frequency (Passes/ Hour)	(8) Average Number of Preventive Patrol Hours per Outside Crime
A	4.5	5	0.8	0.00	1.2	0.11	1.66	51.7
B	6.0	6	4.6	1.44	2.2	0.51	0.74	2.9
C	6.1	6	3.8	0.57	2.1	0.42	1.09	9.3
D	10.3	10	6.0	0.06	1.5	0.40	2.03	5.4
E	7.3	7	7.2	5.09	2.6	0.69	0.48	4.1
F	5.8	6	5.6	3.94	2.7	0.62	0.55	5.7
G	10.0	10	7.7	0.35	4.9	0.51	0.23	6.3
H	13.6	14	5.9	0.00	3.9	0.28	0.57	15.7
I	7.1	7	5.1	0.75	5.2	0.49	0.17	7.0
J	5.8	6	5.4	3.40	4.1	0.60	0.26	4.7
K	2.5	3	0.1	0.00	2.1	0.03	1.18	24.7
L	6.0	6	5.5	3.51	2.6	0.61	0.66	5.5
M	8.8	9	8.8	2.34	2.6	0.66	0.53	5.7
T	8.6	9	7.6	0.87	2.7	0.56	0.59	5.1
S	5.0	5	2.0	0.15	2.4	0.27	0.62	7.9
R	5.5	6	4.6	1.42	2.9	0.51	0.56	5.7
Q	3.4	3	2.2	5.78	4.1	0.49	0.30	10.3
P	20.3	20	11.6	0.00	4.7	0.39	0.35	11.3
O	9.8	10	7.0	0.17	4.5	0.46	0.29	9.8
N	12.5	13	3.4	0.00	6.8	0.18	0.30	31.2

side crime that occurs during the tour. Twelve other precincts, however, provide 20 or more hours of preventive patrol for each outside crime.

Each of the variables appears to provide different and useful information regarding precinct operation. As an example, the variables *patrol frequency* and *preventive patrol hours per outside crime* reflect different characteristics of patrol operation. One precinct that provides only 0.9 hour of patrol per outside crime is characterized by a not particularly low patrol frequency of 0.26 patrol per hour. (There are 12 precincts with patrol frequencies less than this amount.) This behavior results from the fact that, during the Saturday evening tour, the precinct is characterized by a rather high outside crime rate per street mile. On the other hand, a second precinct (which is predominately residential) is characterized by a relatively low patrol frequency (0.14 patrol per hour) but a relatively high number of patrol hours per outside crime (9.0 hours of patrol per outside crime). This precinct has a relatively large number of street miles (147) and a relatively low crime rate per street mile.

Although a fair amount of time is required to interpret all these figures for 77 precincts, eventually all the apparently conflicting behavior can be understood easily. Also, interpretation of each of the separate variables (effectiveness measures) provides an understanding more related to the physical operation of the patrol force than does a weighted formula that combines all factors in some arbitrary manner.

Model-Derived Saturday Operation

Now we reexamine RMP operation during Saturday evenings and derive a precinct-by-precinct allocation that best achieves a set of policy objectives. To obtain a specific set of objectives, one chooses to reduce the wide variations in policy variables that are observed to be characteristic of actual Saturday evening operations. The policy objectives will be as follows: Allocate RMP units to precincts so that

1. There are 4 or more hours of crime-preventive patrol for every outside crime which is reported;

2. The frequency of patrols is at least 0.25 per hour (or, equivalently, the average time between patrol passings is not greater than $1/0.25 = 4$ hours);

3. The average time required to travel to the scene of the incident is no greater than 6 minutes;

4. Independent of 1, 2, and 3, at least 4 RMP units are allocated to each precinct.

Also, if there are additional available RMP units, besides those needed solely to satisfy objectives 1 to 4, allocate them to precincts so as to minimize city-wide average queue delay at the dispatcher's position due to unavailability of RMP units in a precinct.

In actual operations, objective 1 was not fulfilled in 12 precincts, and 2 was not achieved in 10 precincts. In addition, average travel time (objective 3) exceeded 6 minutes in 4 precincts. Only two precincts did not satisfy the administrative minimum.

The model-derived allocations for the 20 illustrative precincts of Table 5.2 are given in Table 5.3. Column 2b now contains the *algorithm*-derived number of RMP units to assign to each precinct. Column 9 indicates the constraint that determines the minimum possible number of RMP units to assign to the precincts so that all constraints are satisfied. Otherwise, the column entries in Table 5.3 correspond identically to those in Table 5.2. The total number of RMP units is set equal to 609, which is identical to the number allocated in actual operations.

Over all 77 precincts, it was found that 577 RMP units are required solely to satisfy constraints. Thus, there are only 609 − 577 = 32 additional units to assign, beyond those required by constraints, in order to minimize city-wide average dispatcher queue delay. Even so, this average delay has been reduced from the predicted 3.5 minutes in actual operations to 0.67 minute with the algorithm-derived allocation. The precinct-by-precinct variation of queue delays is considerably reduced over that predicted for the actual system; the maximum average dispatcher queue delay in the algorithm-derived system is only 2.46 minutes, whereas the maximum in the actual system is considerably larger. In addition, all stated objectives are now satisfied.

To gain insight into the allocation procedure, it is helpful to examine several of the precincts identified in Table 5.3. The allocation level of Precinct E, for instance, is increased from 7 to 9 units, decreasing the average dispatcher queue delay from 5.09 minutes to 0.62 minute. Since the precinct did not violate any of the stated constraints with 7 units assigned (Table 5.2), the additional two units are assigned specifically to reduce dispatcher queue delay. The allocation to Precinct N is increased from 13 to 16 units, solely to satisfy the average travel time constraint. The average queue delay in Precinct N is negligible with either assignment of units.

In Precinct P, the allocation is reduced from 20 to 17 units, which represents the minimum number necessary to satisfy the patrol frequency constraint. The allocation to Precinct H is also reduced in this way. Throughout all 77 precincts, there were 12 precincts for which the net change of assigned

Table 5.3 Model-Derived Operation: Saturday Evening Tour (Average dispatcher queue wait, city-wide = 0.67 minutes; total RMP units allocated = 609 units)

(1)	(2) Number of RMP Units		(3)	(4)	(5)	(6)	(7)	(8)	(9)
Precinct	(a) Average Number Actually Allocated	(b) Model-Derived Number to Be Allocated	Average Number of Radio Runs per Hour	Average Dispatcher Queue Wait Due to Car Unavailability (Minutes)	Average Travel Time (Minutes)	Fraction of Time Busy Servicing Radio Runs	Average Patrol Frequency (Passes/Hour)	Average Number of Preventive Patrol Hours per Outside Crime	Restrictive Constraint Code
A	4.5	4	0.8	0.03	1.3	0.14	1.28	40.1	M
B	6.0	8	4.6	0.12	1.7	0.38	1.25	4.9	C
C	6.1	5	3.8	2.17	2.4	0.50	0.78	6.6	C
D	10.3	9	6.0	0.19	1.6	0.44	1.69	4.5	C
E	7.3	9	7.2	0.62	2.1	0.53	0.91	7.8	C
F	5.8	7	5.6	1.23	2.4	0.53	0.79	8.3	C
G	10.0	11	7.7	0.12	4.5	0.47	0.28	7.6	P
H	13.6	9	5.9	0.18	5.5	0.44	0.28	7.9	P
I	7.1	9	5.1	0.07	4.2	0.38	0.27	11.0	P
J	5.8	7	5.4	1.06	3.6	0.52	0.37	6.7	P
K	2.5	4	0.1	0.00	1.8	0.02	1.59	33.2	M
L	6.0	7	5.5	1.09	2.3	0.52	0.94	7.9	C
M	8.8	10	8.8	0.90	2.4	0.59	0.70	7.5	C
T	8.6	9	7.6	0.87	2.7	0.56	0.59	5.1	C
S	5.0	4	2.0	0.82	2.8	0.34	0.45	5.7	M
R	5.5	6	4.6	1.42	2.9	0.51	0.56	5.7	C
Q	3.4	4	2.2	1.08	3.2	0.36	0.50	16.9	M
P	20.3	17	11.6	0.01	5.3	0.46	0.26	8.5	P
O	9.8	10	7.0	0.17	4.5	0.46	0.29	9.8	P
N	12.5	16	3.4	0.00	6.0	0.14	0.39	39.9	T

units equaled 3 or more. On the other hand, the algorithm-derived allocation and the average actual allocation differed by 1 unit or less[8] in 39 precincts.

Aggregating by borough, we obtain the breakdown of Table 5.4. Thus, the big changes occur in boroughs B4 and B3. Borough B4 loses 22 units while B3 gains 23 units. Within each borough, it is useful to see in Table 5.5 the number of precincts to which units are added, and the number from which units are subtracted. As we see, precincts in Borough B4 consistently lose units to precincts in B3. Changes in other boroughs are significant but appear to be internal shifts of resources within the borough.

5.4.4. The Sunday Day Tour

The allocation algorithm was first applied to the Sunday tour keeping the total number of units constant at 634. This application resulted in such a small average dispatcher queue delay (less than 0.02 minute) that it was felt that a reasonable allocation could be achieved with considerably fewer RMP units. It was chosen to allocate 500 units city wide, representing a reduction of 134 compared to the actual allocation in 1968.

Employing the allocation method, the derived allocation increased the average city-wide dispatcher queue delay to only 0.14 minute (from 0.09

Table 5.4 Borough Allocations (Saturday Evening Tour)

Borough	Old Allocation	New Allocation	Net Additional Units
B1	150	157	+ 7
B2	104	97	− 7
B3	162	185	+23
B4	153	131	−22
B5	40	39	− 1

Table 5.5 Borough Changes (Saturday Evening Tour)

Borough	Number of Precincts Obtaining Additional Units	Number of Precincts Losing Units	Number of Precincts Retaining the Same Number of Units
B1	10	9	2
B2	4	3	4
B3	16	4	8
B4	1	8	5
B5	1	1	1

8. The average actual allocation, computed over an 8-week period, was usually not an integer. Thus, it was possible for the (integer) derived allocations to differ from the average actual allocations by less than one unit.

minute). In addition, in each precinct all objectives were satisfied, whereas two precincts did not satisfy objectives in actual operations. The maximum average dispatcher queue delay was only 0.56 minute, compared to 1.4 minutes in actual operations.

Although 134 units are removed from the total force, 8 of the 77 precincts were allocated additional RMP units. Aggregating by borough, we obtain the breakdown of Table 5.6. Within each borough, a breakdown is obtained from Table 5.7. Thus it appears that the system objectives can be fulfilled with considerably fewer RMP units assigned to the Sunday day tour.

The above procedures could be carried out for each period of the day, each day of the week, incorporating a richer data base, to arrive at a very reasonable city-wide allocation of patrol units.

5.5. Summary

The allocation method developed and applied in this chapter appears to offer several advantages, compared to a subjective hazard formula. Each defined variable or effectiveness measure that is thought to be important appears individually either as a constraint or in the objective function. Rather than linearly affecting overall allocations in proportion to a subjective weighting factor, the nonlinear behavior of each variable is incorporated and any can

Table 5.6 Borough Allocations (Sunday Day Tour)

Borough	Old Allocation	New Allocation	Net Additional Units
B1	152	124	−28
B2	108	75	−33
B3	178	157	−21
B4	155	109	−46
B5	41	35	− 6

Table 5.7 Borough Changes (Sunday Day Tour)

Borough	Number of Precincts Obtaining Additional Units	Number of Precincts Losing Units	Number of Precincts Retaining the Same Number of Units
B1	2	16	3
B2	0	11	0
B3	5	16	7
B4	0	14	0
B5	1	2	0

be a determining factor in the allocation to a particular precinct. In addition, the models themselves fully incorporate the stochastic nature of the police response system, rather than assume a deterministic system.

The illustrative computational results indicate the advantages of basing allocations on a set of objectives to be fulfilled, rather than on some weighted hazard score. In sparsely settled communities (for example, Staten Island), a certain number of units are required simply to maintain the travel time constraint. In heavily settled residential communities, a certain number of units are required to maintain constraints relating to preventive patrol coverage. In densely populated core areas, the number of units required depends almost solely on the rate of calls for service. During busy weekend evenings, the results suggest that relatively more units should be allocated to the core areas, thereby often reducing average dispatcher queue delays due to car unavailabilities in these areas by 30 minutes or more; the algorithm indicates how units can be drawn from other areas so as to maintain adequate coverage to fulfill all stated objectives. Such complicated interactions are handled easily by a computer algorithm but are ignored in hazard formulas.

In addition to aggregate command-by-command allocations, the algorithm can be supplied with hourly data to help determine the needed time scheduling of personnel. Hazard formulas are usually not used for this purpose. In fact, there have been a remarkably large number of cities in the United States whose 24-hour pattern of manpower allocation has been close to a uniform allocation, thereby ignoring the marked differences in demands for service that occur at different times of the day. The numbers of calls for service per hour over a typical 24-hour period are shown in Figure 5.1. (Also see Figures 4.1 and 4.2.) It is not unusual for the peak hour to incur ten times as many calls as the least busy hour. And this variation can be much greater when the particular day of the week is considered (for example, comparing 10:00 to 11:00 P.M. Friday to 6:00 to 7:00 A.M. Sunday).

To schedule the assignments of police personnel effectively over a given time period (say a week), it is first necessary to estimate these hourly demands for police services. Given such an estimate, personnel should be scheduled to satisfy policy objectives in an effective manner. But the problems of determining *demand for services* as reflected in 24-hour histograms and determining *demand for personnel* are distinct. To satisfy certain effectiveness criteria in the best way possible (within given constraints), it is usually necessary to schedule personnel assignments in a way which is *not* propor-

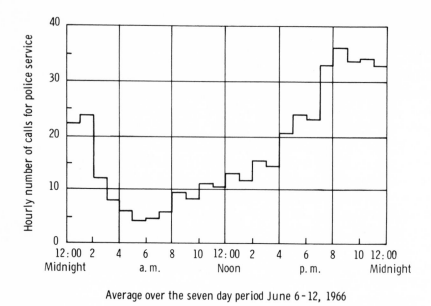

Average over the seven day period June 6-12, 1966

Boston, Massachusetts

Figure 5.1 Number of calls per hour from citizens requiring police service.

tional to demand for services (see Section 1.3). The resource allocation algorithm of this chapter can assist in determining the demand for personnel, both by time of day and region of the city.

After determining demand for police personnel, it is necessary tp try to match this demand by some reasonably simple tour or shift structure which does not violate administrative, contractual, or legal constraints. Finding such a tour structure can be a very difficult problem. One approach breaks down the problem into two subproblems: In the first, the number and starting times of tours are determined. For instance, it may be decided that four tours, each starting at prescribed times and each manned by certain numbers of officers, would adequately approximate the hourly demand for police personnel. Then the second problem is one of finding an algorithm for assigning patrolmen to the tours in such a way that all patrolmen are treated equally and that the total assignment at any time approximately equals that computed in the first stage of the problem. The output of such an algorithm is often displayed on a *tour assignment chart*. Although this problem will not be further addressed in this book, we refer the reader to Heller's work[9] in determining tour assignment algorithms.

In New York City, methods of allocation similar to those of this chapter helped to demonstrate the extent to which effectiveness of the patrol force was lower at times of high demand than at times of low demand.[10] This demonstration was a major impetus behind efforts of the mayor and the police commissioner to modify the state's "three-platoon statute" and to obtain a fourth platoon, which now operates from 6:00 P.M. to 2:00 A.M. This is an example in which quantitative tools can be used to explore the effects of revising constraints, even if the revision requires changes in the law.

Hazard formulas were especially useful when police allocations had to be computed by hand. Now that more and more departments are obtaining a digital computation capability, the requirement of hand calculation is becoming outdated. We should expect to see very soon a tendency toward more sophisticated allocation procedures, based on much more detailed data bases than were possible with hand calculations.

The use of a computer algorithm to assign patrol units will probably become standard practice. In addition, other algorithms will be developed to reassign and redeploy units in real time, as the state of the system evolves. This type of application is further discussed in Chapter 8.

In the subsequent chapters the patrol system is examined operating in modes that are different from those usually observed today.

9. N. Heller, "Proportional Rotating Schedules," Ph.D. dissertation, Operations Research, University of Pennsylvania, 1969.
10. The New York City Rand Institute, *First Annual Report* (New York City Rand Institute, 1970), p. 26.

6

The Simulation Model

In the previous chapters current modes of police patrol force operations were considered as well as one proposed algorithm for the control of these operations. It was shown how to model various patrol and emergency response activities and how to use the models to arrive at a reasonable method of allocation. In the remaining chapters, alternative modes of system operation are examined. Changes are included in the operating rules of the patrol and dispatch system that could result simply by revising administrative procedures (for example, placing a priority structure on the input stream of calls) or they may result from implementation of a hardware system (for example, an automatic car locator system).

A simulation model of the dispatch-patrol system is most helpful in the comparison of alternative operating policies, particularly when complexity of total system operation precludes development of analytical models. This chapter describes and applies the simulation model that was developed for these studies. The model is designed for general use and can be applied to study police patrol operations in any city. It has been programmed for use in a computer time-sharing environment; thus, the state of the system can be monitored by a program operator as it evolves, and control parameters can be changed when and if desired. The model is currently being applied to study specific operational problems in several large urban police departments.

The purpose in this chapter is twofold. First, considerable time is spent in Section 6.1 outlining the logic of the simulation model and capabilities of the computer program.[1] We wish to indicate the structure of a model that can simulate a rather large number of operating systems. Several detailed dispatch and reassignment procedures are developed, not to suggest that they encompass all procedures of interest but rather to illustrate what can be studied with a simulation model. An administrator may suggest his own procedures that are easily inserted into the computer program. Second, Section 6.2 illustrates the use of the model. A simple 9-car command is used for this pur-

Part of the material in this chapter was presented at the 37th National Meeting of the Operations Research Society of America, "A Simulation Model for Spatially Distributed Urban Service Systems," April 1970.
1. The reader who wishes to observe only the use of the model may wish to skip directly to Section 6.2.

pose.[2] Many of the issues raised by this application of the model (for example, the extent of intersector assignments) are reexamined in later chapters. In addition, the simulation results suggest methods of operation that appear to offer advantages over systems which are popular today. For instance, they suggest that urgent calls can be handled much more efficiently with a priority structure imposed on calls and with an accompanying set of administrative rules regarding dispatching procedures.

As illustrated in Chapter 2 for the hypothetical city of Simtown, administrators in any city should find simulation models valuable for the following purposes:

1. They facilitate detailed investigations of operations throughout the city (or part of the city);

2. They provide a consistent framework for estimating the value of new technologies;

3. They serve as training tools to increase awareness of the system interactions and consequences resulting from every day policy decisions;

4. They suggest new criteria for monitoring and evaluating actual operating systems.

A summary of definitions used in the chapter is found in Table 6.1. A chapter summary is given in Section 6.3.

6.1. Description of the Simulation Model

The simulation model works in the following way: Incidents are generated throughout the city, randomly in time and space. Each incident has an associated priority number, the lower numbers designating the more important incidents.[3] As each incident becomes known, an attempt is made to assign (dispatch) a patrol unit to the scene of the incident. In certain cases this assignment cannot be performed because the congestion level of the force is too high; then, the incident report joins a queue of waiting reports. The queue is depleted as patrol units become available.

2. Many of the described capabilities of the program are not illustrated by sample computer runs. It is our purpose here to indicate what can be done to study specific systems, but we do not want to fill pages with computer outputs of various systems, each exhibiting its own set of peculiarities. The complexity of the model is such that "general" results are rarely obtained. When its very many parameters are matched to a particular police department's situation, the model readily allows one to explore the consequences of alternative policies.
3. Low-priority incidents have priority numbers that are greater in magnitude than those of high-priority incidents; we say that an incident of priority i is less important than an incident of priority i' if $i' < i$.

Table 6.1 Summary of Definitions for Chapter 6

N_A	Number of geographical atoms in a city.
$T_{\max}$	Equivalent real time of a simulation run.
k	Index denoting type of event.
T	Equivalent real time during the simulation.
$T(k)$	The next scheduled time for event type k to commence.
λ	Average rate at which calls for service are received (throughout the city).
$P_A(a)$	Probability that any particular call for service originates in geographical atom a, where $a = 1, 2, \ldots, N_A$.
i	Index denoting priority type.
N_P	Total number of priority types.
$P_I(i\|a)$	Probability that a randomly selected reported incident is priority type i, given the incident originated in geographical atom a; where $i = 1, 2, \ldots, N_p$ and $a = 1, 2, \ldots, N_A$.
STATUS(j)	Priority level of the current activity of patrol unit j, where STATUS(j) = $1, 2, 3, \ldots$
PREEMP(i)	An integer designating the least important priority class of activity that cannot be preempted by a priority i call for service, where $i = 1, 2, \ldots, N_p$ and PREEMP(i) $\geqslant i$.
PRICAR(j)	Equivalent status of patrol unit j while it performs preventive patrol.
$[x(j), y(j)]$	Actual position coordinates of patrol unit j.
$[\hat{x}(j), \hat{y}(j)]$	Estimated position coordinates of patrol unit j.
(x, y)	Actual position coordinates of an incident.
$(\hat{x}, \hat{y})$	Estimated position coordinates of an incident.
$R_1(i)$	Maximum allowable estimated travel distance to a priority i incident for a unit on preventive patrol.
$R_2(i)$	Maximum allowable estimated travel distance to a priority i incident for a unit just completing service on a previous assignment.
$R_3(i)$	Maximum allowable estimated travel distance to a priority i incident for a unit commencing preventive patrol.
$P(a\|j)$	Probability that patrol unit j selects atom a to patrol, where $j = 1, 2, \ldots, J$, and $a = 1, 2, \ldots, N_A$.

Table 6.1 Summary of Definitions for Chapter 6 (continued)

σ	Resolution of automatic car locator system.
(x_j^0, y_j^0)	Center-of-mass coordinates of sector j, where $j = 1, 2, \ldots, J$.
$[x^0(a), y^0(a)]$	Center-of-mass coordinates of atom a, where $a = 1, 2, \ldots, N_A$.
F_I	Fraction of assignments that are intersector assignments.
ρ	Utilization factor.
$\hat{d}_j$	Estimated travel distance of unit j to an incident.
$\overline{W}(i)$	Average wait in dispatcher queue of priority i calls.
$\overline{t_r}(i)$	Average patrol car travel time for priority i assignments.
$v(i)$	Patrol car response speed to priority i assignments.
$\hat{d}_j/B(i)$	The weighted distance metric for a priority i incident, estimated to be a distance $\hat{d}_j$ from patrol unit j.

The model is designed to study two general classes of administrative policies:

1. The patrol deployment strategy
2. The dispatch and reassignment policy.

The patrol deployment strategy determines whether patrol units are assigned to nonoverlapping sectors, which sectors constitute a precinct, and which areas are more heavily patrolled than others. The dispatch and reassignment[4] policy specifies the set of decision rules the dispatcher follows when attempting to assign a patrol unit to a reported incident. Included in the dispatch policy are the priority structure, rules about cross-precinct dispatching, the queue discipline, and so forth.

There are several important measures of operational effectiveness that the model tabulates. These include statistics on dispatcher queue length, patrol unit travel times, workloads of individual patrol units, the amount of intersector dispatches, and so on.

The simulation program is organized to reflect the spatial relationships inherent in patrol operations, as well as the sequential time nature of events which is common to all simulations. First the spatial or geographical structure is discussed, then the time sequence of events.

---

4. We distinguish between a "dispatch," which is the immediate assignment of a car to a reported incident, and a "reassignment," which is the assignment of a car (which has just completed servicing a previous incident) to an incident that had been placed in queue.

6.1.1. Atoms, Sectors, Precincts, and Divisions

The city, of arbitrary shape, is partitioned into a set of "geographical atoms." Each atom is a polygon of arbitrary shape and size.[5] The atoms are sufficiently small so that any probability density function over the atom (for example, a pdf describing positions of reported incidents) can be considered uniform over the atom. This does not restrict accuracy of results, because the atoms can be arbitrarily small. It is not necessary to subdivide atoms further into sets of rectangular cells or other quantizing units. Those parts of the city with nearly uniform spatial attributes over large areas would be characterized by relatively large geographical atoms. Other parts with markedly varying attributes would be characterized by correspondingly smaller atoms. However, no unnecessary quantization is introduced, thereby conserving computer processing time and storage requirements.

A patrol unit's *sector* is a collection of atoms. The atoms in the collection need not be contiguous (spatially) or consecutive (in the numerical ordering of atoms). In general, each atom may belong to any number of (overlapping) patrol sectors.

A *precinct* (or a *division*) is also a collection of atoms. However, unlike sectors, the set of precincts must be mutually exclusive and collectively exhaustive (spatially). In addition, each precinct must fully contain all patrol sectors that have any area in common with the precinct. That is, each sector must be fully contained within a precinct. The set of divisions also must be mutually exclusive and collectively exhaustive. In addition, each precinct must be fully contained within a division. These relationships are illustrated in Figure 6.1.

6.1.2. Point-Polygon Method

The technique that is essential if one is to structure the geographical data in the way described is the *point-polygon* method. This method answers the following question: "Given a point (x,y) and a polygon specified by its I clockwise ordered vertices $(x_1,y_1), (x_2,y_2), \ldots, (x_I,y_I)$, is the point (x,y) contained within the polygon?" The basic idea of the method, which is fully discussed by S. Nordbeck, is to extend a ray in any direction from the point in question; if the ray intersects the sides of the polygon an *odd* (*even*) number of times, the point *is* (*is not*) within the polygon.[6] Figure 6.2 illustrates

---

5. Each polygon is composed of an arbitrary number of sides and need not be convex.
6. S. Nordbeck, *Location of Areal Data for Computer Processing*, Lund Studies in Geography, Ser. C. General and Mathematical Geography, No. 2, The Royal University of Lund, Sweden, Department of Geography (Lund, Sweden: C. W. K. Gleerup Publishers, 1962). Also see J. Jacobsen, "Geographical Retrieval Techniques" (Gaithersburg, Maryland: International Business Machines, 1967), and S. H. Brownstein, "Some

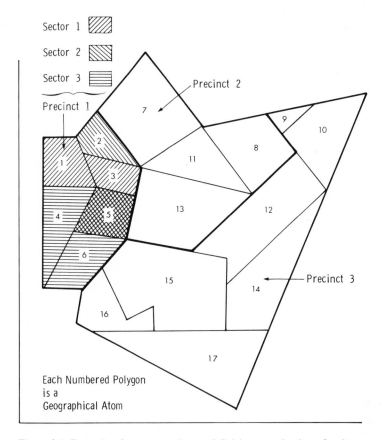

Figure 6.1 Example of sector, precinct and division organization of a city.

this idea. The method is completely general and does not require any special properties (for example, convexity) of the polygon. It is particularly well suited for machine implementation, since the tests for intersection are quickly performed on a computer.

In the simulation model the point-polygon method provides a convenient way to generate samples (x,y) uniformly distributed over a geographical atom. The atom, which is a polygon of arbitrary shape, is enclosed in the smallest rectangle fully containing it. Then, using two random numbers, a candidate point that has a uniform distribution over the rectangle is obtained. If this point is also within the polygon, it is accepted as the sample value;

Concepts and Techniques for Constructing and Using a Geographically-Oriented Urban Data Base," *Socioeconomic Planning Sciences* 1 (1968), pp. 309–325.

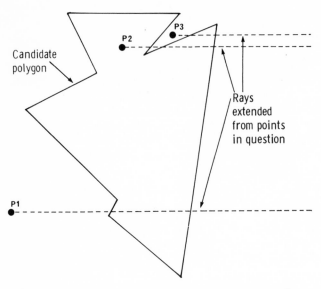

Candidate
polygon

Rays
extended
from points
in question

- Rays from P 1 and P 3 intersect polygon an even number of
  times and thus P 1 and P 3 are not within polygon.
- Ray from P 2 intersects polygon an odd number of times,
  and thus P 2 is within polygon.

Figure 6.2 Point-polygon method.

otherwise it is rejected and new points are generated until one is accepted.
The probability that any candidate point will be accepted is equal to the ratio
of the area of the polygon (A_P) to the area of the rectangle (A_R). The number of candidate points that have to be generated until one is accepted is a
geometrically distributed random variable with mean A_R/A_P. For reasonably
compact polygons, this number, reflecting sampling efficiency, is usually less
than 2 (and often quite close to 1).

The point-polygon method is also helpful in answering the question, "Given
a point (x,y), in which a geographical atom is it contained?" Clearly, this
question can be answered by straightforward application of the method to
each atom in turn, until a positive result is obtained. If the polygons to be
tested have a relatively large number of sides, the computer time for this
search can be reduced considerably by again embedding each atom in the
smallest rectangle that contains it. For any particular atom, denote the respective vertices of this rectangle as follows: (x_{min}, y_{min}), (x_{max}, y_{min}),
(x_{max}, y_{max}), (x_{min}, y_{max}). For the point (x,y) to be within the atom, the fol-

lowing inequalities must be satisfied:

$$x \leqslant x_{max} \tag{6.1a}$$

$$y \leqslant y_{max} \tag{6.1b}$$

$$x \geqslant x_{min} \tag{6.1c}$$

$$y \geqslant y_{min} \tag{6.1d}$$

For large cities, the test indicated by Inequality 6.1a fails about 50 percent of the time, causing immediate rejection of the atom in question. If Inequality 6.1a is satisfied, Inequality 6.1b also has a rejection rate of approximately 50 percent. The complete point-polygon procedure need be carried out only for those atoms which satisfy Inequalities 6.1a to 6.1d, thus greatly decreasing the search time spent on obvious bad choices. If even greater speed is required, contiguous polygons (atoms) can be grouped together and entire groups can be eliminated by procedures similar to those already described.

6.1.3. Time Sequence of Events

The simulation is an *event-paced* model. That is, once a certain set of operations associated with one event is completed, the program determines the next event that occurs and updates a simulation clock by adding to the present time the time until the next event. The program then proceeds with the set of operations associated with that event. Once the clock reaches some maximum time (T_{max}), the simulation is terminated and summary statistics are tabulated and printed out. One completed run of the simulation entails inputing data, initialization of simulation status variables, executing the program for an equivalent real time T_{max}, and printing the summary statistics. In this chapter, only the program execution (the actual simulation of system operation) is discussed further.

First consider the time ordering of events. Designate the kth type or class of event by the index k. Real time is denoted by the variable T. Associated with event type k there is a time $T(k) > T$ that, at time T, is the next scheduled time for event type k to begin. The array that contains all entries $T(k)$ is called the simulation *time-table*. Say that the operations associated with one event which occurred at time T are completed, then the clock is updated to

$$T + \min_{k} [T(k) - T] = \min [T(k)],$$

which is the time at which the next scheduled event occurs. Of course, the operations associated with one event k may require changing several entries in the simulation time table.

6.1.4. Calls for Service

Event type 1 is a report of an incident requiring police service, or more succinctly, a call for police service.[7] The time between successive calls for service is a negative exponential random variable with mean λ^{-1}. That is, the call-for-service process is, in time, a simple homogeneous Poisson process with rate parameter λ. If one wished to simulate time-varying demands, it is straightforward to allow λ to vary with time T.

Once the time of a reported incident is known, its *spatial position* and *priority* must be determined. This is done by first selecting a sample from the probability mass function $P_A(a)$, where

$A \equiv$ atom number of a randomly selected reported incident, and

$$P_A(a) \equiv P\{A = a\},$$

where $a = 1, 2, \ldots, N_A$ = number of geographical atoms. The priority of the incident I is then determined from the conditional probability mass function

$P_I(i|a) \equiv P$ {a randomly selected reported incident is priority type i| the incident originated in geographical atom a}, where $i = 1, 2, \ldots, N_P$ and $a = 1, 2, \ldots, N_A$.

Finally, the (x, y) position coordinates of the incident are determined by obtaining a sample from a uniform pdf over the geographical atom selected.[8]

Once the position and priority of the incident are known, the program executes a DISPATCH algorithm that attempts to assign a patrol unit to the incident. The specific rules of the algorithm are governed by the dispatch policy chosen. Several dispatch policies are available as follows:

1. Only assign a unit whose patrol sector includes the geographical atom containing the incident (a sector policy).
2. Only assign a unit whose precinct designation is the same as that of the incident (a precinct policy).
3. Only assign a unit whose division designation is the same as that of the incident (a division policy).

The particular option on a given run is specified at the start of the run.[9]

6.1.5. Determination of Dispatch Availability

We now indicate how a patrol unit is determined *available*, or *eligible* for dispatch to an incident. Two considerations seem to be important: (1) the pri-

7. A *call for police service* is said to occur whenever a reported *incident* is generated somewhere in the city. Undetected or unreported incidents are not treated in the model.
8. The point-polygon procedure is used to obtain the sample.
9. By using the interactive feature, the dispatch policy can be changed easily during the course of a run if desired.

ority level of the incident and of the activity in which the unit is currently engaged; (2) the estimated travel distance between the unit and the incident.[10] We denote the priority level of the current activity of unit j by the integer STATUS(j). Now, if the reported incident is of high enough priority (that is, low enough priority *number*), unit j can be *preempted* from its current activity of priority STATUS(j) and assigned to the more important incident. Specifically, to priority level i incidents we assign an integer PREEMP(i) (PREEMP(i) $\geqslant i$) such that all units engaged in activities *less important* then priority PREEMP(i) activities are considered *equally eligible* for assignment to the incident. As an example, suppose

$$j = 1$$
$$i = 3$$

PREEMP(3) = 4

STATUS(1) = 10.

Then, unit 1 would be considered available for dispatch to this priority 3 incident since priority level 10 activity is less important than PREEMP(3) = 4 level activity. Clearly, maximum preemption would be achieved by setting

PREEMP(i) = i, $i = 1, 2, \ldots, N_P$,

and no preemption would be achieved by setting

PREEMP(i) $> N_P$, $i = 1, 2, \ldots, N_P$.

The reader may ask, "What is the priority associated with preventive patrol?" The answer is that the user of the program can specify for each unit j ($j = 1, 2, \ldots, J$) an integer PRICAR(j) which is the equivalent priority of preventive patrol activity for that unit. Thus, when unit j is performing preventive patrol, its status is PRICAR(j). This flexibility allows the operator of the simulation to provide a certain continuous level of preventive patrol coverage (for example, if PRICAR(j) = 1, unit j is never assigned to a call for service).

   The second condition for dispatch is that an available unit be estimated sufficiently close to the scene of the incident. The estimated coordinates of unit j are designated by $[\hat{x}(j), \hat{y}(j)]$. The actual coordinates are $[x(j), y(j)]$. For some types of dispatch policies, the exact position of the incident, designated by coordinates (x, y), may not be considered; thus, an estimated posi-

10. Estimated travel time could also be used.

tion of the incident, $(\hat{x},\hat{y})$ is also specified. The operator specifies a maximum distance $R_1(i)$ such that if unit j is estimated to be further than $R_1(i)$ from a priority i incident, it is *not* eligible for dispatch to that incident.

In summary, a unit j is considered available or eligible for dispatch to a priority $i(i = 1,2, \ldots, N_p)$ incident originating at (x,y) if and only if the following conditions are met:

1. $\text{STATUS}(j) > \text{PREEMP}(i)$

2. $|\hat{x}(j) - \hat{x}| + |\hat{y}(j) - \hat{y}| < R_1(i)$.

6.1.6. Addition to a Queue of Unserviced Incidents

If no unit satisfies these conditions, the reported incident is inserted at the end of a queue of other unserviced incidents. Queues are designated by precinct and priority number. That is, associated with each precinct there are, in general, N_P queues of unserviced incidents.

6.1.7. Assignment to an Incident

If at least one unit satisfies the eligibility conditions, the one judged *closest* is assigned to the incident.[11] If a unit is assigned, its status is changed as follows:

$\text{STATUS}(j) = i$

$x(j) = x$

$y(j) = y$.

If assignment of this unit resulted in preemption of service on a less important incident, the preempted incident is placed *first in queue* in its priority class in its designated precinct.

6.1.8. Return from Service

When patrol unit j completes servicing an incident, a type $j + 1$ event is said to occur. A REASSIGNMENT algorithm is then executed that either (1) reassigns the returning unit to an unserviced incident or (2) returns the unit to preventive patrol. The eligibility conditions regarding priorities, travel distances, and administrative areas, which are necessary to specify a dispatch policy, are also an integral part of the reassignment policy. In addition, it is necessary to specify how one unserviced incident is given preference over another. This part of the reassignment policy, called the *reassignment preference policy*, parallels the *queue discipline* in ordinary queuing systems.

11. Clearly this assignment policy can be generalized. A more general policy would somehow combine estimated travel distance, the priority of the incident, and the status of each vehicle. Such a policy is easily inserted into the program.

In practice, reassignment procedures vary considerably among cities. Some cities attempt reassignment immediately following service completion of a previous incident, reassigning the unit while it is still at the scene of the previous incident. In other cities, the unit may not notify the dispatcher of job completion until it has resumed preventive patrol in its sector.[12] Often, one system will exhibit both types of behavior. To allow for both types of reassignments, the REASSIGNMENT algorithm executes two *interrogations* (or searches) for nearby unserviced incidents, one centered at the (estimated) position of the previous incident and the other centered about the estimated position of the unit, after it has resumed preventive patrol. The sequence of interrogations is further described later in this section.

In this model, the reassignment policy is partially specified by the dispatch policy. For instance, if the dispatch policy is a *sector* policy (policy 1, Section 6.1.4.), then only unserviced incidents that originated in the *sector* of the returning unit are eligible for assignment to the unit. Or, if the dispatch policy is a *precinct* (or *division*) policy, then only those unserviced incidents that originated in the *precinct* (or *division*) of the returning unit are eligible for assignment to the unit. Thus, the dispatch policy specifies the administrative area from which a list of eligible calls can be generated.

Once the algorithm determines all incidents in eligible administrative areas, it deletes from the eligible list those incidents that are not sufficiently important and·those that are judged too distant from the unit. The former condition implies that a priority i incident is *not* deleted only if

$PRICAR(j) > PREEMP(i).$

That is, an unserviced incident must be sufficiently important to preempt preventive patrol. The latter condition requires that an unserviced incident be estimated within a certain travel distance of the unit. Since two interrogations are allowed to take place, the first centered at the (estimated) position of the previous assignment and the second centered at the estimated position after resuming patrol, also two maximum allowable travel distances are permitted.

An example of this interrogation procedure is shown in Figure 6.3. In the example, unit j is terminating service on an earlier assignment at an estimated position $[\hat{x}_1(j), \hat{y}_1(j)]$. An interrogation about that point then follows. Any priority i incident judged to be within a distance $R_2(i)$ of the unit is con-

12. This often occurs in cities that require the patrol unit to travel to the precinct station house to complete reports before returning to preventive patrol or before being reassigned to an unserviced incident.

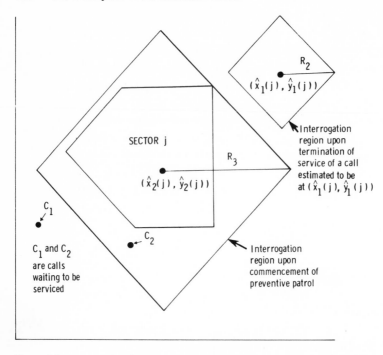

Figure 6.3 An example of reassignment procedures.

sidered eligible. None are found, so the unit tentatively resumes preventive patrol. Another interrogation follows, centered about the estimated position coordinates of the patrolling unit $[\hat{x}_2(j), \hat{y}_2(j)]$. Any priority i incident judged to be within a distance $R_3(i)$ is considered eligible. In the figure, incident $c2$ is estimated to be the only unserved incident sufficiently close, and the unit is reassigned to this incident.

Thus, during the first interrogation, a priority i incident judged to be waiting at $(\hat{x}, \hat{y})$ is eligible for assignment to unit j, which is estimated to be at $[\hat{x}(j), \hat{y}(j)]$, only if

$$|\hat{x}(j) - \hat{x}| + |\hat{y}(j) - \hat{y}| < R_2(i).$$

And, during the second interrogation,[13] a priority i incident judged to be waiting at $(\hat{x}, \hat{y})$ is eligible for assignment to unit j, which is estimated to be at $[\hat{x}(j), \hat{y}(j)]$, only if

$$|\hat{x}(j) - \hat{x}| + |\hat{y}(j) - \hat{y}| < R_3(i),$$

where $[\hat{x}(j), \hat{y}(j)]$ are now the estimated coordinates of the unit as it resumes

13. In the simulation, it is assumed that the time between the second and third interrogations is second order, compared to an average service time, and is thus set equal to zero.

patrol. The reason all of these coordinates are allowed to be estimated rather then the true coordinates is that, even if the true coordinates are known, they may not be used in a dispatch decision (for example, as in strict center-of-mass dispatching).[14]

Finally, after the list of eligible unserviced incidents is generated, the unit is reassigned to the incident selected by the reassignment preference policy. The simulation employs one of two policies, which may be succinctly thought of as (1) first-come, first-served, (FCFS), or (2) closest-car, closest-incident.[15] The two policies are described as follows:

Policy 1: From the list of eligible unserviced incidents, form one sublist for each nonempty queue represented. From each sublist, only consider eligible for reassignment that incident which has been waiting longest. Of all such eligible incidents, reassign the unit to that incident which is judged closest, according to a distance metric that may vary with priority.

Policy 2: Of all eligible incidents, reassign the unit to that incident which is judged closest, according to a distance metric that may vary with priority.

The major difference between the two policies is that policy 2 does not consider length of time in queue, whereas policy 1 does. We further explain the distance metric in Section 6.1.10.

6.1.9. Return to Patrol

Finally, if no eligible incidents are found, once the unit returns to patrol, then the unit assumes patrol status indefinitely. The unit is removed from patrol status only by assignment to an incident that may be reported some time in the future.

The coordinates of the patrolling unit j are determined in two steps. First, a sample is selected from the probability mass function

$P(a|j) = P\{\text{unit } j \text{ selects atom } a \text{ to patrol}\};$

$j = 1, 2, \ldots, J;$

$a = 1, 2, \ldots, N_A.$

That is, first the geographical atom of patrol is determined. Then, the actual coordinates $[x(j), y(j)]$ are determined by obtaining a uniform sample over the atom selected.

A rather general class of patrol deployment strategies is permitted with this

14. For the case of reassignment, as well as many other operations in the program, a setting of parameters to extreme values will, in effect, eliminate certain procedures. For instance, setting $R_2(i) = 0$ ($i = 1, 2, \ldots, N_p$) eliminates searching for nearby waiting incidents from the position of a serviced incident.
15. The policy definitions indicate that these names only partially describe the respective policies.

logical structure. For instance, the New York City Police Department assigns each patrol sergeant to patrol a zone, which comprises four or more usual sectors. Such a zone strategy is easily simulated with this model.

6.1.10. A Priority-Weighted Distance Metric

When reassigning a unit to an eligible waiting incident, the estimated travel distance $\hat{d}_j$ may be divided by an importance factor $B(i)$ associated with a priority i incident. If such weighting factors are employed, the reassignment algorithm reassigns the patrol unit to that unserviced incident with minimum value of $\hat{d}_j/B(i)$, a weighted distance metric. Otherwise, the unit is reassigned to that eligible waiting incident estimated to be closest to the unit, regardless of priority.

Qualitatively, one would expect the values of $B(i)$ (where $i = 1, \ldots, N_P$) to be ranked by priority. That is, one would expect

$$B(i-1) \geqslant B(i) \geqslant B(i+1), \quad i = 2,3,\ldots,N_p - 1.$$

Such a ranking implies that units should be reassigned to a more important incident, even if the incident is judged farther from the unit than some less important incident. Clearly, if

$$B(i-1) \gg B(i) \gg B(i+1), \quad i = 2,3,\ldots,N_p - 1,$$

then the most-important eligible incident is nearly always given preference over a less-important incident, regardless of estimated travel distance. This policy resembles an FCFS discipline *by priority*. Thus, in effect, the weights $B(i)$ (where $i = 1,2,\ldots,N_p$) allow a combination of FCFS by priority and assignment to closest waiting incident.[16]

6.1.11. Car Location

We have distinguished between the actual coordinates of the unit $[x(j),y(j)]$ and the estimated coordinates of the unit $[\hat{x}(j),\hat{y}(j)]$. In some cases (for example, when the unit is servicing a call) the position of the unit is known with certainty; if this information is used,

$$\hat{x}(j) = x(j)$$

$$\hat{y}(j) = y(j).$$

However, if not all available position information is used or if the unit is performing preventive patrol, the method of estimation of patrol car position must be specified. Two methods are distinguished, one that uses an automatic car locator system and one that does not.

---

16. The *weighted distance metric* is one arbitrary but reasonable weighting scheme. The program can easily be altered to explore policies based on other metrics.

Automatic Car Locator System

If the simulated system has an automatic car location capability, the accuracy of the estimated position depends on the resolution σ of the locator system. In particular, if unit j is on preventive patrol and is actually positioned at $[x(j), y(j)]$, then the coordinates $[\hat{x}(j), \hat{y}(j)]$ are determined by obtaining a sample from a circularly symmetric Gaussian pdf with standard deviation equal to σ and mode $[x(j), y(j)]$. The Gaussian pdf is truncated at the boundaries of sector j. That is, it is assumed that patrol unit j is somewhere within its assigned sector. (See Section 7.4 for a more complete description of the car locator model.)

Strict Center-of-Mass Strategy

With a strict center-of-mass strategy (Section 3.4.1) the exact position of neither the unit nor the incident is considered in making a dispatch (or reassignment) decision, even if either or both are known. As has been indicated, this strategy closely simulates dispatch operations as they are actually carried out.

With this strategy, a unit j on patrol is guessed to be at the center of mass of its assigned patrol sector, (x_j^0, y_j^0). The coordinates (x_j^0, y_j^0) are actually generated by averaging the positions obtained by successively and independently placing the unit on patrol many times. That is, Monte Carlo trials are used[17] in determining (x_j^0, y_j^0).

A strict center-of-mass policy does not use the exact position of the incident, even though it may be known. Assuming the incident is located in atom a (where $a = 1, 2, \ldots, N_A$), the position used in dispatch (reassignment) decisions is $[x^0(a), y^0(a)]$, where these are the *center-of-mass* coordinates of atom a. They are obtained by averaging the positions obtained by independently sampling from a uniform pdf over the atom.

Now, consider the case in which the patrol unit is positioned in atom b ($b = 1, 2, \ldots, N_A$) on a *previous assignment*. (Atom b may or may not be within the patrol sector of the unit.) Then, the coordinates for the unit used in dispatch (reassignment) decisions are $[x^0(b), y^0(b)]$, where these are identical to the center-of-mass coordinates of atom b, which was defined earlier.

In summary then, for a strict center-of-mass policy, if an incident is reported from atom a, the estimated center-of-mass travel distance between

---

17. This procedure prohibits certain sectors with peculiar shapes (for example, a doughnut-shaped sector), but such sectors are rarely of interest.

unit j and the incident is

1. $|x_j^0 - x^0(a)| + |y_j^0 - y^0(a)|$, if unit j is performing preventive patrol; or

2. $|x^0(b) - x^0(a)| + |y^0(b) - y^0(a)|$, if unit j is on a previous assignment in geographical atom b.

Modified Center-of-Mass Strategy

With a modified center-of-mass strategy (Section 3.4.1) a dispatcher uses more of the position information available, even though there is no complex automatic car location system.

When on patrol, the estimated coordinates of unit j are (x_j^0, y_j^0), which are the same as those used with a strict center-of-mass strategy. However, since all other positions are known with certainty, the exact coordinates are used in making dispatch (reassignment) decisions.

In particular, if an incident is generated at position (x,y), the estimated distance between unit j and the incident is

1. $|x_j^0 - x| + |y_j^0 - y|$, if unit j is performing preventive patrol; or

2. $|x(j) - x| + |y(j) - y|$, if unit j is on a previous assignment at $[x(j), y(j)]$.

6.1.12. Simulation Variables

The simulation program can tabulate statistics on any algebraically defined variable. The variables that were most often recorded in our studies were

1. Total time required to service an incident, that is travel time plus time at the scene.

2. Workload of each patrol unit (measured in total job assignments).[18]

3. Fraction of services preempted.

4. Travel time of a unit to reach the scene of the incident.

5. Number of unserviced incidents waiting in queue at the time of arrival of a report of an additional incident.

6. The wait in queue before a patrol unit is assigned to the incident.

7. The fraction of dispatch and/or reassignment decisions for which the car position was *estimated*, rather than known exactly.

8. The fraction of dispatches and reassignments that were to incidents located in the *same sector* as the patrol unit normally patrols.

9. The fraction of dispatch decisions which were nonoptimal, in the sense that there was at least one available unit closer to the scene of the incident.

10. The extra distance traveled as the result of a nonoptimal dispatch assignment.

---

18. It would also be straightforward to record workload in total hours spent servicing incidents.

On any given run only one or several of these variables may be of interest. Thus, the user specifies on each run which variables he wishes to have tabulated.

6.2. A Nine-Unit Command
In this section we illustrate the use of the simulation model for the simple 9-unit command illustrated in Figure 6.4.

From the command, incidents are generated in time by a Poisson process with rate λ incidents per hour. We deliberately keep λ as a parameter in order to study how the system operates under different workloads. The positions of incidents are uniformly distributed throughout the command and all positions are mutually independent.[19] This study of this command is divided into

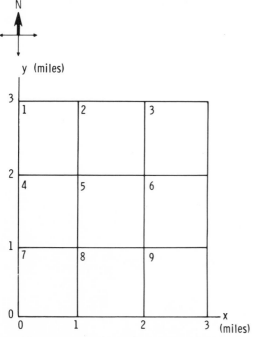

• The number of each sector is given in the upper left-hand corner of the sector

Figure 6.4 A nine-unit command.

19. This choice is made for simplicity in interpreting the results. Other spatial distributions of incidents or time dependencies among calls could be inserted, if desired.

three parts:

1. Tracing the simulated operation, incident by incident, for a 2-hour period;

2. Comparing three modes of operation, each with no priority structure; and

3. Examining system operation with a priority structure imposed on the input stream of calls.

The tracing of actual operation is helpful in developing an intuitive understanding of how the simulation works. The three modes of nonpriority operation that are compared are

1. Strict center-of-mass dispatching, FCFS reassignments;

2. Modified center-of-mass dispatching, FCFS reassignments;

3. Modified center-of-mass dispatching, closest-car, closest-incident reassignments.

Finally, we see how important calls are handled more effectively in the third study.

The use of the simulation model is further illustrated in Chapter 7, in which automatic car locator systems are studied.

6.2.1. Tracing the Simulation

Here we trace the system operation for 2 hours, starting with no queues of waiting calls and with all units assigned to preventive patrol. The parameters relating to input rate and service times are as follows:

λ = nine calls received per hour (on the average)

$\mu^{-1} = \dfrac{2}{3}$ hour required (on the average) to service a call, once at the scene of the call

v = 15 mph response speed.

The value λ = nine calls per hour was chosen so that each car, on the average, would be dispatched (or assigned) once each hour. Since the average service time is 40 minutes, the utilization factor[20] is high at approximately 0.67.

Cars are assigned to mutually exclusive sectors (Figure 6.4), with the position of each car chosen from a uniform pdf over the sector of the car. A strict center-of-mass dispatch and reassignment policy is used. Any queue that forms is depleted in an FCFS manner. Command-wide dispatching and reassignment are allowed; that is, any car is eligible for assignment to any call and

---

20. The average utilization rate is actually slightly greater than 0.67 because of the time required to travel to the scene of the incident.

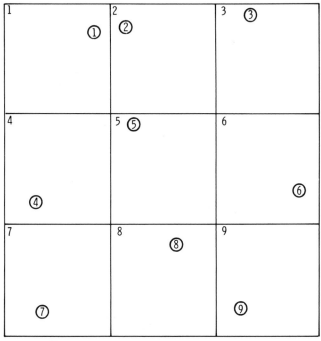

- The sector number is given in the upper left-hand corner of each sector.
- The position of each (free) patrol unit is shown by a circle, enclosing the number of the unit.

Figure 6.5 Initial positioning of patrol units in their respective sectors at time $T = 0$.

there is no maximum limit on estimated travel distances. For this command, sectors and geographical atoms are equivalent.

At time $T = 0$, the cars are positioned in their respective sectors (Figure 6.5).

Time Sequence of Events

The time sequence of operations for the following 2 hours is summarized in Figure 6.6. This figure indicates whether each unit is on patrol or busy servicing a call, and if busy, whether in its own sector or in some other sector. In addition, the total number of patrolling units (or the number of waiting incident reports) is shown as a function of time.

The figure indicates how the transient behavior, because all cars are initially on patrol, subsides in about 1 hour. Note that most initial assignments (within the first hour) are to units within their own sectors. But, as a congestion situation approaches (the second hour), a great fraction of assignments require the assigned unit to leave its usually assigned sector. Queues form during four different periods, starting at $T = 0.94$ hour.

Queues exist for a total 0.47 hour. All units are simultaneously busy servicing calls a total of about 0.6 hour; thus, about 30 percent of the time there is *no preventive patrol* coverage in the command.

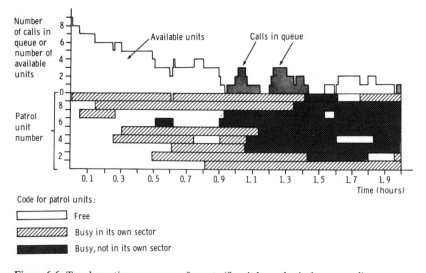

Figure 6.6 Two-hour time sequence of events (9-unit hypothetical command).

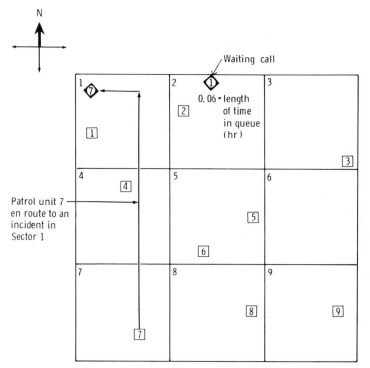

●The sector number is given in the upper left-hand corner of each sector.
●The position of each busy patrol unit is shown by a square, enclosing the number of the unit.
● There are no free patrol units.

Figure 6.7 Snapshot of the system at time T = 1 hour.

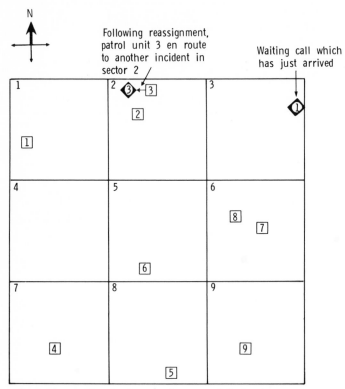

- The sector number is given in the upper left - hand corner of each sector.
- The position of each busy patrol unit is shown by a square enclosing the number of the unit.
- There are no free patrol units.

Figure 6.8 Snapshot of the system at time $T = 2$ hours.

Snapshots of the System

In conjunction with Figure 6.6, it is helpful to examine spatial "snapshots" of the system. These are given in Figures 6.7 and 6.8 for times $T = 1$ and $T = 2$, respectively. At time $T = 1$, we know (from Figure 6.6) that all units are busy and one call is waiting in queue. From the snapshot of the system, we see how the busy units are distributed. Only one of the units (unit 6) is in a sector other than its own. Another unit (7) is traveling from its assigned sector an incident in the N–W corner of sector 1; the required travel time of this assignment is 12.15 minutes. The waiting call is located in the northern portion of sector 2 and has been in queue for 0.06 hour.

At time $T = 2$ (Figure 6.8), again all units are busy but only three of the units are located in their own sectors. As a result of intersector assignments, a situation arises in which units 7 and 8 are in sector 6, but unit 6 is in sector 5, while unit 5 is in sector 8. In a somewhat unusually good dispatch decision for this system, unit 3 is traveling a very short distance (in sector 2) to an unserviced incident, also in sector 2. One incident is unserviced in the N–E corner of sector 3.

Summary Statistics

As previously discussed, the program tabulates and prints out summary statistics of system operation. For the simulated 2-hour period, the system variables assumed the following values:

Total calls generated = 26

Mean total service time per call = 0.73 hour

Maximum workload = 4 assignments (units 4, 9)

Minimum workload = 1 assignment (unit 1)

Mean travel time = 5.01 minutes

Mean number of calls in queue = 0.27

Mean wait in queue = 0.03 hour

Fraction of assignments (dispatches and reassignments) that are dispatches = 0.68

Fraction of assignments that are assignments to units in their own sectors = 0.48

Fraction of dispatch assignments for which a unit other than the closest unit was dispatched = 0.0.

The last value is somewhat remarkable for a strict center-of-mass dispatching policy, because there is a good chance (at least with low or moderate utilization systems) that a car other than the sector car is closest to the scene.

All of these statistics tend toward a steady-state value as the simulated time period grows larger. A better estimate of the fraction of nonoptimal dispatch assignments will be obtained in the next section, in which larger time periods are simulated.

6.2.2. A Comparison of Three Modes of Operation

Now the simulation model is used to compare system operation under these different strategies:

Strategy 1: Strict center-of-mass dispatching, FCFS reassignments;

Strategy 2: Modified center-of-mass dispatching, FCFS reassignments;

Strategy 3: Modified center-of-mass dispatching, closest-car, closest-incident reassignments.

We would expect the average travel time of system 2 to be less than that of system 1, provided that the utilization rate is high enough so that a non-negligible fraction of all dispatches occur when the sector car associated with the incident is busy, thus allowing the formulation of an interrogation strategy. However, if the utilization factor is too great (that is, near 1), then a large fraction of assignments are made from a queue, and one would expect systems 1 and 2 to exhibit nearly equal travel time characteristics.

On the other hand, for small utilization factors, we would expect systems 2 and 3 to exhibit nearly identical behavior. But, as the utilization rate nears unity, the advantages of closest-car, closest-incident reassignments should become apparent. Then the mean travel time of system 3 should be less than that of system 2.

Identical Demand Sequences

In order to reduce variability in the results due to random fluctuations in occurrence times and positions of calls and in service times of calls, we repeatedly use the same sequences of calls and only change by a constant factor the time between calls. That is, say in one run with average demand rate λ, the ith call occurred at time t_i from position $[x(i), y(i)]$ and required a time $t_s(i)$ to service (at the scene); then in another run with average demand rate λ_2 the ith call would occur at a time $(\lambda_1/\lambda_2) t_i$ from position $[x(i), y(i)]$ and would require a time to service $t_s(i)$. This control is not only helpful in examining one system under different workloads, but it also facilitates the comparison of alternative systems, each responding to the same sequence of demands for service.

For each run used to develop results in the following subsections, the same sequence of 909 calls for service was used.

Travel Distance versus Workload

Plotted in Figure 6.9 are average patrol car travel times (in minutes) versus utilization factor ρ. The three curves in the figure represent

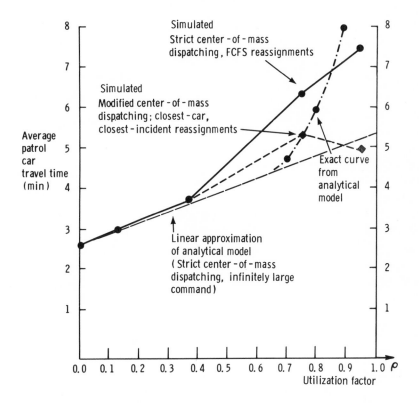

Figure 6.9 Relationship between patrol car travel time and utilization factor (nine-sector hypothetical command).

1. Simulation results of a system using strategy 1 (strict center-of-mass dispatching, FCFS reassignments)

2. Simulation results of a system using strategy 3 (modified center-of-mass dispatching; closest-car, closest-incident reassignments)

3. Analytical results for average travel time of a strict center-of-mass system and infinitely large command. Both the exact result (Equation 3.34) and the linear approximation (Equation 3.38) are plotted.

The mean travel times of a strategy-2 system are only slightly less those of a strategy-1 system, and therefore are not plotted in the figure. Apparently for this 9-sector command the reduced travel time advantages of a modified center-of-mass strategy, compared to a strict center-of-mass strategy, are not very large. In a larger command, the difference would probably be more noticeable since more alternative dispatch choices are possible.[21]

The two simulated strategies that are plotted behave approximately as one expects. They exhibit virtually identical average travel times for $0 \leqslant \rho \leqslant 0.4$, and agreement with the analytical model is nearly perfect. However, at higher utilization rates the differences between the two simulated systems become more apparent. At $\rho = 0.75$, for instance, the average travel time of the strategy-1 system is 6.3 minutes, compared to 5.3 minutes for the strategy-3 system, and compared to 5.2 minutes derived from Equation 3.34. For $\rho = 0.95$, the average travel time of the strategy-3 system drops below previous values, and one would expect it to drop to zero as ρ approaches 1. The average travel time of the strategy-1 system approaches 8 minutes, which is that of *one car assigned to a single square sector*[22] *of area 9*. Finally, the average travel time predicted from the analytical model becomes increasingly large as ρ approaches 1, since the model assumes an infinitely large command (and no limit on maximum allowable travel distance).

Overall, these curves indicate the validity of the earlier analytical model for utilization factors equaling approximately 0.5 or less but also reveal the need for more precise models for higher utilization rates. For this reason, it is helpful to return to the study of FCFS and closest-car, closest-incident reassignment strategies in Chapter 7.

Number of Intersector Assignments versus Workload

In Figure 6.10 is plotted the fraction of assignments (either dispatches or reassignments) that are intersector for the strategy-1 system as a function of

21. In larger commands, nearly every sector is completely surrounded by other sectors within the command; in a 9-sector command, only the center sector is completely surrounded in this way.
22. See Equation 3.4.

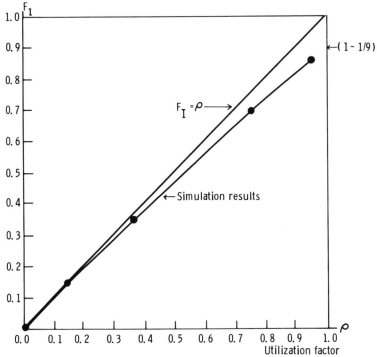

- F_I = Fraction of assignments which are intersector assignments
- An assignment is either a dispatch or a reassignment
- The line $F_I = \rho$ is given for reference
- Approx. 900 calls for service were generated in each simulation run

Figure 6.10 Relationship between fraction of assignments that are intersector and utilization factor (nine-sector hypothetical command), strict center-of-mass dispatching, FCFS reassignments.

utilization factor ρ. Strategy-2 and strategy-3 systems exhibit nearly identical behavior. Note that the fraction increases nearly linearly with ρ, approaching $^8/_9$ at $\rho = 1$, indicating that a unit receives an equal number of assignments (on the average) from each of the sectors.

Because of the strong implications of these results to so-called sector identity arguments, this behavior is examined further in Section 7.6.4 and Section 8.1.

Dispatch Errors versus Workload

In Figure 6.11 the probability is plotted that a dispatch will be in error (that is, that another available unit is closer to the scene) versus utilization factor for a strategy-1 system. Note that the error probability is about 0.27 at $\rho = 0$,

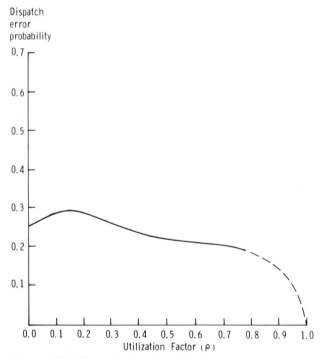

•Approx. 900 calls for service were generated in each simulation run.

Figure 6.11 Relationship between dispatch error probability and utilization factor (nine-sector hypothetical command).

then increases to about 0.3 at $\rho = 0.14$, and then[23] gradually decreases to about 0.13 at $\rho = 0.95$.

A strategy-2 or strategy-3 system reduced the error probability for moderate values of ρ by about 10 to 20 percent.

In Figure 6.12 the conditional distribution is plotted of *extra distance traveled due to dispatch error, given that error occurs*. To illustrate interpretation of the curves, at $\rho = 0.0$, for instance, about 40 percent of all erroneous dispatches cause an extra distance of at least 0.3 mile to be traveled;

Probability that the extra distance
traveled due to an incorrect dispatch
is greater than d (sector lengths),
given that the dispatch is in error

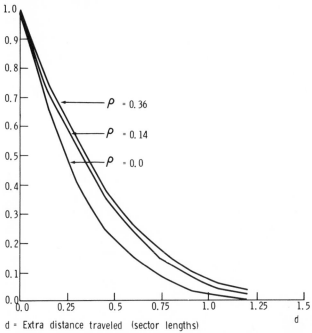

d = Extra distance traveled (sector lengths)

• Approx. 900 calls for service were generated on each simulation run

Figure 6.12 Distribution of extra distance traveled due to dispatch error.

23. For ρ near 0.95, the steady-state error probability may actually be less than 0.13. Statistics on dispatch errors in the model are maintained from $T = 0$, at which time all units are on preventive patrol and no queues exist. As saturation occurs, the likelihood of error decreases.

(or equivalently with probability 0.4, the extra distance traveled is 0.3 mile or more, given that dispatch error occurs.) Only three values of ρ were plotted ($\rho = 0.0, 0.14, 0.36$). For ρ larger than 0.36, the curve for $\rho = 0.36$ is a good approximation.

The *average* extra distance traveled, given dispatch error, is approximately 0.3 mile for $\rho = 0$, and about 0.4 mile for $\rho \geqslant 0.1$. For moderate values of ρ, a change to a strategy-2 or strategy-3 system reduced this average value by about 25 percent.

6.2.3. Priorities on Calls

The 9-sector command is now reconsidered with calls classified into one of three priority groups. Priority 1 calls, which represent 5 percent of all calls, are the most urgent class; they represent reported crimes in progress, officers in trouble, serious auto accident, and so on. Response time is critical for this class. Priority 2 calls, which comprise 45 percent of all calls, represent reported crimes which occurred in the past, miscellaneous disturbances, family disputes, and so forth. Priority 3 calls, comprising 50 percent of all calls, are the lowest-priority class; typically, they include open fire hydrants, parking violations, lock outs, and so on. Clearly, response time is least important for this class of calls.[24]

Parameters of the System

The controllable parameters of the system are set to reflect the relative importance of the various priority classes. These parameters specify the maximum acceptable dispatch radii associated with each class and the manner in which units completing service are reassigned to unserviced calls.

Recall that there are three occasions when a maximum allowable dispatch radius must be specified. These are the following:

1. Dispatch from preventive patrol;
2. Reassignment from the point of a previous assignment;
3. Reassignment after tentative resumption of preventive patrol.

Each radius can, in general, be a function of priority number. For priority 1 calls, one can set

$$R_1(1) = R_2(1) = R_3(1) = \infty;$$

that is, there will be no limit on dispatch distance for Priority 1 calls. For priority 2 calls, one sets

---

24. This percentage breakdown is typical of that found in large cities in which the stated policy is to dispatch police to nearly all citizen requests for police service.

$R_1(2) = \infty$

$R_2(2) = 1$ mile

$R_3(2) = 2$ miles,

and for priority 3 calls,

$R_1(3) = 2$ miles

$R_2(3) = 0$ miles

$R_3(3) = 2$ miles.

Thus, for priority 2 calls, a unit can be reassigned if the call is in the immediate vicinity of the unit when it terminates service on a previous incident. No such immediate reassignment is allowed for priority 3 calls. After tentative return to preventive patrol, units may be reassigned to priority 2 or 3 calls anywhere within an estimated two sector lengths of the unit. This set of values of dispatch radii tends to save or hold less-important calls for the unit associated with the sector of the call.

When determining which call to assign to a newly available unit, we allow different weighting factors $B(i)$ to be used for each of the priority classes, $i = 1, 2, 3$. We will set

$B(1) = 100$

$B(2) = 10$

$B(3) = 1$,

which would closely approximate a FCFS *by priority* queueing discipline.

Regarding other parameters, the following hold:

No preemption is allowed.

A modified center-of-mass dispatching strategy is used.

A closest-car, closest-incident reassignment policy is used (incorporating a distance metric which is a function of priority).

The equivalent priority of preventive patrol is greater than 3 for all units.

The response speeds are lower for less urgent calls,

$v(1) = 15$ mph

$v(2) = 12$ mph

$v(3) = 10$ mph.

The same time and space sequence of calls was generated as in the previous simulations, but for each call a priority was chosen by a Monte Carlo trial, reflecting the percentage breakdown of calls into priority classes.

The administrative conditions that we have imposed do not affect system operating characteristics at low utilization rates. Their benefits become increasingly more apparent at higher utilization rates. For this reason, we select a 0.95 utilization rate and compares the present priority system to the simple strategy-2 system (Section 6.2.2).

Average Travel Time

For the strategy-2 system, average travel time is 5 minutes (assuming 15 mph response speed for *all* calls). For the priority system, the average travel times (by priority) are as follows:

$\bar{t}_r(1) = 7.5$ minutes

$\bar{t}_r(2) = 4.8$ minutes

$\bar{t}_r(3) = 6.0$ minutes.

Thus, the mean travel time is actually *increased* for the most urgent calls.[25] The mean travel time of priority 2 calls is below that of the strategy-2 system, even though response speed is 3 mph less than that of the strategy-2 system.

Average Wait in Queue

For the strategy-2 system, the average wait for all calls in the dispatcher queue (prior to dispatch) is 20 minutes. For the priority system, the queue waits are as follows:

$\overline{W}(1) = 3.6$ minutes

$\overline{W}(2) = 20$ minutes

$\overline{W}(3) = 42$ minutes.

Adding the mean wait in queue to the mean travel time, one obtains an approximation for the entire police response time,

$\overline{W}(1) + \bar{t}_r(1) = 11.1$ minutes;

$\overline{W}(2) + \bar{t}_r(2) = 24.8$ minutes;

$\overline{W}(3) + \bar{t}_r(3) = 48$ minutes.

These figures clearly indicate the advantage of the priority dispatching procedures.

Amount of Intersector Assignments

The maximum dispatch radii imposed for priority 2 and 3 calls should tend to save these calls for the unit assigned to the sector of the call. Recall that

25. This results from the reassignment strategy that reassigns units to high priority calls first, (almost) regardless of estimated travel distance.

for the strategy-2 system, the fraction of assignments that were intersector assignments was 0.83. For the priority systems, these fractions (by priority) are as follows:

$F_I(1) = 0.85$

$F_I(2) = 0.66$

$F_I(3) = 0.52.$

Averaged over priorities, the fraction of total assignments that are intersector assignments is 0.59. Again, the advantages of the priority structure and accompanying administrative procedures becomes apparent.

6.3. Summary

In this chapter we have described a general simulation model of police dispatch-patrol operations, and we have applied the model to a simple 9-sector command. The model could be briefly summarized as follows:

The city is partitioned into a set of geographical atoms.

A patrol sector is a collection of atoms; patrol sectors are allowed to overlap.

A precinct (division) is a collection of sectors (precincts).

Calls for service arrive in a Poisson manner at a rate λ.

There is an arbitrary number of priority classes.

Demands for service need not be spatially homogeneous.

Patrol deployment need not be spatially homogeneous.

An equivalent priority number is given to preventive patrol activity; each patrol unit can be assigned a different number.

Three dispatch strategies are permitted as follows:
A *sector* strategy;
A *precinct* strategy;
A *division* strategy.

Maximum estimated travel distances are permitted; these may vary with priority. They may also depend on whether the assignment is (1) a dispatch, (2) reassignment from the position of a previous incident, or (3) reassignment from preventive patrol.

Two general reassignment policies are allowed:
A first-come, first served strategy;
A closest-car, closest-incident strategy.

A general preemption capability is provided.

Three methods of position estimation are provided:
Strict center of mass,
Modified center of mass,
Gaussian car locator.

Any algebraically defined variable can be tabulated and statistically analyzed. The program can be rerun with identical demand sequences.

We applied the model to a simple 9-sector command. First we traced an actual system operation for a 2-hour period and showed how saturation caused a large number of intersector assignments. Then we compared three different systems (each without a priority structure) and indicated how certain strategies were better than others. Finally, we examined a system in which calls are categorized into one of three priority classes, with accompanying administrative procedures to guide dispatcher decisionmaking. We saw how such an administrative structure speeds the response to urgent calls, while delaying less important calls.

In the next chapter, we will again employ the simulation model to examine systems with car location information. Also we will reexamine several of the issues posed by the simulation runs.

7

Evaluating Technological Innovations: Automatic Car Locator Systems

There is much current interest in improved police communication systems, real-time command and control systems, automatic car location systems, and other technological innovations. Total evaluation of any proposed system would have to include estimated effects on criteria of performance, officer moràle, community response, crime deterrence, and so forth.

In this chapter we select one proposed innovation—automatic car locator systems—and examine the potential effect on several criteria of performance. We hope to demonstrate that the modeling approach provides a convenient framework for exploring alternative ways of implementing a new technological capability and for predicting many of the quantitative effects of each alternative prior to implementation.

We shall be concerned with the following types of questions:

1. How are the resolution characteristics of a car locator system quantified and modeled?

2. What is the probability of dispatching other than the closest car with present manual dispatching systems?

3. What is the anticipated reduction in travel time that can be obtained with car location information?

4. How do increased utilization rates affect the potential benefits of car locator systems?

5. Does closest-car dispatching *degrade* system performance in any way?

6. What effect does the size of the command have on the value of car location information?

7. What would be the operating characteristics of the dispatch-patrol system if cars were no longer assigned to nonverlapping sectors, but car location information was used to dispatch the closest car?

Again the approach relies on constructing necessarily idealized mathematical models to develop insight into these questions. After discussing some preliminary matters, the plan for the chapter is to examine several different implementations of car locator systems. First we consider traditional nonoverlapping sectors, comparing center-of-mass dispatching with closest car dispatching. As in Chapter 3, the focus is first on linear concatenated sectors for which analytical results can be found. Then the simulation model introduced in the previous chapter is used to examine two-dimensional arrays of sectors. Generally speaking, the response time reduction benefits found for nonoverlapping sector systems are not very large, typically ranging between 10 and 20 percent. For this reason, the operating characteristics are then explored of overlapping sector systems in which the car locator information is used to dispatch the closest car. In comparing an overlapping sector system employing perfect resolution car location information to a nonoverlapping system with center-of-mass dispatching, we find that the two systems exhibit remarkably similar travel time characteristics. This finding is particularly interesting, because there are several arguments based on regional identity and patrol randomness that favor some type of overlapping sector plan.

The chapter concludes with two models that are useful for predicting response times in commands with small numbers of units assigned to overlapping sectors, using either a first-come, first-served reassignment policy or a closest-incident, closest-car reassignment policy.

The probable costs of car locator systems do not appear unreasonable. Knickel estimated about $500 to $1,000 per car for purchase plus somewhat lower annual operating and maintenance costs.[1] Although these costs may appear high for a $2,500 automobile, the salaries and overhead costs of the ten patrolmen required to keep the car staffed continually with two men typically ranges from $100,000 to over $200,000 annually.

While cost considerations are important, no attempt is made in this chapter to perform a cost-benefit analysis of car locator systems. Instead, the interest is in developing models that illustrate the various ways in which car location information can improve (or perhaps degrade) operation. Should one choose to do so, these models could be used in a cost-benefit context to assess the reasonableness of allocating funds for car locator systems. Such an analysis should be done with extreme care, however, since many of the important issues that arise when considering these systems are not easily quantified. These include the following: (1) improved officer safety; (2) improved administrative capabilities; and (3) the psychological effects on officers of operating in a car whose position is continually monitored. These types of issues will probably be resolved only by trial implementations.

A summary of definitions for the chapter is included in Table 7.1.

7.1. A Simple Example

First a simple example is given in which closest-car dispatching, using car location information, would result in assigning a car from outside the sector of

1. E. Knickel, "Electronics Equipment Associated with the Police Car," *Task Force Report: Science and Technology, A Report to the President's Commission on Law Enforcement and Administration of Justice* (Washington, D. C.: U.S. Government Printing Office, 1967), Appendix E.

Table 7.1 Summary of Definitions for Chapter 7

E-W (N-S)	East-west (north-south)
(x^0, y^0)	Position coordinates of an incident
(x_j, y_j)	Position coordinates of patrol unit j
$v_x (v_y)$	Patrol response speed E–W (N–S)
T_r	Time for the dispatched unit to travel to the scene of the incident
D	Distance traveled by the dispatched unit
T_j	Travel time from patrol unit j to the incident
ρ	Utilization rate or fraction of time a patrol unit is busy serving calls $(0 \leqslant \rho < 1)$
σ	Resolution of car locator system
S_i^1, S_i^2	States for the linear concatenated command (see Figure 3.4)
F_I	Fraction of assignments that are intersector
R_N	Travel distance to the closest of N units
$f_{R_N}(\cdot)$	Pdf of R_N
γ	Average number of patrol units per square mile
$p_K (k \mid A)$	Probability that there are k units in a region of area A (completely overlapping sectors), $k = 0, 1, 2, \ldots$
μ^{-1}	Mean total service time
N	Number of patrol units assigned to a command
λ	Average arrival rate of calls for service from a command
P_i	Probability that the system is in state i, where i is the total number of calls in service and in queue.

the incident, even though the sector car is available. (Recall that center-of-mass dispatching always gives first preference to the sector car.)[2]

Consider a square four-car command that is divided into four square patrol sectors (Figure 7.1). The coordinates of an incident generated in sector 1 are (x^0, y^0); the coordinates of the jth patrol unit are designated (x_j, y_j) (where $j = 1,2,3,4$).

2. The term "center-of-mass dispatching" is used to include all four strategies: SCM, $\overline{\text{SCM}}$, MCM, and $\overline{\text{MCM}}$.

Let $v_x(v_y)$ be the response speed of the unit traveling E-W (N-S). The time required for unit j to travel to the incident is

$$t_j = \frac{|x^0 - x_j|}{v_x} + \frac{|y^0 - y_j|}{v_y} .$$

The locus of all points about (x^0, y^0) that require a travel time t to reach (x^0, y^0) is given by the parallelogram obtained from all values of (x, y) satisfying

$$t = \frac{|x^0 - x|}{v_x} + \frac{|y^0 - y|}{v_y} . \tag{7.1}$$

Several sample parallelograms are drawn in Figure 7.1 for the case $v_x = v_y$. For future reference, this figure is called a *time-equidistant parallelogram of size t*. It is used in determining which car is closest (in a travel time sense) to (x^0, y^0).

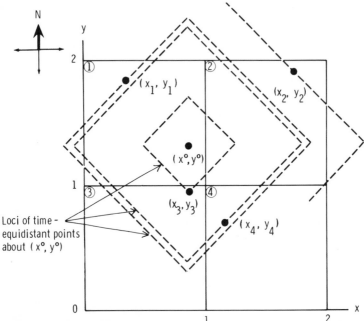

Units: sector lengths
(x^0, y^0) = coordinates of incident
(x_j, y_j) = coordinates of patrol unit j (j = 1, 2, 3, 4)

Figure 7.1 A four-sector command, illustrating time-equidistant parallelograms.

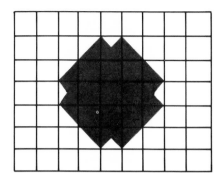

Figure 7.2 Locus of possible optimal dispatch points for a call in sector (0, 0) with full availability of patrol units.

By successively increasing the values of t (Equation 7.1), we see (Figure 7.1) that sector car 3 is closest to the incident. Sector car 4 is second closest, followed by cars 1 and 2. Clearly, the fact that a call is generated from a particular sector does not imply that the corresponding sector car is closest. Thus, if a police dispatcher knew the position coordinates of the cars, he could reduce city-wide travel time by consistently dispatching the closest (available) car.

The possibility that the closest car is one other than the sector car is far from remote. In fact, it is somewhat remarkable that in a large city with a regular[3] square sector pattern (Figure 7.2) and full availability of cars, the *closest* car to dispatch to the scene of a call may be in any one of 21 sectors! This result is not peculiar to the right-angle distance metric; with the Euclidean metric also, the same 21 sectors may contain the closest car. Although a regular square grid pattern for sectors is an idealized model, it is instructive. For instance, 12 of the 21 possible sectors are not contiguous to the sector of the incident. In a situation with full availability of units, dispatching from noncontiguous sectors is a strange idea to most dispatchers with whom the author has talked.

On the other hand, most commands do not contain 21 sectors. New York City, for instance, with 77 precincts and approximately 700 sector cars, averages about 9 sectors per precinct. Thus, with full availability of units in a 9-sector precinct, the choice of the closest car is restricted to a maximum of 9 cars. If several of the cars are unavailable, the choice is even further restricted. Thus, the size of the command (in terms of the number of patrol

---

3. We assume $v_x = v_y$.

units assigned) plays a critical role in determining the potential usefulness of car locator information. It is for this reason that later in the chapter a typical 9-sector command is examined as well as commands having a greater number of sectors.

7.2 Previous Work

A preliminary simulation of an automatic car locator system for police was conducted by M. Bellmore for the Science and Technology Task Force of the President's Commission on Law Enforcement and Administration of Justice.[4] Bellmore simulated a square area containing 144 square sectors, which for practical purposes is nearly infinite in size. Car locations were generated from a uniform pdf over the respective sector of each car.

A utilization rate ρ was chosen for each run.[5] Successive cars were designated to be unavailable for dispatch as a result of independent Bernoulli trials, with ρ being the unavailability probability. Since the area was so large, queues never formed.[6] Travel distance was assumed to be right angle. To determine the resolution of the car locator system, each sector was broken down into K^2 square cells or subsectors. Given that the car was actually in a particular cell, the car locator system would indicate the correct cell with certainty, but the conditional pdf of the car position within the cell was uniform.

After determining which cars were available for dispatch (from the Bernoulli trials), the program generated coordinates of the call for service from a uniform pdf over the entire city. The closest car that was available for service was determined and the travel distance computed. Then the car that the dispatcher thought to be closest (by a center-of-mass strategy) was determined,[7] and if different from the closest car, the difference in travel distance was computed. The conclusion of the study was that nearly no incorrect dispatches were made if $K = 5$ and that $K = 2.5$ appeared to be an acceptable resolution.

The focus in this chapter includes analytical as well as simulation models.

4. President's Commission on Law Enforcement and Administration of Justice, *Task Force Report, Science and Technology* (Washington, D. C.: U.S. Government Printing Office, 1967), pp. 149–151.
5. Recall that the utilization rate ρ is the average fraction of time each unit is busy servicing calls, or equivalently, ρ is the probability that a randomly interrogated unit is busy.
6. The utilization rate ρ was never so close to unity that all 144 cars would be simultaneously busy.
7. The writeup does not indicate which center-of-mass strategy was used.

The model for imperfect resolution appears more realistic than the preliminary one used by Bellmore. In addition, several different sector configurations are examined, including linear sectors and overlapping sectors, and an examination is included of car location information in systems in which queues can form.

Other recent studies have been conducted by R. Adams and S. Barnard,[8] who studied the value of an automated dispatching system for the San Jose Police Department, and by R. A. Bales,[9] who reexamined Bellmore's results using a more realistic model for position estimation errors.

7.3. Types of Car Locator Systems

The suitability of any particular model for car location depends a great deal on the technology of the car locator system. The resolution characteristics in particular would appear to be quite dependent on the type of system to be implemented.

For the President's Commission, Knickel discussed and evaluated four techniques for automatic car location:[10]

1. A system of patrol car emitters and callbox sensors.
2. A modified radar transponder system.
3. A medium-frequency radio-direction-finder system.
4. A car-borne position computation and reporting system.

A more recent study was prepared for the Chicago Transit Authority and the U.S. Department of Transportation.[11] Vehicle monitoring systems considered in the study were placed in three categories:

1. Dead reckoning automatic vehicle monitor (DAVM)
2. Trilateration automatic vehicle monitor (TAVM)
3. Proximity sensing automatic vehicle monitor (PAVM).

A DAVM system is comparable to inertial navigation systems used in military

8. R. Adams and S. Barnard, "Simulation of Police Field Forces for Decision-Making in Resource Allocation," in *Law Enforcement Science and Technology III, Proceedings of Third National Symposium on Law Enforcement Science and Technology* (Chicago, Ill.: Illinois Institute of Technology Research Institute, 1970).

9. R. A. Bales, "A Police Car Simulation Model: Conventional Versus AVM Dispatching," in *Proceedings of the 1970 Carnahan Conference on Electronic Crime Countermeasures* (University of Kentucky and Institute of Electrical and Electronic Engineers, April 16–18, 1970), pp. 1–28.

10. Knickel, "Electronics Equipment."

11. J. D. Garcia (principal investigator), "An Analytic and Experimental Evaluation of Alternative Methods for Automatic Vehicle Monitoring," report submitted to the Chicago Transit Authority and the U.S. Department of Transportation by the Institute of Public Administration, New York, and Teknekron, Inc., 1968.

systems; components of a system would probably include a digital odometer, a bearing indicator, and a simple computer to integrate the distance and direction of travel. A TAVM system uses the principle of electronic ranging; the location of an object can be estimated by measuring the arrival times of radio signals that travel between the vehicle being located and three (or more) receiving stations. PAVM systems incorporate fixed post sensors, spaced throughout an area, and the system updates the estimated position of a vehicle each time the vehicle passes within a few feet of a fixed post.

Specific proposals for these types of systems have appeared in recent years and field tests of several are currently in progress.[12]

Each locator would have different resolution characteristics. Using Knickel's categorization, his systems 1 and 4, for instance, would probably evidence time-varying resolution; that is, for each car these systems would probably accumulate errors as the time increased since the last calibration. His systems 2 and 3 would probably have non-time-varying error characteristics, at least in a city in which communication problems (such as those caused by multipath reflections from skyscrapers) were negligible.

7.4. Assumptions of the Model

This study of car locator systems will use both analytical and simulation techniques. The general model is characterized by the following assumptions:

1. Each patrol unit is assigned to patrol an area (not necessarily mutually exclusive of other areas).

2. The position of any particular unit is a random variable selected from a uniform pdf over the corresponding patrol area. The positions of units are mutually independent.

12. See, for example, "Electronic Eye on Auto Fleets," *Business Week*, no. 2107 (January 17, 1970), p. 88; R. Distler, "An Active Infrared System for Vehicle Tracking and Ranging," in *Law Enforcement Science and Technology I, Proceedings of the First National Symposium on Law Enforcement Science and Technology* (Chicago, Ill.: Illinois Institute of Technology Research Institute, 1967), pp. 913–918; D. Harris, *A Study of the Application of an Automatic Vehicle Monitoring System to the Operation of the Boston Police Department* (Wellesley, Mass.: Urban Sciences, Inc., 1971); H. Heubrocker, "Feasibility of Radar Beacon Techniques for Patrol Vehicle Tracking and Position Display," in *Law Enforcement Science and Technology I, Proceedings of the First National Symposium on Law Enforcement Science and Technology* (Chicago, Ill.: Illinois Institute of Technology Research Institute, 1971), pp. 903–912; C. Rypinski, "Police Message, Status and Location Reporting System," in *Law Enforcement Science and Technology III, Proceedings of the Third National Symposium on Law Enforcement Science and Technology* (Chicago, Ill.: Illinois Institute of Technology Research Institute, 1970); J. Zauderer, "Field Testing of an Automatic Vehicle Monitoring System," in *Law Enforcement Science and Technology III, Proceedings of the Third National Symposium on Law Enforcement Science and Technology* (Chicago, Ill.: Illinois Institute of Technology Research Institute, 1970).

3. Incidents are generated by a Poisson process (in time) and the positions of incidents are generated from a uniform pdf over the total area. Times and positions of all incidents are mutually independent.

4. Travel distance is right-angle.

The analytical work will assume perfect car position resolution.

For nonperfect resolution, assume the estimated position of unit j is given by

$$\hat{X}_j = X_j + X_e$$
$$\hat{Y}_j = Y_j + Y_e$$

(7.2)

where

(X_j, Y_j) are the actual coordinates of unit j

(X_e, Y_e) are additive error terms due to imperfect resolution.

For many systems (see Bales,[13] for instance) it is reasonable to assume that X_e and Y_e are *independent*, *zero-mean* Gaussian random variables with known variance σ^2. The standard deviation σ is a measure of the resolution of the system. The pdf for the error terms is

$$f_{X_e}(x) = f_{Y_e}(x) = \frac{1}{\sqrt{2\pi}\sigma} e^{-x^2/2\sigma^2}, \quad -\infty < x < +\infty.$$

Of particular interest is the *radius of error*,

$$R_e \equiv \sqrt{X_e^2 + Y_e^2}.$$

By straightforward change of variables, one finds the pdf of R_e,

$$f_{R_e}(r) = \frac{r}{\sigma^2} e^{-r^2/2\sigma^2}, \quad r \geqslant 0.$$

(7.3)

This is a Rayleigh[14] pdf with parameter $1/\sigma$. The mean radius of error is

$$E[R_e] = \sigma \sqrt{\frac{\pi}{2}}.$$

(7.4)

The variance is

$$\sigma_{R_e}^2 = \left(2 - \frac{\pi}{2}\right)\sigma^2.$$

(7.5)

13. Bales, "Police Car Simulation."
14. See any introductory book on probability, for instance, A. W. Drake, *Fundamentals of Applied Probability Theory* (New York: McGraw-Hill Book Company, 1967), p. 276.

In simulating this type of car position estimator, one can deal directly with the Gaussian random variables X_e and Y_e, or one can sample from the Rayleigh pdf and use the relations

$$\hat{X}_j = X_j + R_e \cos \theta$$

$$\hat{Y}_j = Y_j + R_e \sin \theta,$$

where θ is a random variable uniformly distributed over $[0, 2\pi]$, independent of R_e.

In these simulation studies, the resolution characteristics of a car-locator system are modeled using the aforementioned Gaussian model, with the additional assumption that each patrolling unit is within its own sector. If the first estimated coordinates $(\hat{x}_j, \hat{y}_j)$ are not within patrol sector j, repeated independent bivariate Gaussian samples[15] are drawn until a set of coordinates $(\hat{x}_j, \hat{y}_j)$ falls within sector j. This set of coordinates is then the guessed position of patrol unit j. In the simulation, if the exact position of the unit is known due to prior assignment, there is no position estimation error. With this model σ does not change with time, so the model more closely resembles systems 2 and 3 under Knickel's categorization than systems 1 and 4.

7.5. Nonoverlapping Sectors, Full Availability

We are ready to examine the effects of car location information in systems with various sector configurations. First we consider nonoverlapping sectors, including linear as well as square sectors. It is convenient to examine first the case for which all units are available (that is, full availability), followed by the partial availability case. Later in the chapter, systems with overlapping sectors are examined.

7.5.1. Linear Sectors

Perhaps the simplest application of car location information would involve concatenated linear or straight-line sectors. Assume that one patrol unit is assigned to patrol uniformly each interval $[i, i + 1]$, i integer. Incidents are distributed uniformly over the entire region of patrol. With center-of-mass dispatching and full availability of units, the unit assigned to interval $[i, i + 1]$ would service all incidents generated in that interval. However, the closest

15. Such repeated sampling could actually occur in implemented type 2 and type 3 systems (using Knickel's categorization) if the original guessed coordinates of the patrol unit placed the unit in an unexpected location. The individual samples would be nearly independent if the car is moving (see Harris, *A Study of the Application*). In fact, multiple samples could be used routinely to increase the sample size, thereby improving the resolution characteristics of the system.

unit to an incident in $[i, i + 1]$ may be in one of the adjacent intervals. With perfect car location information, the dispatcher could always dispatch the closest unit.

For this model it is straightforward to show that the pdf of the travel distance to the *nearest* unit is

$$f_D(d) = \begin{cases} 2 - 4d^2 & 0 < d \leqslant \dfrac{1}{2} \\[2em] 4 - 8d + 4d^2 & \dfrac{1}{2} < d \leqslant 1. \end{cases} \tag{7.6}$$

The mean travel distance to the nearest unit is

$$E[D] = \frac{7}{24}. \tag{7.7}$$

This compares to a mean travel distance of $1/3$ following a center-of-mass dispatching strategy. Thus, *for concatenated linear sectors with full availability of units, perfect resolution car location information reduces mean travel distance by 12.5 percent.*

We are also interested in the probability of dispatching other than the closest unit P_E, the dispatch error probability. Without loss of generality we can assume that the incident is uniformly distributed over $[0, 1/2]$, and we can label units as in Figure 3.4. Given that the incident is located at $x (0 \leqslant x \leqslant 1/2)$ and unit 0 is located at $u (0 \leqslant u \leqslant 1)$, the probability of dispatch error with center-of-mass dispatching is

$P_E(x, u) = P\{$unit 1 is closer to the incident than unit 0| incident at x and unit 0 at $u\}$.

Since unit 1 is uniformly distributed over $[-1, 0]$,

$P_E(x, u) = \max [u - 2x, 0]$.

Eliminating x and u by integration, we find

$$P_E = \frac{1}{6}. \tag{7.8}$$

Thus, *for concatenated linear sectors with full availability of units, perfect resolution car location information would reduce the travel distance of one-sixth of all responses.* The average travel distance reduction for these responses would be 0.25 sector length.

7.5.2. Square Sectors

Next consider a regular lattice of square sectors, each of unit area, assuming $v_x = v_y$. Consider two cases analytically: (1) incident at the *center* of a sector; (2) incident at the *corner* of a sector.

Case 1: Incident at Center of Sector

Referring to Figure 7.3, given the incident is at the center of a sector, we note that the cdf for the travel distance to the nearest car can be written

$$F_D(\ell) = \begin{cases} 2\ell^2 & 0 \leqslant \ell \leqslant \dfrac{1}{2} \\[4mm] 1 - 2(1 - \ell)^2 \left[1 - \left(\ell - \dfrac{1}{2}\right)^2\right]^4 & \dfrac{1}{2} < \ell \leqslant 1. \end{cases} \tag{7.9}$$

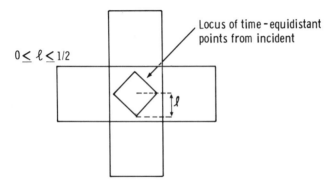

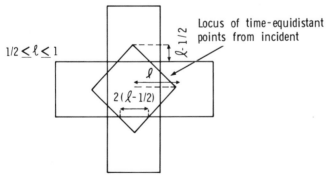

• Distance is measured in sector lengths

Figure 7.3 Closest car strategy, mutually exclusive sectors. Case 1: Incident in center of a sector.

The mean is

$$E[D] \approx 0.49. \tag{7.10}$$

This result compares to a mean travel distance of 0.50 to an incident in the center of the sector, given a system with no car location information, in which case the car assigned to the sector of the incident is always dispatched. Thus, there is almost no difference between the two systems for an incident at the center of a sector.

Case 2: Incident at Corner of Sector

Now, for the case in which the incident is at the corner of a sector, with no car location information the sector car would always be dispatched, resulting in a mean travel distance of 1 sector length. With a perfect resolution car location system, the closest car can be in any one of 12 sectors (Figure 7.4). Clearly, car location information should be most useful in this case.

The cdf of the travel distance to the closest car is

$$F_D(\ell) = \begin{cases} 1 - \left(1 - \dfrac{1}{2}\ell^2\right)^4 & 0 \leqslant \ell \, 1 \\[2ex] 1 - \left[\dfrac{1}{2}(2 - \ell)^2\right]^4 \left[1 - \dfrac{1}{2}(\ell - 1)^2\right]^8 & 1 < \ell \leqslant 2. \end{cases} \tag{7.11}$$

The mean is

$$E[D] \approx 0.58. \tag{7.12}$$

This is about 42 percent less than the corresponding mean travel distance in a system with no car location information. Thus, a perfect resolution car location system would reduce mean travel distance by never more than 42 percent, and the average percentage reduction may be much less.[16]

7.6. Nonoverlapping Sectors, Partial Availability

We now wish to compare center-of-mass dispatching to closest-car dispatching at *arbitrary utilization rates*. Among the questions of interest is, "How does the value of car location information vary with utilization rates?" We first examine linear concatenated sectors, obtaining analytical results to assist our intuition; then we use the simulation model to examine the two-dimensional case.

16. Ideally one would also like the mean travel distance to the closest car not to be conditioned on the incident location. But this mean value is quite tedious to evaluate.

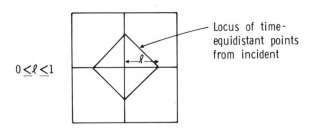

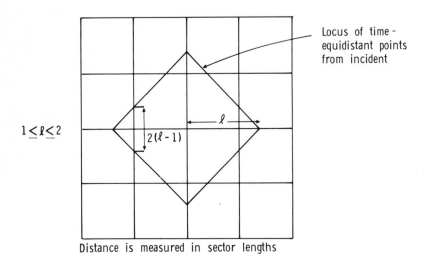

Distance is measured in sector lengths

Figure 7.4 Closest car strategy, mutually exclusive sectors. Case 2: Incident at corner of sector.

7.6.1. Linear Sectors

Referring again to Figure 3.4 we assume that the incident position is selected from a uniform distribution over $[0,1/2]$, each available unit is positioned according to a uniform distribution over its own sector, and each unit is unavailable with probability ρ, independent of the status of all other units. We wish to compute expected travel distance at arbitrary utilization rates, assuming perfect resolution car location information with closest-car dispatching, and to compare the results found for both SCM and MCM dispatching in Chapter 3. We are also interested in dispatch error probabilities at arbitrary utilization rates for both SCM and MCM dispatching.

Let state S_i^2 correspond to all units $0,1,\ldots,i-1$ unavailable and both units i and $i+1$ available. Let state S_i^1 correspond to all units $0,1,\ldots,i-1$ unavailable, unit i available, and unit $i+1$ unavailable. Clearly,

$$P\{S_i^2\} = \rho^i(1-\rho)^2 \qquad i = 0,1,2,\ldots$$
$$P\{S_i^1\} = \rho^{i+1}(1-\rho) \qquad i = 0,1,2,\ldots \tag{7.13}$$

Now, car location information can improve performance over that obtained with center-of-mass dispatching only if the system is in some state where either of two units may be closest, that is, some state S_i^2 and not S_i^1. (For a state S_i^1, either type of center-of-mass dispatching correctly determines that unit i is the closest available unit.) Straightforward probability arguments yield the conditional expected travel distances for each type of state:

$$E[D|S_i^2] = \begin{cases} \dfrac{7}{24} & i = 0 \\[2mm] \dfrac{17}{24} + \dfrac{i-1}{2} & i = 1,2,\ldots \end{cases} \tag{7.14}$$

$$E[D|S_i^1] = \begin{cases} \dfrac{1}{3} & i = 0 \\[2mm] \dfrac{3}{4} + \dfrac{i-1}{2} & i = 1,2,\ldots \end{cases} \tag{7.15}$$

Computing the unconditional expected travel distance, we have for closest-car dispatching

$$E[D] = \frac{7}{24} + \frac{11}{24}\rho + \frac{1}{2}\frac{\rho^2}{1-\rho}. \tag{7.16}$$

This function increases monotonically with ρ and blows up as ρ approaches

1, thus exhibiting similar behavior to the comparable expressions for SCM and MCM dispatching found in Chapter 3.

As in Chapter 3, it is instructive to compare expected travel distances for alternative dispatching strategies by constructing *difference functions*. Let $\epsilon_1(\rho)$ be the difference in expected travel distance between SCM dispatching and closest-car dispatching, given a utilization rate of ρ. Let $\epsilon_2(\rho)$ have a similar definition for MCM dispatching. Examining $\epsilon_1(\rho)$ first, using Equations 3.24 and 7.16, we find

$$\epsilon_1(\rho) = \frac{1 + 6\rho - 7\rho^2}{24(1 + \rho)}.$$

(7.17)

This function has the following properties:

At $\rho = 0$ the difference is 1/24 sector length, a result in agreement with Equation 7.7;

At $\rho = 1$ the difference is zero, indicating no difference between SCM and closest-car dispatching;

The function is unimodal, reaching a maximum at $\rho \approx 0.309$, at which point $\epsilon(0.309) \approx 0.0696$, or approximately 67 percent greater than $\epsilon(0)$.

Compared to SCM dispatching, we see that the value of closest-car dispatching is maximum at a moderately low but nonzero value of ρ.

Switching now to MCM strategies, using Equations 3.16 and 7.16, we find

$$\epsilon_2(\rho) = \frac{1}{24}(1 - \rho).$$

(7.18)

This surprisingly simple result indicates that, when compared to MCM dispatching, the maximum value is obtained from car position information at $\rho = 0$.

We are also interested in dispatch error probabilities for arbitrary ρ for both SCM and MCM dispatching. Let $P_E^1(\rho)$ be the probability of dispatching other than the closest available car, given a utilization rate of ρ and SCM dispatching. Let $P_E^2(\rho)$ have the identical definition for MCM dispatching. Let E denote the event of dispatching other than the closest available car.

Consider SCM dispatching first. If the system is in some state S_i^2 ($i = 1,3,5, \dots$), then the dispatcher using an SCM strategy is equally likely to assign unit i or unit $i + 1$, even though the incident is located in the interval $[0,1/2]$; the conditional probability of dispatch error is 1/2. If the system is in some state S_i^1 ($i = 0,1, \dots$), then the dispatcher will correctly assign unit i. Finally, if the system is in some state S_i^2 ($i = 0,2,4, \dots$), the dispatcher will always assign unit i; but the techniques that led to Equation 7.8 reveal that unit $i + 1$

is closer than unit i with probability 1/6. Summarizing these results, we have

$$P(E|S_i^2) = \frac{1}{6} \quad i = 0,2,4,\ldots$$

$$P(E|S_i^2) = \frac{1}{2} \quad i = 1,3,5\ldots$$

$$P(E|S_i^1) = 0 \quad i = 0,1,2,\ldots \tag{7.19}$$

Using Equations 7.13 and 7.19 to compute the unconditional probability, we find for SCM dispatching

$$P_E^1(\rho) = \frac{(1-\rho)(1+3\rho)}{6(1+\rho)}. \tag{7.20}$$

This is a unimodal function which reaches a maximum value at $\rho = -1 + 2\sqrt{3}/3 \approx 0.155$, at which point $P_E(0.155) \approx 0.179$, or about 7.2 percent greater than $P_E(0)$.

  Similar reasoning for MCM dispatching yields

$$P(E|S_i^2) = \frac{1}{6} \quad i = 0,1,\ldots$$

$$P(E|S_i^1) = 0 \quad i = 0,1,\ldots \tag{7.21}$$

Computing the unconditional probability, we find for MCM dispatching

$$P_E^2(\rho) = \frac{1}{6}(1-\rho). \tag{7.22}$$

Again for MCM dispatching, we see the value of car location information is maximum at $\rho = 0$ and decreases linearly to zero at $\rho = 1$.

7.6.2. Square Sectors

We now use the simulation model described in Chapter 6 to examine how car location information affects operating characteristics of a command comprising a regular pattern of square sectors.[17] Reflecting the size of typical commands, the primary focus is on the 9-sector command introduced in Section 6.2. To illustrate sensitivity of results to command size, we often compare to results obtained from a 49-sector command comprising a 7 X 7 array of square sectors. In all cases the dispatching algorithm assigns to an incident the available car judged closest. For the case of a reassignment to a waiting call, the unit is reassigned to the waiting call judged closest.

17. Certain dispatch error characteristics for a strategy-1 system (Section 6.2.2) have already been summarized in Figures 6.11 and 6.12.

For a *perfect resolution* 9-sector system, the average travel time as a function of ρ is given in Figure 7.5. In comparison to a strict center-of-mass strategy, the average travel time is reduced from 2.64 minutes to 2.34 minutes at $\rho = 0$, an 11 percent reduction; at $\rho = 0.14$, average travel time is reduced from 3.03 minutes to 2.58 minutes, an 18 percent reduction. In comparing Figure 7.5 to Figure 6.9, there is successively less to be gained (in travel time reduction) from the car location information as ρ becomes larger than about 0.25. At $\rho = 0.75$, there is no significant difference in average travel time between a strict center-of-mass system and a perfect resolution system.

The dispatch error probability for SCM dispatching follows a unimodal curve, as discovered previously for straight-line sectors. This probability equals 0.26 at $\rho = 0$, reaches a maximum of about 0.28 between $\rho = 0.1$ and $\rho = 0.2$, and falls off very gradually to zero as ρ approaches unity. For MCM dispatching the dispatch error probability drops monotonically from 0.26 at $\rho = 0.0$ to 0 at $\rho = 1.0$, but the decrease is not linear (as was found for straight-line sectors). For $\rho \geqslant 0.1$, the dispatch error probability for MCM dispatching is typically 0.03 less than that for SCM dispatching; for instance, at $\rho = 0.5$, dispatch error probability for SCM dispatching equals 0.22 in contrast to 0.19 for MCM dispatching. For values of ρ between 0.1 and 0.8, the average extra distance traveled due to inaccurate position estimation is consistently about 25 to 35 percent greater for SCM dispatching than that for MCM dispatching.

These results are modified somewhat for a 49-sector command. At $\rho = 0$, the average travel time is reduced from 2.64 minutes to 2.23 minutes, a 15.5 percent reduction. The amount of travel reduction remains greater than the comparable amount for the 9-sector command for all values of ρ. Even at $\rho = 0.7$, perfect resolution car location information saves an average of 29 seconds for each response. At this utilization, 25 percent of all dispatches resulting from a strict center-of-mass strategy are in error; for these dispatches, the car location information reduces average travel time by nearly 2 minutes.

For a 49-sector command with SCM dispatching, dispatch error probability again follows a unimodal curve, but for each value of ρ the error probability is greater than that for the 9-sector command. This reflects the greater number of dispatch alternatives in the 49-sector command. The error probability starts at 0.32 at $\rho = 0$, reaches a maximum of about 0.36 between $\rho = 0.1$ and $\rho = 0.2$, and decreases very slowly to zero as ρ approaches one. The corresponding probabilities for MCM dispatching are typically 0.04 below those

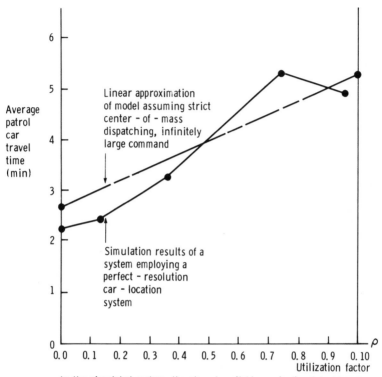

In the simulated system , the closest available car is dispatched to an
incident (if at least one car is available); cars completing service
are reassigned to the closest waiting call (if there is a queue of
waiting calls).
Travel speed assumed to be 15 mph.
Approx. 900 calls for service were generated in each simulation run.

Figure 7.5 Relationship between patrol car travel time and utilization factor, assuming
perfect car position information (9-sector hypothetical command).

Table 7.2 Car Locator Resolution and Dispatch Error Characteristics (9-Sector hypothetical command; utilization rate $\rho = 0.0$)

	Strict Center-of-Mass Dispatching	$\sigma = 0.25$	$\sigma = 0.15$	$\sigma = 0.1$	$\sigma = 0.0$
Probability of dispatch error	0.27	0.23	0.17	0.11	0.0
Average extra travel distance, given dispatch error	0.31	0.23	0.15	0.12	0.0
Unconditional average extra travel distance	0.084	0.053	0.025	0.013	0.0

Note: Distance units are sector lengths = miles. Each table entry is based on a simulation run in which approximately 900 calls for service were generated. Dispatch error occurs if the assigned unit is not the closest available unit to the scene of the call. The "extra travel distance" is the difference between the distance traveled by the dispatched unit and the travel distance of the closest available unit. Here, σ = resolution (miles) of car locator system.

for SCM dispatching. The average reduction in travel distance that could be obtained by dispatching the closest car is typically 20 to 30 percent greater for the 49-sector command than that for the 9-sector command.

7.6.3. Resolution Characteristics[18]

For a 9-sector system with $\rho = 0$, for several values of resolution Table 7.2 contains (1) the probability of dispatch error; (2) the average extra distance traveled, given dispatch error; and (3) the average extra distance traveled, averaged over all dispatches. For $\sigma = 0.25$, we observe that dispatch error probability 0.23 is nearly equal to that of a center-of-mass system. The conditional extra distance traveled, given error, is reduced from 0.31 for a center-of-mass system to 0.23 mile. Thus, for $\sigma = 0.25$, the average extra distance traveled on a random dispatch caused by inexact car location information is (0.23) · (0.23) ≈ 0.053 mile. A higher resolution system ($\sigma = 0.1$) is still characterized by a moderate dispatch error probability (0.11), but the additional distances traveled due to error are quite small.

Again these results are modified slightly for a 49-sector system. For $\sigma = 0.25$, the probability of dispatch error is increased to 0.27 and the average extra distance traveled given error is increased to 0.27 mile. For $\sigma = 0.1$, there is no significant difference between the 9-sector and the 49-sector systems.

7.6.4. Amount of Intersector Assignments versus ρ

Since a car other than the sector car may be closer to the scene of the incident, one would expect a *greater amount* of intersector dispatching in a sys-

18. See Section 7.4 for a discussion of imperfect resolution.

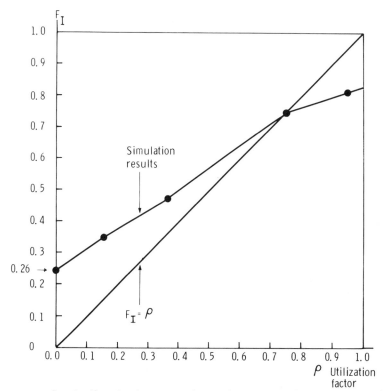

- F_I = fraction of assignments which are intersector assignments
- An assignment is either a dispatch or a reassignment
- The line $F_I = \rho$ is given for reference
- Approx. 900 calls for service were generated in each simulation run

Figure 7.6 Relationship between fraction of assignments that are intersector and utilization factor, assuming perfect car position resolution (9-sector hypothetical command); closest available car dispatching; closest-car, closest-incident reassignments.

tem with perfect car position information and closest car dispatching. This conjecture is verified in Figure 7.6. At $\rho = 0$, for instance, the fraction of assignments which are intersector assignments is $F_I = 0.26$, compared to $F_I = 0$ in a center-of-mass system. For a 49-sector system, this is increased to $F_I = 0.32$.

This completes the simulation analysis of square sectors with car locators. Overall, it is observed that in a command of typical size (for example, 9 sectors), the reduction in mean travel time caused by car position information is not particularly large (usually less than 20 percent, depending on the utilization factor). To accomplish this reduction, the amount of intersector assignments is increased beyond that observed in center-of-mass systems, thus further decreasing a patrol unit's contact with its own sector.

We would expect car location information to be more useful in providing the capability to implement different patrol strategies that were previously impractical or infeasible. In the remainder of the chapter we investigate one promising alternative strategy, that of assigning patrol cars to overlapping sectors.

7.7. Closest Car Strategy: Overlapping Sectors
7.7.1. Two Units per Sector

Here the probability distribution of the travel distance to the closest unit is determined, given that two units patrol one unit-area square sector uniformly and independently. We assume full availability of both units and equal response speeds E–W and N–S.

Let $D_j (j = 1,2)$ be the travel distance from unit j to the position of a reported incident. That is, if (X_j, Y_j) are the coordinates of unit j and if (X, Y) are the coordinates of the incident, then

$$D_j = |X - X_j| + |Y - Y_j|.$$

The probability density function for D_j is given by Equation 3.27.

The distance to the closest unit is

$$R_2 = \min [D_1, D_2].$$

Conditioned on the values of the incident coordinates $(X = x, Y = y)$, we determine the cumulative distribution function for R_2 by writing

$$F_{R_2}(r|X = x, Y = y) = 1 - \left[\int_r^\infty f_D(v|X = x, Y = y)\, dv \right]^2.$$

Carrying out the computations for an incident at the sector center, we obtain

$$F_{R_2}(r|X=0,Y=0) = \begin{cases} 1 - (1 - 2r^2)^2 & 0 \leqslant r \leqslant \frac{1}{2} \\ 1 - (2 - 4y + 2r^2)^2 & \frac{1}{2} \leqslant r \leqslant 1. \end{cases} \qquad (7.23)$$

The mean travel distance is $E[R_2] \approx 0.38$ sector length. Compared to a mean travel distance of 0.50 for a single unit located in a square sector of unit area, adding a second unit to the sector reduces the mean travel distance by approximately 23 percent. Or, if the area of the sector is doubled (so that, on the average, there is one car per unit area), the mean travel distance to the closest unit is $(0.38)\sqrt{2} \approx 0.53$ sector length. This compares to a mean distance of 0.50 for a unit-area square sector with one car assigned, or a difference of about 6 percent. The same percentage comparisons are found for an incident located at a corner of the sector. Thus, with full availability and car location information, assigning two units to one double-size sector does not cause a significant degradation in mean travel distance, compared to single-car sectors and no car location information.

This behavior is investigated for a large number of completely overlapping sectors and the same general property is found to hold. First, we must determine the limiting behavior of the minimum travel distance as the number of units patrolling the same area becomes increasingly large.

7.7.2. Many Units per Sector: Asymptotic Behavior

Consider a square command with N units distributed uniformly and independently throughout the command. Assume that, on the average, there is one patrol unit per unit area (that is, $\gamma \equiv$ patrol unit density $= 1$ per unit area). We wish to show that as the command becomes increasingly large and additional units are added so that γ is always unity, the exact distribution of travel distance between an incident and the nearest unit tends to a Rayleigh with parameter 2. In the next section we show the physical significance of this result.

For simplicity in the derivation we assume that the incident is located at the center of the command, although the general result holds for any incident position. Let D_j be the distance between an incident and the jth patrol unit. It is straightforward to show that

$$f_{D_j}(d) = \begin{cases} 4\dfrac{d}{N} & 0 \leqslant d \leqslant \sqrt{N}/2 \\[2mm] \dfrac{4}{\sqrt{N}} - \dfrac{4d}{N} & \sqrt{N}/2 < d \leqslant \sqrt{N}. \\[2mm] 0 & \text{otherwise} \end{cases} \qquad (7.24)$$

The random variables $D_1, D_2, \ldots, D_N$ are mutually independent and identically distributed according to Equation 7.24. It must be shown that the asymptotic distribution of

$$R_N = \min \left[D_1, D_2, \ldots, D_N \right]$$

is Rayleigh with parameter 2, that is, $F_{R_N}(r)$ approaches

$$F(r) = 1 - c^{-2r^2}, \qquad r \geqslant 0. \tag{7.25}$$

Or, equivalently, using the complementary cumulative distribution, we must show that $\log \left[1 - F_{R_N}(r) \right]$ approaches

$$\log \left[1 - F(r) \right] = -2r^2. \tag{7.26}$$

From Equation 7.24, we have for $0 \leqslant r \leqslant \sqrt{N}/2$,

$$F_{D_j}(r) = 2 \frac{r^2}{N}, \qquad 0 \leqslant r \leqslant \sqrt{N}/2. \tag{7.27}$$

The probability that the minimum of N samples from Equation 7.24 is less than or equal to r is

$$F_{R_N}(r) = 1 - \left[1 - F_{D_j}(r) \right]^N. \tag{7.28}$$

Since it is clear that $F_{R_N}(\sqrt{N}/2) \longrightarrow 1$ as $N \longrightarrow \infty$, we need only consider the interval $0 \leqslant r \leqslant \sqrt{N}/2$. Using Equations 7.27 and 7.28, we write

$$1 - F_{R_N}(r) = \left[1 - 2\frac{r^2}{N} \right]^N, \qquad 0 \leqslant r \leqslant \sqrt{N}/2 \tag{7.29}$$

Now one takes the logarithm of Equation 7.29 and observes its limiting behavior os N becomes large. We obtain

$$\log(1 - F_{R_N}(r)) = N \log \left[1 - 2\frac{r^2}{N} \right], \qquad 0 \leqslant r \leqslant \sqrt{N}/2. \tag{7.30}$$

For $-1 < x < 1$, recall that

$$\log(1 + x) = x - \frac{1}{2}x^2 + \frac{1}{3}x^3 - \frac{1}{4}x^4 + \cdots.$$

Thus, we rewrite Equation 7.30 as

$$\log \left[1 - F_{R_N}(r) \right] = N \left[- 2\frac{r^2}{N} - \frac{1}{2} \left(2\frac{r^2}{N} \right)^2 + \ldots \right], 0 \leqslant r \leqslant \sqrt{N}/2.$$

We obtain for large N,

$$\lim_{N \to \infty} \left[\log(1 - F_{R_N}(r)) \right] = -2r^2, \tag{7.31}$$

the desired result.

In the next section, we use this result to examine the travel distance behavior in a very large command with patrol units distributed independently
and uniformly throughout and with very low utilization rate. Then we use
the result to approximate the travel distance behavior in a command of arbitrary size and arbitrary utilization rate.

7.7.3. Spatial Poisson Process Model

We consider the case of a very large command with negligibly low utilization
rate and derive the probability law for travel time to the nearest car, allowing
the possibility of different speeds E–W and N–S. The approach relies on the
fact that the positions of the units can be considered to be generated by a
spatial Poisson process. Once the probability law is obtained, the agreement
of the result with that of Section 7.7.2 is shown. We then compare statistics
of the travel time for this system to a strict center-of-mass system with nonoverlapping sectors.

The assumptions are as follows:

1. Patrol units are distributed at random uniformly throughout the geographical command. On the average, there are γ patrol units per square mile.

2. All units are fully available for dispatch (that is, $\rho = 0$).

3. Car location information is perfect (that is, $\sigma = 0$).

4. Travel speed E–W is v_x; travel speed N–S is v_y.

5. The unit that requires the least time to travel to the scene of the incident is
always dispatched.

First, one obtains the probability $p_K(k|A)$ that there are k patrol units in an
arbitrary region of area A. We ignore end effects at the boundaries of the
command by considering the command to be infinitely large. Then, the spatial distribution of patrol units constitutes a homogeneous spatial Poisson
process[19] with parameter γ ($\equiv$ average number of patrol units per unit area),
and the probability that k units are in any region of area A is

$$p_K(k|A) = \frac{(\gamma A)^k \, e^{-\gamma A}}{k!}, \qquad k = 0, 1, 2, \dots . \tag{7.32}$$

This very useful result allows us to examine many properties of the system.

We are primarily interested in the distribution of travel time from the position of a reported incident to the nearest available car. Using Equation 7.32,
we can easily obtain the cumulative distribution function of this travel time
T_r. We need the fact that the area of a time-equidistant parallelogram of size t
is $2t^2 v_x v_y$ (Figure 7.1). Since the position of the call for service is chosen in-

19. S. Karlin, *A First Course in Stochastic Processes* (New York: Academic Press, 1966),
pp. 336–43.

dependently of the positions of patrol units, the probability that there are exactly k patrol units in a time-equidistant parallelogram of size t, centered at the position of the call, is $p_K(k|2t^2 v_x v_y)$. Thus, the cumulative distribution function for the travel time is

$$F_{T_r}(t) = 1 - p_K(0|2t^2 v_x v_y)$$
$$= 1 - e^{-[\gamma 2t^2 v_x v_y]}, \quad t \geq 0.$$

Taking the derivative with respect to t, we obtain the probability density function for the travel time to the nearest unit,

$$f_{T_r}(t) = 4\gamma t v_x v_y \, e^{-[\gamma 2 t^2 v_x v_y]}, \quad t \geq 0. \tag{7.33}$$

This is a Rayleigh probability density function with parameter $2\sqrt{\gamma v_x v_y}$. The mean and the variance are as follows:

$$E(T_r) = \frac{1}{4}\sqrt{\frac{2\pi}{\gamma v_x v_y}}, \tag{7.34a}$$

$$\sigma_{T_r}^2 = \left(2 - \frac{\pi}{2}\right)\frac{1}{4\gamma v_x v_y}. \tag{7.34b}$$

These results can be used to compare the operation of a perfect resolution system with completely overlapping sectors to a system with mutually exclusive sectors, no car location information, and strict center-of-mass dispatching. For simplicity in the comparison, we assume $v_x = v_y = 1$. The comparison between the two systems is shown in Table 7.3. The mutually exclusive sector case is characterized by a mean travel distance 6 percent greater than the no sector (perfect resolution) case, and a variance 4 percent greater.

Thus, at least at low utilization rates, if there are reasons to want overlapping sectors (even to the extent of having no sectors at all), there would be no degradation in travel time characteristics of the overlapping sector system,

Table 7.3 Comparison of Two Systems

	Mutually Exclusive Sectors, No Car Position Information	No Sectors, Perfect Car Position Information
Mean travel distance	$\frac{2}{3}\sqrt{\frac{1}{\gamma}} \approx 0.667\gamma^{-1/2}$	$\frac{1}{4}\sqrt{\frac{2\pi}{\gamma}} \approx 0.627\gamma^{-1/2}$
Variance of travel distance	$\frac{1}{9\gamma} \approx 0.111\gamma^{-1}$	$\left(2 - \frac{\pi}{2}\right)\frac{1}{4\gamma} \approx 0.107\gamma^{-1}$

compared to a strict center-of-mass system, provided perfect car position information is available. In fact, the average travel time (or distance) of a fully
overlapping sector system with car position information is slightly less than
that of a strict center-of-mass system. Apparently the prepositioning advantages gained by assigning units to mutually exclusive sectors are more than
completely recovered by knowing exact car positions in a system with no
deliberate spatial prepositioning.

Isotropy, Revisited

One can develop some intuition for this result by reconsidering the distribution of Ψ, the angle at which the street grid is rotated with respect to the
straight line between the incident and the initial position of the assigned patrol unit. (See Section 3.6.1.) The distribution of Ψ determines the distribution of R, the ratio of the right angle and Euclidean travel distances. Recall
from Section 3.6.1 that for an isotropic situation in which Ψ is uniformly
distributed over $[0,\pi/2]$, $E[R] \approx 1.273$, and for responses within square sectors whose sides are parallel to directions of travel, $E[R] \approx 1.274$. Given that
patrol units are distributed as a homogeneous spatial Poisson process and
that the closest unit will be assigned, the initial position of the assigned unit is
uniformly distributed over some equidistant parallelogram of size t, where t is
the travel time. For simplicity, assume $v_x = v_y$, so the parallelogram is a
square rotated at $45°$. Simple geometrical arguments lead to the cumulative
distribution of Ψ.

$$F_\Psi(\psi^0) = \frac{1}{2}\left[1 + \tan\left(\psi^0 - \frac{\pi}{4}\right)\right] \qquad 0 \leqslant \psi^0 \leqslant \frac{\pi}{2}. \qquad (7.35)$$

Proceeding as in Section 3.6.1, one finds the cumulative distribution of R,

$$F_R(v) = 1 - \frac{\sqrt{2 - v^2}}{v}, \qquad 1 \leqslant v \leqslant \sqrt{2}. \qquad (7.36)$$

In particular,

$$E[R] = \sqrt{2}\,\log(1 + \sqrt{2}) \approx 1.246. \qquad (7.37)$$

Thus, the average value of the ratio of the right angle and the Euclidean distances is about 2.2 percent less for the case of no sectors and closest car dispatching, compared to square sectors and center-of-mass dispatching. This implies that dispatching the closest unit with no sectors results in responses
which are closer to straight-line responses than those of square sectors with
center-of-mass dispatching. This at least partially explains the smaller mean
travel distances for closest car dispatching.

Comparison to Asymptotic Distribution

As we would expect, the result of Section 7.7.2 states that the limiting distribution of the minimum of N independent travel distances, each distributed according to Equation 7.24, tends to that obtained by distributing the units according to a homogeneous spatial Poisson process.

From the earlier comparison with the center-of-mass strategy, we see that the spatial Poisson approximation for the mean travel distance for the case of one car per sector is about 6 percent in error. We will tolerate this amount of error to arrive at an approximate description of travel distance for a small command with arbitrary utilization rate. The method employed can easily be adapted to make the approximation errors arbitrarily small.

7.8. Arbitrary Utilization Rate: First-Come, First-Served Reassignments, Overlapping Sectors

In this section we consider a geographical command of finite area A, with N patrol units assigned, and characterized by an arbitrary utilization rate ρ. Again, *there are no sectors and car position information is perfect.* The primary new feature of the developed model is the provision for queuing; it is assumed that queued calls are serviced in a strict first-come, first-served manner. The major focus is the discovery of how queuing affects the travel distance behavior of the system.

The general queuing assumption made is that the state of the geographical command is specified by the number of calls both in service and in queue in the command. It is assumed that service time, once at the scene of the incident, is a negative exponential random variable with mean μ^{-1}. Also, it is assumed that the time to travel to the scene is second-order, compared to the service time, so that the state probabilities can be closely approximated by just assuming negative exponential service time with mean μ^{-1}, ignoring the travel time. Similar assumptions are made in the next section in which behavior of a "closest-car, closest-incident" dispatch and reassignment policy is approximated.

The approximation we use from the previous sections is that travel distances are distributed as Rayleigh random variables. Specifically, with n units ($n > 0$) available in the command, the probability density function of the travel distance to the closest available unit is approximated to be Rayleigh with parameter $2\sqrt{n/A}$. The largest error is introduced when the number of units available is small. The error is typically 6 or 7 percent.[20] The assumptions and approximations are as follows:

1. The geographical command is a square of area A.

2. Demands for police service arrive in a Poisson manner at rate λ.

3. There are N patrol units assigned to the command. Each patrols the entire command in a uniform manner, independent of other units.

4. The service time distribution is negative exponential with mean μ^{-1} where $\rho = [\lambda/N\mu] < 1)$.

5. With n ($N \leqslant n < 0$) units available in the command, the probability density function for the travel distance to the closest available unit is Rayleigh with parameter $2\sqrt{n/A}$.

6. From a queue of waiting calls, units completing service on a previous assignment are reassigned to waiting calls in first-come, first-served manner.

The further observation can be made that the respective positions of an incident in queue and the assigned unit are mutually independent and uniformly distributed throughout the entire command. Thus, the probability density function for the travel distance of a reassigned unit to the scene of a call is the same as that of a single square sector of area A.

The system constitutes a well-known birth and death process. The probability that the system is in state i (that is, i calls in service and in queue) is[21]

$$P_i = \frac{\left(\frac{\lambda}{\mu}\right)^i \Big/ i!}{\sum_{i=0}^{N-1} \left(\frac{\lambda}{\mu}\right)^i \Big/ i! + \left[\left(\frac{\lambda}{\mu}\right)^N \Big/ N!\right]\left[\frac{1}{1-\rho}\right]} \qquad i = 0, \ldots, N-1$$

$$P_i = \frac{\left(\frac{\lambda}{\mu}\right)^N \rho^{i-N} \Big/ N!}{\sum_{i=0}^{N-1} \left(\frac{\lambda}{\mu}\right)^i \Big/ i! + \left[\left(\frac{\lambda}{\mu}\right)^N \Big/ N!\right]\left[\frac{1}{1-\rho}\right]} \qquad i = N, N+1, \ldots$$

(7.38)

Thus, the probability density function for the travel distance of a unit to an arbitrary incident is given by

20. If further accuracy is desired, exact results can be used for the cases in which the number of units is small. The exact results would be substituted into Equations 7.39 and 7.40.

21. See, for example, R. Syski, *Introduction to Congestion Theory in Telephone Systems* (London: Oliver & Boyd Ltd., 1960), pp. 340–43.

$$f_{R_N}(\ell) = \sum_{i=0}^{N-1} P_i \, 4 \frac{N-i}{A} \ell e^{-\left[2\ell^2\left(\frac{N-i}{A}\right)\right]} + f_{D_r}(\ell,A) \sum_{i=N}^{\infty} P_i, \tag{7.39}$$

where $f_{D_r}(\ell,A)$ is given in Equation 3.27, scaled for a sector of area A, and the P_i are from Equation 7.38.

Using Equations 7.34a and 7.39, we note that the mean is

$$E[R_N] = \sum_{i=0}^{N-1} P_i \, \frac{1}{4} \sqrt{\frac{2\pi A}{N-i}} + \frac{2}{3}\sqrt{A} \sum_{i=N}^{\infty} P_i. \tag{7.40}$$

This function is plotted in Figure 7.7. In order to normalize the results, for each different value of N, the area A of the command was chosen so that $A = N$, or equivalently, so that $\gamma = 1$. A unit of distance is an equivalent sector length, which is the length of a sector if all cars were assigned to mutually exclusive, collectively exhaustive square sectors. Since $\gamma = 1$, an equivalent sector length is equal to $\sqrt{\gamma} = 1$. In the figure, note that as ρ nears unity, the mean travel distance approaches that of a single car assigned to an area A, as we would expect because most assignments are from a queue, following an FCFS policy. Note also that for $\rho < 0.5$, the mean distance is nearly independent of N.

7.9. Arbitrary Utilization Rate: Closest-Car, Closest-Incident Reassignments, Overlapping Sectors

As previously indicated, a reassignment policy preferable to that of first-come, first-served is one in which a car just having completed an assignment on a previous call is reassigned to the nearest waiting call (if there is one). Such a policy is called a "closest-car, closest-incident" policy. This policy is examined in the following discussion.

To approximate the travel distance behavior of this system, it is necessary to extend the application of the Rayleigh probability density function to the case of waiting calls. With m calls in queue, the distance from a car just completing an assignment to the next (closest) assignment is the minimum of m random variables, each distributed independently[22]; that is, the travel distance D, given m calls in queue, is

$$(D|m) = \min [D_1, D_2, \ldots, D_m]$$

22. In extreme saturation conditions, each car would tend to remain within a very small area answering calls. Calls that arrive and are distant from any unit may never be answered; in such cases one would expect the set of random variables $[D_1, D_2, \ldots, D_m]$ to be *biased* toward greater travel distances than the average obtained from a spatial Poisson assumption. It would be interesting to study this behavior using simulation techniques.

Distance
(in equivalent
sector lengths)

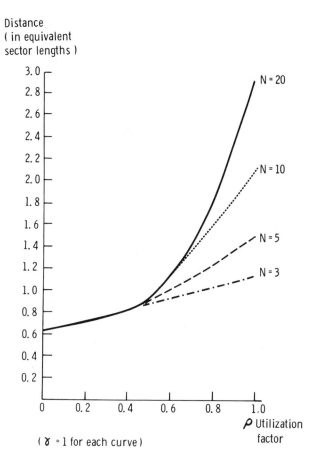

(γ = 1 for each curve)

Figure 7.7 Relationship between mean travel distance and utilization factor for commands with totally overlapping sectors and perfect car position information; first-come, first-served reassignment policy.

where the pdf for D_i $(i = 1, 2, \ldots, m)$ is given by an equation analogous to Equation 7.24, which conditions the set of D_i on the car location.

From Section 7.7.2 we know that the probability density function of the random variable $(D_r|m)$ can be approximated by a Rayleigh with parameter $2\sqrt{m/A}$. This approximation is used in addition to the approximation that the probability density function of the travel distance between a call and the closest of n available cars is Rayleigh with parameter $2\sqrt{n/A}$.

We can succinctly state the assumptions as follows:

1. The geographical command is a square of area A.

2. Demands for police service arrive in a Poisson manner at rate λ.

3. There are N patrol units assigned to the command. Each patrols the entire command in a uniform manner, independent of other units.

4. Service time distribution is negative exponential with mean μ^{-1} where $(\rho = \lambda/N\mu) < 1$.

5. With $n(N \geqslant n > 0)$ unit available in the command, the probability density function for the travel distance to the closest available unit is Rayleigh with parameter $2\sqrt{n/A}$.

6. From a queue of waiting calls, units completing service on a previous assignment are reassigned to the closest waiting call.

7. If there are m calls in queue, the distance from a unit completing service on a previous assignment to the next assignment is distributed as a Rayleigh random variable with parameter $2\sqrt{m/A}$.

The unconditional probability density function of the travel distance of a closest-car, closest-incident reassignment system is[23]

$$f_{R_N}(\varrho) = \sum_{i=0}^{N-1} P_i 4\left(\frac{N-i}{A}\right) \varrho\, e^{-\left[2\left(\frac{N-i}{A}\right)\varrho^2\right]}$$

$$+ \sum_{i=N}^{\infty} P_i 4\left(\frac{i+1-N}{A}\right) \varrho\, e^{-\left[2\left(\frac{i+1-N}{A}\right)\varrho^2\right]}. \tag{7.41}$$

The mean is

$$E[R_N] = \sum_{i=0}^{N-1} P_i \frac{1}{4}\sqrt{\frac{2\pi A}{N-i}} + \sum_{i=N}^{\infty} P_i \frac{1}{4}\sqrt{\frac{2\pi A}{i+1-N}}. \tag{7.42}$$

This function is plotted in Figure 7.8 in such a way that Figures 7.7 and 7.8 are directly comparable. As is expected, as ρ nears unity, the mean travel dis-

23. As in Section 7.8, these results can be made more accurate by substituting exact distributions for the cases in which n or m is small. For the purposes here, such fine-grain accuracy is not required.

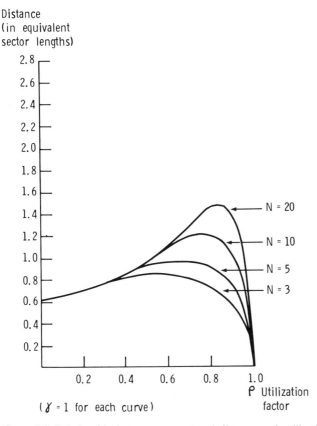

Distance
(in equivalent
sector lengths)

Figure 7.8 Relationship between mean travel distance and utilization factor for commands with totally overlapping sectors and perfect car position information; closest-car, closest-incident reassignment policy.

tance approaches zero (because of closest incident reassignments), rather than a maximum value (Figure 7.7).

It is interesting to observe that maximum mean travel distance is obtained for increasingly larger values of ρ as the command becomes larger, thus including more patrol units. This results from a decreasing probability of a queue forming, for a fixed value of ρ, as N is increased; thus, the travel time benefits of closest-car, closest-incident dispatching are not as apparent in a command with a large number of patrol units, compared to a command with a smaller number.

As an example, a command with five patrol units and a utilization factor 0.8 experiences a mean travel distance of 1.28 with FCFS reassignments, compared to a distance of 0.91 with closest-car, closest-reassignments. The latter represents a 29 percent reduction over the former. On the other hand, a command with 20 patrol units and a 0.8 utilization factor is characterized by a mean travel distance of 1.81 with an FCFS policy, compared to 1.46 with a closest-car, closest-incident policy. This is a reduction of approximately 19 percent.

When average queue delay is added to average travel time, one would still expect mean total response time to become smaller as N increases (for a fixed value of ρ).

In Section 3.2.3, we observed that mean right-angle travel distance is not very sensitive to exact sector shape, given a sector area constraint. We would expect this same insensitivity to apply to the models of this and the previous section; thus Equations 7.39, 7.40, 7.41, and 7.42 should be useful for obtaining approximate results in commands of fairly arbitrary shapes.

7.10. Summary and Discussion
This chapter has illustrated the types of models one may construct when investigating the potential effects of a technological innovation. The particular focus was on the travel time reduction properties of a car locator system.

The results are summarized by addressing each of the seven questions posed at the beginning of the chapter, as follows:

1. The resolution characteristics of a car locator system would depend strongly on the technology of the particular system used. If the estimated position coordinates of unit j are $(\hat{X}_j, \hat{Y}_j)$ and the actual coordinates are (X_j, Y_j), then the estimated coordinates are

$$\hat{X}_j = X_j + X_e$$
$$\hat{Y}_j = Y_j + Y_e$$

where X_e and Y_e are additive error terms. For several types of systems it would be reasonable to assume that X_e and Y_e are independent zero-mean Gaussian random variables with known variance σ^2. This model was used to simulate nonperfect resolution car-locator systems, with the additional constraint that each car while on patrol must be within its own sector.

2. The probability of dispatching other than the closest car (P_E) with present manual dispatching systems depends on sector geometries, utilization factors, and on the type of position estimation used. Assuming the position of each patrol unit is selected from a uniform distribution over its respective sector and that incidents are uniformly distributed over the entire region of

patrol, independent of patrol or other incident positions, we found the following: At $\rho = 0$, for an infinite number of linear concatenated sectors, $P_E = 1/6$; for a 3 X 3 array of square sectors, $P_E \approx 0.27$; for a 7 X 7 array of square sectors, $P_E \approx 0.32$. *Assuming SCM dispatching*, $P_E(\rho)$ is a unimodal function reaching a maximum at $\rho \approx 0.155$ for linear concatenated sectors and between $\rho = 0.1$ and $\rho = 0.2$ for an array of square sectors. *Assuming MCM dispatching*, for linear concatenated sectors $P_E(\rho)$ decreases linearly with ρ, reaching zero at $\rho = 1.0$; for an array of square sectors $P_E(\rho)$ decreases monotonically with ρ, with values typically 0.03 less than the corresponding value with SCM dispatching. Finally, *with nonperfect car location resolution*, we found $P_E \approx 0.23$ for a 3 X 3 array of square sectors at $\rho = 0$ and a resolution of one-quarter sector length. This probability decreased as resolution improved; with a resolution of one-tenth sector length, $P_E \approx 0.11$. For a 7 X 7 array at $\rho = 0$, with one-quarter sector length resolution $P_E \approx 0.27$ and with one-tenth sector length resolution P_E is approximately equal to that found for a 3 X 3 array.

3. The reduction in travel time that can be obtained with car location information depends on the same factors cited for P_E earlier, with typical reductions averaging between 10 and 20 percent. Making the same assumptions for patrol and incident positions as stated in question 2, we found the following: *At $\rho = 0$*, for an infinite number of *linear concatenated sectors*, the mean travel distance with perfect resolution car location information and closest-car dispatching is 7/24 sector length; compared to center-of-mass dispatching, this represents a reduction of 1/24 sector length, or 12.5 percent. The conditional average reduction in travel distance, given that dispatch error would have occurred with a center-of-mass policy, is 0.25 sector length. For a *3 X 3 array of square sectors at $\rho = 0$*, the average reduction in travel distance is 0.08 sector length; *for a 7 X 7 array*, the average reduction is 0.10 sector length.

At arbitrary utilization rates, we let $\epsilon(\rho)$ be the average amount of travel distance reduction achievable by perfect resolution car location information, given a utilization rate of ρ. *Assuming SCM dispatching*, it was found for linear concatenated sectors that $\epsilon(\rho)$ is a unimodal function, reaching a maximum at $\rho \approx 0.309$; for a 3 X 3 array of square sectors, $\epsilon(\rho)$ remains between 0.10 and 0.12 sector length for most values of ρ; for a 7 X 7 array, $\epsilon(\rho)$ is typically 0.02 sector length greater than the corresponding value for the 3 X 3 array. *Assuming MCM dispatching*, we found for linear concatenated sectors that $\epsilon(\rho)$ is a linear decreasing function of ρ, reaching 0 at $\rho = 1.0$; for an array of square sectors, $\epsilon(\rho)$ is typically 25 percent smaller than the corresponding value for SCM dispatching. Finally, *with nonperfect car location resolution*, we found $\epsilon(0) \approx 0.053$ for a 3 X 3 array of square sectors and a resolution of one-quarter sector length. This value becomes smaller as resolution improves; with a resolution of one-tenth sector length, $\epsilon(0) \approx 0.013$. For a 7 X 7 array at $\rho = 0$, the first value is increased to 0.073 and the second is not measurably changed.

4. The effects of increased utilization rates on the potential benefits of car locator systems are summarized in questions 2 and 3. Generally speaking, the *value* of a car locator system compared to an SCM system increases to a maximum at a moderately low value of ρ, then drops to zero as ρ approaches 1. Compared to an MCM system, this value drops monotonically to zero as ρ approaches 1.

5. If increased out-of-sector responses are accepted as undesirable, then closest-car dispatching degrades system performance in that it results in greater amounts of intersector dispatching. At $\rho = 0$, assuming closest-car dispatching, the fraction of dispatches that are intersector dispatches is 1/6 for linear concatenated sectors, 0.26 for a 3 X 3 array of square sectors, and 0.32 for a 7 X 7 array. For most values of ρ, this fraction remains greater than ρ.

6. The effect of the size of the command on the value of car location information is discussed in questions 2, 3, and 5. Generally speaking, car location information is more valuable in larger commands that allow more dispatch alternatives than smaller commands.

7. If sectors were eliminated and each car were to patrol uniformly one large area, independently of other cars, and if perfect resolution car location information were used to dispatch the closest available car, then the travel time characteristics of this overlapping sector system are nearly identical to those of an SCM system with nonoverlapping sectors.

For small commands with arbitrary utilization rates, an FCFS reassignment policy was compared to a closest-car, closest-incident policy, assuming in both cases completely overlapping sectors and uniform independent patrol. For large utilization rates the latter policy reduces average travel distance considerably. For low utilization rates, both systems exhibit nearly identical travel distance characteristics.

A central idea of this chapter is that car locator systems may provide maximum benefit by facilitating operational policies previously infeasible. One such policy that appears to offer several advantages over traditional methods (Sections 2.7.2 and 4.3.1) is to assign units to overlapping sectors.

However, many of the issues addressed in this chapter, such as overlapping sectors, will require experimental test. For instance, a critical assumption in the analysis of overlapping sectors is that patrol cars are positioned *independently* of each other. But overlapping sectors could result in certain units informally *pairing* with others, thereby tending to *cluster* the positions of units. Such clustering would result in increased travel times. Statistical tests to detect clustering would be straightforward to devise and could even be implemented as standard practice in any operating system that records car locations.

In any actual implementation of car locators, additional features such as priorities and time-varying demands would probably warrant simulation tests prior to implementation. For instance, there are many ways to implement an overlapping sector plan using car locators, including the following:

A system with roving *stacking units;* each of the stacking units would eventually answer low priority stacked, or queued calls from anywhere in the command. Other units may be stationed in mutually exclusive sectors.

A system in which two adjacent sectors are merged to form one large sector. Two units independently patrol the larger area, and the closer available unit is assigned to each call.

A system with a completely overlapping sector plan, in which the closest available unit is assigned to each call.

A *fluid patrol* system with no fixed sector boundaries.[24] One or more units would be assigned to patrol particular regions as the need became apparent, and these assignments could change dynamically over the course of a tour.

When the complexities of each alternative plan and the geographical features of the particular city are included, the detailed operating characteristics of the system can only be investigated by simulation. But simpler analytical models as illustrated in this chapter (and throughout the book) should be useful in guiding intuition, indicating the level of detail required, and pointing to those factors and parameters which require careful attention.

24. See, for example, K. Bergstrom, "The Fluid Patrol System," paper prepared for the Traffic Police Administration Training Program, Traffic Institute, Northwestern University, 1966.

8

Intersector Cooperation and Repositioning

In this concluding chapter there are several issues that we wish to revisit, and there are several that we outline requiring further research. The central theme is intersector cooperation and interaction. In current systems most dispatchers will immediately assign an out-of-sector patrol unit to an incident if the sector unit is unavailable and other units in the command are available. This is a frequently occurring form of intersector cooperation. Yet most sectors are laid out with the idea that the unit patrolling that sector performs most of the work in the sector. Sector designs are based on reducing *intrasector* travel time (or travel distance). Given the high call-for-service workloads of many present-day police departments, however, it is not unusual on a given tour for a patrol unit to respond to more calls *outside* its own sector than inside. This type of behavior was illustrated by the simulation results (Chapters 2, 6, and 7). Thus, one subject of primary concern in this chapter is examining intersector dispatching in more detail and exploring some possible consequences of current high levels of intersector dispatching. The effects on intersector dispatching of equal workloads, time-varying demands, closest-car dispatching (using a car locator system), and command saturation (causing queuing delays) are examined analytically. The predicted high levels of intersector dispatching have been substantially verified in practice, and they carry strong implications about traditional philosophies of assigning each car to its own sector. Alternatives include overlapping sectors and various types of fluid patrol.

Next the problem of sector geometry is reexamined, assuming intersector cooperation. For illustrative purposes, we consider the case in which two or four units are teamed up to handle cooperatively calls from one area of a command. If a call arrives from a sector whose unit is unavailable, the dispatcher gives first preference to one of the cooperating units if one is available. In order to anticipate such cross-sector assignments, the available unit may reposition itself to be closer to possible calls arriving from the busy unit's sector. Certain simple properties of such intersector cooperation are found, indicating the general way in which results focusing on single sectors are modified. Of fundamental importance is the fact that the type of intersector cooperation determines the best geometry for sectors, and this is usually different from that obtained from simple single-sector designs.

The final topic involves *global repositioning,* a type of intersector cooperation in which one or more available patrol units are temporarily reassigned to
areas in other commands. This type of cooperation is required to relieve
temporary congestion in these areas. Such global repositioning has been
standard practice in large urban fire departments for many years, particularly
because one large fire is a very clear and visible signal of the need for large-
scale repositioning. But congestion in police departments usually arises from
the accumulation of many smaller incidents, so signals indicating oncoming
congestion are more subtle. This discussion of global repositioning only de-
fines the problem, pointing to the directions requiring further research. Many
of the repositioning ideas proposed for fire operations by the New York City
Rand Institute should be applicable to repositioning in police operations.

A detailed chapter summary is given in Section 8.5. A summary of definitions is given in Table 8.1.

8.1. The Amount of Intersector Dispatching

Police administrators are often heard to argue against overlapping sectors or
fluid patrol or spatial repositioning or other schemes that would remove the

Table 8.1 Summary of Definitions for Chapter 8

$\lambda_i(t)$	Average rate at which calls for service are generated in a Poisson manner from sector i at time t
$\rho_i(t)$	Probability that patrol unit i is unavailable for dispatch at time t
μ^{-1}	Average total time required for a patrol unit to service a call
F_I	Fraction of dispatches which are intersector dispatches.
$a_i(t)$	Probability that unit i is assigned to a call that arrives from sector i at time t, given unit i is available.
d_1, d_2	Dimensions of a two-sector configuration (Figure 8.3)
p_0	Probability that neither unit of two cooperating units is busy
p_1	Probability that exactly one unit of two cooperating units is busy
$P_M(j/A)$	Probability that exactly j calls are being serviced in a region of area A, $j = 0, 1, \ldots$
N_c	Number of patrol units assigned to command c
$P\{S_c\}$	Probability that command c is saturated

patrol officer from his own uniquely assigned sector. The primary motivation for this one-unit, one-sector concept is the establishment on the part of the officer of a *sector identity*. The well-known police administrator V. A. Leonard says that the beat (or sector) "is the ultimate unit upon which the structure of police organization is reared . . . [Within the beat] the officer is held responsible for the total delivery of police service, including . . . the protection of life and property, the prevention and suppression of crime and vice, traffic regulation and control and the preservation of law and order."[1] According to O. W. Wilson, "The highest quality of patrol service results from the permanent assignment of an officer to a beat . . . . Frequent changes of beat assignments make it difficult to place responsibility for unsatisfactory conditions. Procedures that interfere with the application of the important rule that an officer should be held responsible for the performance of his duties must not be tolerated."[2] However, while an officer is theoretically responsible for the delivery of police services within his own sector, the physics of radio-dispatched patrol operation often causes an officer to leave his sector to respond to calls in other sectors within his command. With the high call-for-service rates experienced by many cities, it is not unusual for an officer to spend more time outside of his sector than inside; in such a situation, it is likely that the majority of calls for service within his sector are serviced by patrol units from other sectors in the command. Thus, the one-man, one-sector concept often breaks down in practice, thereby making it difficult to assign responsibility for the delivery of services in the sector.

In this section the amount of intersector dispatching is examined more closely, assuming the currently popular nonoverlapping sector arrangement. Intersector dispatch probability is found to be sufficiently high to warrant planning for intersector dispatching as part of normal operations, perhaps involving local repositioning, and in the longer run, to warrant critical re-examination of the whole concept of individual sectors.

For a given command with I patrol units assigned, the following parameters are important in determining the amount of intersector dispatching:

$\lambda_i(t)$ = average rate (calls/hour) at which calls for service are generated in a Poisson manner from sector i at time t, $i = 1, 2, \ldots, I$, where $0 \leq t \leq T$;

1. V. A. Leonard, *Police Patrol Organization* (Springfield, Ill.: Charles C Thomas Publisher, 1970), p. 19.
2. O. W. Wilson, *Police Administration*, 2nd ed. (New York: McGraw-Hill Book Company, 1963), p. 252.

$\rho_i(t)$ = probability that patrol unit i is unavailable for dispatch[3] at time t, $i = 1,2,\ldots,I$, where $0 \leqslant t \leqslant T$;

$$\lambda = \frac{1}{T} \int_0^T \sum_{i=1}^I \lambda_i(t)\, dt;$$

μ^{-1} = average total time[4] required for a patrol unit to service a call.

Given a call that arrives from sector i, we assume the dispatching algorithm is as follows:

1. Dispatch car i, if available;
2. Otherwise, dispatch some car $j, j \neq i$, where the particular choice depends on the state of the system.

We assume that the probability that all units are simultaneously unavailable is negligibly small.

Given the assumptions, it is easy to see that the probability that a random dispatch which occurs in $[0,T]$ will be an intersector dispatch is

$$F_I = \frac{1}{T} \int_0^T \sum_{i=1}^I \rho_i(t) \frac{\lambda_i(t)}{\lambda}\, dt. \tag{8.1}$$

Some interesting special cases of Equation 8.1 provide insight into system operation.[5]

8.1.1 Non-Time-Varying System

If $\lambda_i(t) = \lambda_i$ and $\rho_i(t) = \rho_i$, Equation 8.1 reduces to

$$F_I = \sum_{i=1}^I \rho_i \frac{\lambda_i}{\lambda}. \tag{8.2}$$

Consider the following three applications of Equation 8.2:

3. In general, a unit may be "unavailable" because of a prior dispatch assignment, a meal break or any number of other activities (Sec. 1.1). If there should be a sector i with no patrol unit assigned, then we use the convention $\rho_i(t) \equiv 1$.
4. Including travel time as well as service time at the scene.
5. It should be clear that the $\rho_i(t)$, the $\lambda_i(t)$, and the dispatching strategy are integrally related. For instance, given the dispatcher's automatic first preference for the sector unit, $\lambda_i(t)$ and $\rho_i(t)$ cannot be specified independently over the entire possible range of both parameters. But adjustment of the out-of-sector dispatching strategy allows some flexibility in determining $\rho_i(t)$ independently of $\lambda_i(t)$. When one sets $\lambda_i(t)$ and $\rho_i(t)$ equal to particular values, one assumes that sector i has been designed to yield that value of $\lambda_i(t)$ and that the out-of-sector dispatching strategy has been devised to yield that value of $\rho_i(t)$.

Case 1.

If each unit is unavailable *an equal fraction of time*, that is, if

$$\rho_i = \rho$$

then

$$F_I = \rho \sum_{i=1}^{I} \frac{\lambda_i}{\lambda} = \rho. \tag{8.3}$$

That is, regardless of the average rate of calls from sector i, λ_i, if each unit is unavailable an equal fraction of time ρ, then the fraction of dispatches that are intersector dispatches equals ρ. Furthermore, if units can only be unavailable for call answering duties,

$$F_I = \frac{\lambda}{I\mu}. \tag{8.4}$$

Case 2.

If each sector has *an equal share of the call volume*, that is, if

$$\lambda_i = \frac{\lambda}{I},$$

then

$$F_I = \frac{1}{I} \sum_{i=1}^{I} \rho_i \equiv \overline{\rho} = \text{average fraction of time units are unavailable.} \tag{8.5}$$

That is, regardless of the actual fraction of time that unit i is unavailable, ρ_i, if the call rates λ_i from each sector are equal, then the fraction of dispatches which are intersector dispatches *equals* the command-wide average fraction of time units are unavailable. Furthermore, if units can only be unavailable for call answering duties, then

$$F_I = \frac{1}{I} \sum_{i=1}^{I} \frac{\lambda_i^*}{\mu} = \frac{\lambda}{I\mu}, \tag{8.6}$$

where λ_i^* = average rate at which unit i is dispatched to calls.[6]

Case 3.

Focusing on nonuniform distributions of workloads and call rates, if we have

6. In general the times of dispatch of unit i are not selected according to a Poisson process, so λ_i^* is not the parameter of a homogeneous Poisson process.

$$\left\{\begin{matrix} \rho_i \geqslant \bar{\rho} \\ \rho_i \leqslant \bar{\rho} \end{matrix}\right\} \text{ whenever } \left\{\begin{matrix} \lambda_i \geqslant \dfrac{\lambda}{I} \\ \lambda_i \leqslant \dfrac{\lambda}{I} \end{matrix}\right\}, \text{ then}$$

$$F_I \geqslant \frac{1}{I}\sum_{i=1}^{I}\rho_i. \tag{8.7}$$

That is, if greater-than-average call rates in a sector imply greater-than-average unavailability rates for the corresponding sector car (and conversely), then the fraction of dispatches that are intersector dispatches is greater than or equal to that which would be obtained with a uniform distribution of either workloads or call rates. This is proved by writing $\rho_i = \bar{\rho} + \Delta\rho_i$ and $\lambda_i = \lambda/I + \Delta\lambda_i$, substituting into Equation 8.2, and observing that $\Delta\rho_i \, \Delta\lambda_i$ is always nonnegative. If units can only be unavailable for call answering duties, then

$$F_I \geqslant \frac{\lambda}{I\mu}. \tag{8.8}$$

Case 1 is important because sector assignments are often designed to distribute workload uniformly (that is, equal workload assignments). Equation 8.3 states that if each unit works an equal fraction of time ρ, and if the system is non-time-varying, then the fraction of dispatches that are intersector assignments equals ρ. Case 2 is important because administrators may design sectors so as to distribute the call volume uniformly, thinking the resulting workloads will all be equal. In general, they will not be equal.[7] Still, Equation 8.5 states that if call volumes are all equal and if the system is non-time-varying, then the fraction of dispatches that are intersector dispatches equals the command-wide average fraction of time units are unavailable. If units can only be unavailable for call answering duties, Equations 8.4 and 8.6 imply that either method of attempting to achieve equal workloads results in the same amount of intersector dispatching. However, Case 3 suggests that if neither workloads nor call rates are distributed uniformly, the amount of intersector dispatching is increased beyond that observed for Cases 1 and 2. These results suggest that an equal workload design of sectors, where workload can be measured in either of two ways (call volumes or fractions of time busy), minimizes the command-wide amount of intersector dispatching. From an equity point-of-view, Case 1 is preferred, because it results in each

7. See discussion in chapter summary (Section 8.5).

patrol sector having the same proportion (ρ) of calls serviced by out-of-sector units and in each patrol unit working an equal fraction of time.

8.1.2. Time-Varying System

Referring again to Equation 8.1, if the system is time-varying (that is, if $\lambda_i(t) \neq \lambda_i$ and $\rho_i(t) \neq \rho_i$), then in general F_I could be greater or less than that which would be achieved by a non-time-varying system with

$$\lambda_i = \frac{1}{T} \int_0^T \lambda_i(t)\, dt,$$

$$\rho_i = \frac{1}{T} \int_0^T \rho_i(t)\, dt.$$

At one extreme, if meal breaks of unit i were scheduled to coincide with periods of zero demand from sector i, then during such intervals one would have

$$\lambda_i(t) = 0$$

$$\rho_i(t) = 1$$

$$\lambda_i(t)\, \rho_i(t) = 0.$$

When averaged with other periods for which $\lambda_i(t) \neq 0$ and $\rho_i(t) \neq 0$, it is possible to have

$$\lambda_i \rho_i > \frac{1}{T} \int_0^T \lambda_i(t)\, \rho_i(t)\, dt,$$

resulting in a reduced amount of intersector dispatching.

On the other hand, for many operating systems it is not unreasonable to assume that $\rho_i(t) \geqslant \rho_i$ when $\lambda_i(t) \geqslant \lambda_i$ or that $\rho_i(t) \leqslant \rho_i$ when $\lambda_i(t) \leqslant \lambda_i$. Heuristically, these assumptions imply that when the call volume from sector i is

$\left\{\begin{matrix} \text{greater} \\ \text{less} \end{matrix}\right\}$ than average, then the probability that unit i will be busy is

$\left\{\begin{matrix} \text{greater} \\ \text{less} \end{matrix}\right\}$ than average. If these assumptions are valid, then one can show that

the amount of intersector dispatching is at least as great as that which would be obtained if the system were non-time-varying, that is,

$$F_I \geqslant \sum_{i=1}^{I} \rho_i \frac{\lambda_i}{\lambda}. \tag{8.9}$$

To obtain Equation 8.9, let

$$\rho_i(t) = \rho_i + \rho_i^{\Delta}(t)$$

$$\lambda_i(t) = \lambda_i + \lambda_i^{\Delta}(t).$$

From Equation 8.1, we have

$$F_I = \frac{I}{\lambda T} \sum_{i=1}^{I} \int_0^T \{\rho_i\lambda_i + \rho_i\lambda_i^{\Delta}(t) + \lambda_i\rho_i^{\Delta}(t) + \rho_i^{\Delta}(t)\,\lambda_i^{\Delta}(t)\}\,dt.$$

Since the second and third terms in the integrand integrate to zero,

$$F_I = \sum_{i=1}^{I} \rho_i \frac{\lambda_i}{\lambda} + \frac{1}{\lambda T} \sum_{i=1}^{I} \int_0^T \rho_i^{\Delta}(t)\,\lambda_i^{\Delta}(t)\,dt.$$

Now, since

$$\mathrm{sgn}\,[\rho_i^{\Delta}(t)] = \mathrm{sgn}\,[\lambda_i^{\Delta}(t)],$$

we have

$$\int_0^T \rho_i^{\Delta}(t)\,\lambda_i^{\Delta}(t)\,dt \geqslant 0,$$

and thus Equation 8.9 must be true.

8.1.3. A Generalized Dispatching Algorithm

In deriving Equation 8.1, we assumed that car i would be dispatched to any call arriving from sector i, provided car i is available. In other words, the sector car was always given first preference. This is a good model for center-of-mass dispatching systems. However, for a system in which the dispatcher has car location information, he may prefer to assign an out-of-sector car that is closer to the scene than the sector car. Thus, in general, the sector car would not always be given first preference.

The analysis is easily generalized to allow for this type of behavior. Let

$a_i(t)$ = probability that unit i is assigned to a call that arrives from sector i at time t, given unit i is available.

Then, Equation 8.1 becomes

$$F_I' = \frac{1}{T} \int_0^T \left[\sum_{i=1}^{I} \rho_i(t) + (1 - \rho_i(t))\,(1 - a_i(t)) \right] \frac{\lambda_i(t)}{\lambda}\,dt. \qquad (8.10)$$

Carrying out analyses similar to those done for Equation 8.1, one usually finds that $F_I' > F_I$. This result corroborates our observation of increased inter-sector dispatching in simulated systems which employ car location information. (See Chapter 7).

8.1.4. Cases When a Queue Forms

The practical significance of these results does not change if one allows a queue to form, provided the reassignment policy does not favor assigning units to calls in their own sectors.

For instance, consider an FCFS reassignment policy for a system approaching saturation. Assume non-time-varying system parameters in which the call rate from sector i is λ_i. In near saturation conditions, each patrol unit i services an equal fraction $1/I$ of the calls, regardless of λ_i. The probability that a random assignment is an *intrasector* assignment is

$$\sum_{i=1}^{I} \frac{1}{I} \frac{\lambda_i}{\lambda} = \frac{1}{I}, \tag{8.11}$$

or that obtained by chance alone.

8.1.5. Discussion

An operationally significant conclusion of the results (Equations 8.1 to 8.11) is the following: *In most cases it is not unreasonable to estimate the fraction of dispatches which are intersector dispatches to be equal to or greater than the average fraction of time that units are unavailable.* Due to possible imbalances in workloads or demands for services among sectors, this result does not imply that each individual patrol unit with utilization rate ρ_i spends at least a fraction of time ρ_i outside its own sector. But, averaged over the entire command, one can state the following to a police administrator: "If your patrol units are busy 60 percent of the time (a typical value), then approximately 60 percent or more of all dispatch assignments cause the assigned patrol unit to leave its own patrol sector. Thus, 60 percent or more of all citizen contact occurring while responding to calls-for-service takes place in sectors other than the unit's own sector."

The predicted amount of intersector dispatches (called *flying* by some patrolmen) has been substantially verified both by the author's own work and by the research of others. For instance, in a report by McCormack and Moen[8] (both law enforcement officers supported as Office of Law Enforcement

8. R. J. McCormack and J. L. Moen, *San Francisco's Mission Police District: A Study of Resource Allocation*, A Report for the Center for Planning and Development Research, Institute of Urban and Regional Development, University of California, Berkeley, 1968.

Assistance Fellows),[9] the following observations based on analysis of a one-week sample of radio dispatches from the San Francisco Mission Police District are reported [italics added]:

On most tours the sector cars were responding to one call after another *irrespective of their assigned areas*, and that with the exception of the 12 p.m. to 8 a.m. tour there was little time for preventive patrol.[10]
It was found that in almost 50% of the cases, a unit *from another area* (sector) answered the call."[11]

The 50 percent figure checks roughly with that predicted by analysis. (The Mission District cars were busy during the sample week a percentage of time slightly greater than 50 percent.)[12]

A much more detailed test[13] using data from the borough of Queens (New York City) yielded similar results. The data showed that the amount of intersector dispatching is never significantly less than the percentage of time unavailable, and it may be significantly more. Intersector dispatches ranged from 37 to 57 percent of the total.

As discussed earlier, the amount of intersector dispatching brings into question the philosophy behind nonoverlapping sectors. Instead of a sector identity, perhaps it would be better to establish a regional identity concept in each officer, with nearby regions overlapping in some way. Such a regional identity might be accompanied by various forms of intersector cooperation to anticipate intersector dispatches. Local repositioning is one such form of intersector cooperation.

9. The Office of Law Enforcement Assistance (OLEA) was set up in the Department of Justice as a result of the 1965 Law Enforcement Assistance Act. With the passage of the 1968 Omnibus Crime Control and Safe Streets Act, OLEA was dissolved; the new administrative agency is the Law Enforcement Assistance Administration (LEAA). College-level education of law enforcement officers is now sponsored by LEAA under the Law Enforcement Education Program (LEEP). See *LEAA*, 1970 (Washington, D.C.: U.S. Government Printing Office, 1970), pp. 52–56.
10. McCormack and Moen, *San Francisco's Mission Police*, p. 32.
11. *Ibid.*, p. 42.
12. It is difficult to check the model exactly because McCormack and Moen do not report all the relevant data (for example, time spent on meal breaks or hourly distribution of calls) and they could compute only a lower bound estimate of the percentage of calls requiring intersector dispatch: "An exact figure for 'out of sector response' was prohibited because the sector boundaries divide the statistical plots in many cases. Only those transmissions (dispatches) which clearly indicated an 'out of sector' response were used in this analysis, and the results indicated that at least 46% of the calls were in areas other than the assigned area." (From McCormack and Moen, *San Francisco's Mission Police*, p. 42.)
13. R. C. Larson, *Measuring the Response Patterns of New York City Police Patrol Cars*, R-675 (New York City Rand Institute, 1971).

8.2. Some Simple Cases of Local Repositioning

In this section simple probabilistic models are used to obtain a qualitative understanding of the effect of local repositioning on average travel times. For simplicity, one assumes right-angle response with $v_x = v_y$ and thus we can deal directly with travel *distances*.[14]

In the simplest possible case, consider two adjacent square sectors (Figure 8.1). We will assume that the units assigned to these sectors cooperate in the following way: *If a call arrives from one sector whose patrol unit is unavailable, the other patrol unit will respond to the call if it is available.* The question of interest is, "At the moment when one of the units becomes busy, is there any advantage to repositioning the remaining available unit? If so, how should this be accomplished?"

To illustrate the approach, make the assumptions that (1) demands for service are uniformly distributed over the area of the two sectors; and (2) each unit patrols in a uniform manner over the area of its sector whenever the other unit is available. Whenever one unit becomes unavailable, consider the following three alternatives for the free unit:

Alternative 1: The free unit continues patrolling in the usual manner (that is, no repositioning).

Alternative 2: The free unit patrols both sectors uniformly (that is, uniform repositioning).

Alternative 3: The free unit assumes a position on the boundary line between the sectors at the north-south halfway point (that is, fixed-point repositioning).

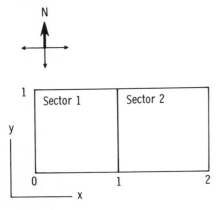

Figure 8.1 Two adjacent cooperating sectors.

14. It is straightforward to generalize the results to the case $v_x \neq v_y$.

For each alternative one now finds the average travel distance for the case in which one unit is busy:

Alternative 1: If the incident is in the patrol unit's sector, the average travel distance is 2/3 sector length; otherwise, the average travel distance is 1/3 N–S plus 1 E–W, or 4/3 sector lengths.[15] Thus, the unconditional average travel distance for the case in which one unit is busy is 1/2 [2/3 + 4/3] = 1 sector length.

Alternative 2: Regardless of the sector of the incident, the average travel distance is 1/3 N–S plus 2/3 E–W, or 1 sector length.

Alternative 3: Regardless of the sector of the incident, the average travel distance is 1/4 N–S plus 1/2 E–W, or 3/4 sector length.

Thus, in an average travel distance sense, uniform patrol repositioning (Alternative 2) offers no advantage over no repositioning (Alternative 1). On the other hand, fixed-point repositioning offers a 25 percent reduction in average travel distance when compared to Alternatives 1 and 2.

In Table 8.2 the results are displayed of the same type of reasoning applied to the four-sector case shown in Figure 8.2. Again we obtain a comparison of (1) no repositioning, (2) repositioning while maintaining uniform patrol coverage, and (3) fixed-point repositioning. The comparison is done for each possible number of units busy (0, 1, 2, or 3). Note again that in no case does Alternative 2 offer a reduction of average travel distance, compared to Alter-

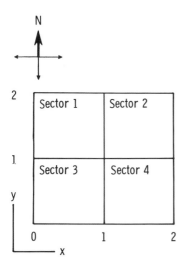

Figure 8.2 A region of four cooperating square sectors.

15. See Section 3.4.2 and Equation 3.30 in particular.

Table 8.2 Average Travel Distances for a Four Sector Region with Various Types of Repositioning Strategies (Distances given in sector lengths)

No. of Units Busy	No Repositioning	Uniform Patrol Repositioning	Fixed-Point Repositioning
0	$\dfrac{2}{3}$	$\dfrac{2}{3}$	$\dfrac{2}{3}$
1	$\dfrac{2}{3} \cdot \dfrac{3}{4} + \dfrac{4}{3} \cdot \dfrac{1}{4} = \dfrac{5}{6}$	$\dfrac{2}{3} \cdot \dfrac{1}{2} + \dfrac{3}{3} \cdot \dfrac{1}{2} = \dfrac{5}{6}$	$\dfrac{2}{3} \cdot \dfrac{1}{2} + \dfrac{3}{4} \cdot \dfrac{1}{2} = \dfrac{17}{24}$
2a	$\dfrac{1}{2} \cdot \dfrac{2}{3} + \dfrac{1}{2} \cdot \dfrac{4}{3} = 1$	1	$\dfrac{3}{4}$
2b	1	1	$\dfrac{3}{4}$
3	$\dfrac{2}{3} \cdot \dfrac{1}{4} + \dfrac{4}{3} \cdot \dfrac{1}{2} + 2\dfrac{1}{4} = \dfrac{4}{3}$	$\dfrac{4}{3}$	1

Case 2a: 2 adjacent sectors busy
Case 2b: 2 diagonal sectors busy

Uniform Patrol Repositioning

Units busy	
1	A unit adjacent to the busy sector patrols both sectors uniformly
2	The two free units each patrol two sectors uniformly
3	The free unit patrols all four sectors uniformly

Fixed-Point Repositioning

Units busy	
1	A unit adjacent to the busy sector is stationed at the halfway point between the sectors
2	Both units are stationed at halfway points
3	The free unit is stationed at the intersection of all four sectors

native 1. Alternative 3 offers successively greater reductions in average travel distance as the number of busy units increases.

The results suggest that any local repositioning (among nearby sectors) is advantageous in a travel distance sense only if patrol is concentrated near the boundaries of the appropriate sectors. In practice, strict fixed-point repositioning may not be advisable because of lost preventive patrol coverage; still, if the free unit must remain patrolling, a large part of the travel distance reduction can be retained provided the patrol occurs near the appropriate sector boundaries. In fact, the author has heard patrolmen remark that on an informal basis two units will occasionally agree to cover both sectors when the other unit is unavailable; this covering usually takes the form of concentrated patrol near the common sector boundary. To gain travel distance reductions when such covering occurs, it is necessary that the dispatcher be aware of the identity of the cooperating units so that he can assign the covering unit to a call in the busy unit's sector.

8.3. Sector Geometry with Intersector Cooperation

If internal repositioning or other types of intersector cooperation are to be incorporated into operating policy, perhaps a redesign of sector boundaries is in order. Previously sector designs have been explored for single area-constrained sectors, allowing for rectangular, elliptical, or diamond-shaped geometries.[16] Assuming right-angle response and uniformly, independently distributed incident and patrol unit positions, we showed that a sector design which equalizes average E–W and N–S travel times results in minimum average intrasector travel time. With cooperation among sectors, the design that minimizes average intrasector travel time is usually not optimal for the entire system of cooperating sectors.

As an example, consider again the two-sector case in which the sectors are to be of equal size and cover a total area A, with boundaries parallel to street directions. Referring to Figure 8.3, we assume that each sector has dimensions $d_1/2$ E–W and d_2 N–S ($d_1 d_2 = A$). We assume for simplicity that calls arriving when both units are busy are serviced by units outside of this two-sector region. Let $p_0(p_1)$ be the probability that neither unit (one unit) is busy when a call arrives that will be serviced by one of the units ($p_0 + p_1 = 1$). Again we assume center-of-mass dispatching, uniform demand, and uniform patrol over any area in which a unit is assigned to patrol. Finally, we assume that the time required to accomplish local repositioning is negligibly small.

The task is now to derive the sector dimensions which minimize average travel time. Again we set $v_x = v_y$ and deal directly with travel distance.

8.3.1. No Repositioning

For the case of no repositioning, the average travel distance to a random call that is serviced by one of the two units is

16. See Section 3.3.

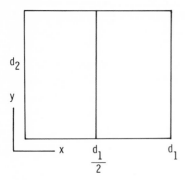

•Area Constraint: $d_1 d_2 = A$

Figure 8.3 Two cooperating sectors to be designed for minimum average travel distance.

$$E[D] = p_0[\tfrac{1}{3}d_2 + \tfrac{1}{6}d_1] + p_1[\tfrac{1}{3}d_2 + \tfrac{1}{3}d_1]. \tag{8.12}$$

Substituting the constraint $d_2 = A/d_1$ and taking the derivative with respect to d_1, we obtain the optimal[17] E-W dimension of the two sectors

$$d_1^* = \sqrt{\frac{2A}{2 - p_0}}. \tag{8.13}$$

For $0 < p_0 < 1$, we find $\sqrt{A} < d_1 < \sqrt{2A}$; in contrast to the single sector results of Chapter 3, which recommend square sectors when $v_x = v_y$, this result implies (1) neither sector itself should be square and (2) the two-sector configuration should not be square.

8.3.2. Uniform Patrol Repositioning

A moment's reflection indicates that Equation 8.12 also applies to the case of uniform patrol repositioning. Thus, the optimal sector design for the case of uniform patrol repositioning is identical to that obtained for the case of no repositioning (Equation 8.13).

8.3.3. Fixed-Point Repositioning

For the case of fixed-point repositioning, the average travel distance is

$$E[D] = p_0[\tfrac{1}{3}d_2 + \tfrac{1}{6}d_1] + p_1[\tfrac{1}{4}d_2 + \tfrac{1}{4}d_1]. \tag{8.14}$$

Proceeding as before, we find the optimal E–W dimension:

$$d_1^{**} = \sqrt{\frac{A(3 + p_0)}{3 - p_0}}. \tag{8.15}$$

---

17. The second derivative is positive, and thus a minimum is obtained.

Again, for $0 < p_0 < 1$, we find $\sqrt{A} < d_1 < \sqrt{2A}$, indicating nonsquare sectors. Also it is easy to verify that

$$d_1^{**} \geqslant d_1^* .$$

These results are intuitively appealing. With increased intersector dispatching, the common sector boundary (of length d_2) becomes elongated. This reduces the average *intersector* travel distance, while increasing the average *intrasector* travel distance. The inequality $d_1^{**} \geqslant d_1^*$ is due to the fact that fixed-point repositioning already reduces intersector travel distance, so that each sector can be better designed to reduce intrasector travel distance.

8.3.4. Numerical Example

Here we consider the case $p_0 = p_1 = 1/2$, $A = 2$, to indicate the approximate magnitude of mean travel distance reduction which is achieved with these sector designs. The standard of comparison is a two-sector system with square sectors and no repositioning, for which the mean travel distance is

$$p_0 \tfrac{2}{3} + p_1 (\tfrac{1}{2} \cdot \tfrac{2}{3} + \tfrac{1}{2} \cdot \tfrac{4}{3}) = \tfrac{5}{6} \approx 0.833 \text{ sector length.}$$

For an optimal two-sector design with no repositioning or with uniform patrol repositioning,

$$d_1^* = \sqrt{\tfrac{4}{3}A}, \qquad d_2^* = \sqrt{\tfrac{3}{4}A},$$

yielding a mean travel distance $E[D] \approx 0.816$, or only about a 2 percent reduction compared to square sectors.

To evaluate fixed-point repositioning with an optimal sector design, we must also compute the mean travel distance with square sectors and fixed-point repositioning. This distance is $17/24 \approx 0.708$, or about 15 percent less than that obtained with square sectors and no repositioning. The optimal sector design with fixed-point repositioning is given by

$$d_1^{**} = \sqrt{\tfrac{7}{5}A}, \qquad d_2^{**} = \sqrt{\tfrac{5}{7}A},$$

yielding a mean travel distance $E[D] \approx 0.697$. Thus, a shift to fixed-point repositioning retaining square sectors yields a 15 percent mean travel time reduction; a subsequent sector redesign further reduces mean travel time by only about 1.6 percent.

These numerical results indicate travel time insensitivities to multisector designs paralleling those found for single sectors in Chapter 3. They also suggest that designing sectors solely to minimize intrasector travel times results in a total system travel time greater than the minimum possible, but the difference is less than we might have expected intuitively.

The optimal design of sectors for an arbitrary number of cooperating sectors and for an arbitrary spatial distribution of demands has not been solved here. Rather, we hope that these elementary considerations will pinpoint relevant factors when designing patrol sectors, as well as help identify future areas of research.

8.4. A Discussion of Global Repositioning

Global repositioning refers to the assignment of one or more units to commands geographically separate from their usual commands. For instance, it could refer to the assignment of several units from one precinct (division) into another precinct (division). Such repositioning is required if the state of the patrol force indicates that one or more precincts are becoming congested relative to the others. Even if forces are properly prepositioned in each precinct at the start of a tour, one would expect that stochastic fluctuations in the number of calls reported and their service times would cause several precincts to become relatively overloaded (and others relatively underloaded) on any given tour.[18]

To obtain an estimate of the probability that saturation occurs in any particular area, we briefly digress to study the spatial distribution of calls being serviced.

8.4.1. The Number of Busy Servers in an Area

Assume that there is some homogeneous region of area A°, from which calls are generated in a Poisson manner at an average rate αA° (calls/hour). Assume that there are sufficiently many patrol units so that no call is delayed in queue. The average total service time for a call is μ^{-1}. Then, invoking a result from the theory of $M/G/\infty$ queues,[19] the steady-state probability $P_M(j/A)$ that there are j calls in service in any subregion of area $A(A \leqslant A^\circ)$ is

$$P_M(j/A) = \frac{(\alpha A/\mu)^j e^{-\alpha A/\mu}}{j!}, \qquad j = 0, 1, 2, \ldots . \tag{8.16}$$

This probability is independent of the numbers of calls in service in any disjoint subregions. Thus, in the steady state, the number of calls in service constitutes a homogeneous spatial Poisson process with parameter α/μ (calls/unit

18. Of course, global phenomena such as weather conditions or extraordinary events such as civil disorders could cause an unexpectedly large (or small) load on all commands during a particular tour.
19. See, for example, L. S. Goddard, *Mathematical Techniques of Operational Research*, (Reading, Mass.: Addison-Wesley Publishing Co., 1963), pp. 146-7.

area). This result can be used to obtain many useful descriptors of system operation.

8.4.2. Command Saturation

We wish to address the problem of saturation of a command. For that purpose, we can replace αA in Equation 8.16 with λ_c, where

λ_c = average rate at which calls are generated from command c, where $c = 1, 2, \ldots, I$.

Also, we need make no assumptions about spatial homogeneity of demand. We assume that command c has N_c units usually assigned. We say that command c is *saturated* if the number of calls in service in the command is equal to or greater than N_c. We will assume that throughout all commands there are sufficiently many patrol units $(\Sigma_c N_c)$ so that the probability that all commands are simultaneously saturated is negligibly small. Then, if a call arrives from command c at a time when there are no available units in the command, we assume that a patrol unit from another command is immediately assigned to the call (so that no call must wait in queue).

A relevant operational question is, "What is the probability that at least one command will be saturated at any given time?" Using Equation 8.16, we note that the probability that command c is saturated is

$$P\{S_c\} = \sum_{k=N_c}^{\infty} \frac{(\lambda_c/\mu)^k e^{-\lambda_c/\mu}}{k!} . \tag{8.17}$$

Thus, the probability that at least one command is saturated at any particular time is

$$P\{S\} = 1 - \prod_{c=1}^{I} (1 - P\{S_c\}). \tag{8.18}$$

As an example, consider a city with $I = 5$ commands, each usually assigned $N_c = 5$ patrol units. Let $\lambda_c = 3.75$ calls per hour ($c = 1, \ldots, 5$) and $\mu^{-1} = 2/3$ hour. Then, the utilization factor ρ (or fraction of time busy servicing calls) is not particularly large, $\rho = 1/2$. But, using Equations 8.17 and 8.18, we see that the probability that at least one command is saturated is approximately

$$P\{S\} \cong 1 - (0.89)^5 \approx 0.44.$$

Thus, for reasonable parameter values, this probability is sufficiently high to warrant consideration of intercommand repositioning prior to saturation to reduce travel times.

8.4.3. Strategies

With global repositioning, two policies must be developed: (1) a set of rules governing when and how to reposition forces outside of their usually assigned commands; (2) a set of rules pertaining to the redeployment of the repositioned units back to their usual commands. The repositioning and redeployment policies parallel the dispatch and reassignment strategies in usual dispatching. However, development of the strategies is considerably more difficult than for usual dispatching, primarily because of the large number of possible ways to accomplish repositioning.

A Time to Act

Of primary importance is the development of criteria for determining when global repositioning is required and when redeployment is needed. Potential signals indicating these needs are not as visible as a received call for service or as a unit notifying the dispatcher that it is again available for assignment. Of course, one possible signal for repositioning is saturation in one region; however, we would hope to accomplish repositioning prior to saturation and thus avoid lengthy travel times.

With the real-time computer aided dispatching systems that are currently planned in several police departments, it would seem desirable to maintain a continuous monitor on the state of the patrol system. By analysis of current input call levels and data describing past operation, a monitoring program could signal the dispatcher when the probability of saturation in a particular area within a time T exceeds some threshold. Then, the program could suggest to the dispatcher several possible repositioning alternatives to reduce saturation probability. The dispatcher could then act, in his new command capacity, and either (1) implement one of the suggested alternatives; (2) choose one of his own; or (3) choose to do nothing.

Similarly, the monitor could signal the dispatcher when the probability of saturation has been reduced sufficiently so that redeployment can occur.

A Possible Criterion

A criterion upon which to base the need for repositioning would probably include in some way the congestion of each region (command). Congestion can be measured in terms of fraction of cars busy, number of call reports in queue, and so forth.

One useful criterion depends on the transient form of the system state probabilities. For command c, let the state n correspond to n calls in the command, either in service or in queue. Let

$P_c\,(n\,|N,m,T)= P$ {command c is in state n at time T | it is in state m at
time 0 and has N patrol units assigned}.

Again assume that λ_c calls are received per hour, on the average, from command c. The total city-wide rate of calls is

$$\lambda = \sum_{c=1}^{I} \lambda_c.$$

Then, the probability that a random call arriving at time T will incur response delay because of saturation is

$$\sum_{c=1}^{I} \frac{\lambda_c}{\lambda} \sum_{n_c=N_c}^{\infty} P_c(n_c\,|N_c,m_c,T), \tag{8.19}$$

given that at time 0 command c is in state m_c with N_c units assigned. One could determine the N_c so that this probability is minimized, thereby developing a criterion for repositioning and redeployment. That is

$$\underset{\{N_c\}}{\text{Min}} \left[\sum_{c=1}^{I} \frac{\lambda_c}{\lambda} \sum_{n_c=N_c}^{\infty} P_c(n_c\,|N_c,m_c,T) \right],$$

subject to the total manpower constraint,

$$\sum_{c=1}^{I} N_c = N^{\circ}.$$

The time T chosen in the criterion function would probably be in the order of 1 to 2 hours (that is, sufficiently large so that units need not be repositioned continuously).

The minimization can be done easily with dynamic programming, once the transient solution is known in analytical form. In fact, the same algorithm suggested in Chapter 5 could be used to perform this minimization.

Selecting Particular Units

Given that a new set of N_c is determined from this procedure, the problem is then to decide which particular units to choose from one region (for which the allocation level is being reduced) and assign to another region (for which the level is being increased). This appears to be a very difficult problem, with many types of intermediate strategies possible. For instance, because of lengthy travel times, it may be desirable to station some of the repositioned units in a command for which the net change of manpower is zero; an equivalent number of units from the command would be sent to a destination where the actual need was occurring. Such a procedure may reduce by 50 percent the actual time to accomplish repositioning (or redeployment).

To reduce the possibility of very complicated *domino-type* effects, caused by successively shuffling the same number of (different) units from one command to the next adjacent command, it would be preferable to assign a cost to moving a unit. Then, the time required to accomplish repositioning would have to be traded off with the cost of moving many units.

Even if no intermediate strategies are permitted, one can see that the number of ways to implement a repositioning scheme is enormous. For instance, if the determination of a set of N_c required moving M specific units to new distinct positions, there are $M!$ different ways to accomplish the repositioning.

In a fire operations context, several approaches have been tried by individuals at the New York City Rand Institute. Swersey[20] divided the repositioning problem into two subproblems: (1) determining which fire houses should be empty and which full, given a specific total amount of available fire apparatus; and (2) determining how to transform the current distribution of apparatus to achieve the desired distribution. The first was formulated as an integer programming model, in which the cost function combined mean travel time to fires and a penalty cost for each unit relocated. Given the solution to this model, Swersey apparently found satisfactory results for the second problem by using a standard "assignment" algorithm.

Walker and Shinnar[21] have tried various techniques to decrease the computer time required to solve Swersey's first model, but unfortunately none has yet been found fast enough to make the model useful to dispatchers on a real-time basis.

The relocation method which is planned for implementation in New York City has been developed by Kolesar and Walker[22] based on a suggestion of Chaiken. Rather than focusing on average travel distances, this algorithm

20. A. Swersey, "A Mathematical Formulation of the Fire Engine Relocation Problem," unpublished mimeograph (New York City Rand Institute, 1970).
21. W. Walker and S. Shinnar, "Approaches to the Solution of the Fire Engine Relocation Problem," unpublished mimeograph (New York City Rand Institute, 1970).
22. P. Kolesar and W. Walker, "A Relocation Algorithm for the MICS," unpublished mimeograph (New York City Rand Institute, 1970).

uses concepts of *minimal acceptable coverage* in order to signal needs for relocation and to recommend how the relocation is to be performed. A point is said to be satisfactorily covered if at least one unit of type i fire apparatus can travel to the point within a specified amount of time T_i (for all i). In New York City, $i = 1$ corresponds to fire engines and $i = 2$ corresponds to ladder trucks. The T_i are important policy parameters whose values are partially determined by current levels of fire activity within the city. The algorithm mandates at least one relocation whenever the collection of available fire apparatus enters a state in which neighborhoods would otherwise remain uncovered for an expected time of, say, 20 minutes or more. It uses approximate methods to determine which empty fire houses need to be filled and which specific engines and ladders should be moved into them. Although no unique optimal solution is found, apparently the resulting relocations are found quite satisfactory by fire dispatchers, who desperately need computer assistance when areas of the city become saturated.

8.5. Summary and Future Research

In this chapter models were developed predicting the amount of intersector dispatching and command-level saturation, thereby indicating the need for both local and global forms of repositioning to reduce travel times. Several simple forms of repositioning were considered, both to introduce certain concepts and to indicate approximate benefits of repositioning.

In Section 8.1 a model was developed predicting the fraction of dispatches which are intersector dispatches. Certain special cases of the model provided insight into system operation. In a non-time-varying environment in which sectors are designed to distribute workload uniformly, it was found that the fraction of dispatches which are intersector dispatches approximately equals the average fraction of time units are not available for dispatch. In a time-varying environment, the amount of intersector dispatching is usually greater than that in the equivalent non-time-varying system. In a system that utilizes car location information, the amount of intersector dispatching is greater than that in the corresponding center-of-mass dispatching system. During near-saturation conditions when queues of waiting call reports are depleted in a first-come, first-served manner, the responding units handle calls almost irrespective of the sector of the call. Most of the predicted results have been verified experimentally and in simulation studies (for instance, see Chapters 2, 6, and 7).

The results of Section 8.1 also provide insights into traditional concepts of patrol and sector workloads, which are usually tied to the number of calls for service generated from within the sector. For instance, O. W. Wilson states, "If one beat has twice the need for police service that another has, the officer assigned to the first beat has twice as much work to do as the officer assigned to the second."[23] But with the amount of intersector dispatching currently prevalent with most radio-dispatched patrol forces, the fact that one sector generates twice the calls for service as another does not imply that one patrol unit works twice as hard as the other. In fact, because of intersector dispatching, they may both work about equally hard. This result has strong implications about traditional ways of tabulating workloads—to assess correctly a unit's call-for-service workload its dispatch assignments must be recorded, not its sector's number of calls for service.

With these ideas in mind, consider a traditional procedure that attempts to distribute call-for-service workload uniformly by designing sectors to have equal rates of calls for service. In general, such an apportionment of call-for-service rates does not yield equal workloads among patrol units. The reason again hinges on dispatching strategies and intersector responses. The particular geometry of any command will probably be such that certain patrol units are preferred more often for intersector dispatches than others. For instance, the unit near the center of a command is not too distant from any point in the command and thus would make a reasonable out-of-sector choice for many calls; thus, such a unit would be preferred more often for out-of-sector dispatches than, say, a unit patrolling near the edge of the command. By being more likely to receive intersector dispatch assignments, the preferred units will incur heavier workloads, even though their own sectors generate no more calls than any other sectors. Thus, extreme care must be taken to consider out-of-sector responses when attempting to balance workloads.

Certain traditional one-man, one-sector concepts are brought to question by the results predicting large amounts of intersector dispatching, and the predicted amounts have been verified experimentally. Perhaps a sector identity should be replaced by a regional identity. Or perhaps the method of assigning units to rigidly defined nonoverlapping sectors should be discarded. Some type of overlapping sector plan would acknowledge that delivery of police service to an area is the responsibility of several units. It would provide a more continuous level of preventive patrol, thereby increasing the deterrent threat (Chapter 4). Also, it would not significantly change anticipated travel times, provided patrol position information is available (Chapter 7).

23. Wilson, *Police Administration*, p. 274.

If sectors are to be retained, a certain amount of regional identity can be achieved by having units in nearby sectors formally cooperate in various ways. As examples, Section 8.2 considered two simple cases of local repositioning to reduce travel times of anticipated intersector dispatches (1) uniform patrol repositioning, and (2) fixed-point repositioning. With uniform patrol repositioning, a unit is assigned to patrol uniformly both its usual sector and one or more contiguous sectors in which the corresponding sector units are busy. With fixed-point repositioning, a unit is assigned to a specific point somewhere near the boundary of its usual sector and one or more contiguous sectors in which the corresponding sector units are busy.[24] Strict center-of-mass dispatching was assumed throughout. We found expected travel distances for each of these strategies for very simple sector configurations. For the examples considered, uniform patrol repositioning offered no reduction of average travel distance over that achieved with no repositioning. However, fixed-point repositioning offered substantial reductions.

We then determined the manner in which intersector cooperation influences sector geometry (Section 8.3). For two contiguous rectangular sectors with uniformly distributed demand, we studied three possible examples of intersector cooperation, each of which entails dispatching an available cooperating unit to any calls in a busy unit's sector. In the first example, the available unit continues patrolling only its own sector when the other unit becomes busy; in the second, the available unit repositions for uniform patrol of both sectors; in the third, the available unit repositions to a fixed point. Of fundamental importance is the fact that the type of intersector cooperation determines the optimal sector design. For these examples, the numerical results indicate that the simple single sector designs of Chapter 3 yield average travel times for the system of sectors quite close to the minimum possible.

The final form of intersector cooperation that we discussed was global repositioning, that is, the temporary assignment of one or more available units to other commands. (Section 8.4) To indicate the need for global repositioning, the steady-state probability distribution of the number of busy units in a region was computed. When the number of busy units exceeds a specified threshold, the region is said to be saturated. Even for cities with apparently underworked patrol forces, it is often likely that at least one command will be saturated under normal operating conditions, thereby indicating the need for intercommand repositioning.

24. These examples are simple, analytically useful approximations for more realistic strategies that might be employed.

Implementation of a repositioning procedure requires a criterion indicating the level of congestion, a threshold signaling that congestion is, or will probably be, too great if units are not repositioned, and an algorithm for selecting particular units to reposition. Some of the ideas suggested for repositioning of fire units should prove applicable to the analogous problem in police patrol.

Clearly the subject of intersector cooperation and repositioning should be a rich one for future research. The potential benefits to be accrued in more effective patrol operations will become particularly apparent with the introduction of computer-supported command and control facilities, which will provide the necessary real-time monitoring and analysis capability.

A partial list of subjects for study would include

1. Methods for improving the design of cooperating sectors (either mutually exclusive or overlapping);

2. Criteria for local and global repositioning and redeployment;

3. Procedures for obtaining the transient state probabilities of the system;

4. Rules for selecting particular units to reposition.

Both simulation programs and analytical models will probably be required in this research.

Glossary

(Words set in italics are defined elsewhere in the glossary)

Beat
An area or region in which one *patrol unit* has *preventive patrol* responsibility. Same as *sector*.

Call for service
A communication to police originating from a citizen, an alarm system, a police officer, or other detector, reporting the need for on-scene police assistance. Used interchangeably with *reported incident*.

Car locator system
A method or device which provides the *dispatcher* with improved estimates of the positions of available *patrol units*. This is to be distinguished from usual manual position estimation methods which usually entail guessing an available unit's position, using a *center-of-mass* criterion.

Car position resolution
The precision of the *car locator system*. A high resolution system is characterized by small errors in position estimation.

Center-of-mass
That point in a *sector* or a *geographical atom*, respectively, which is the statistically average position of the patrolling unit or the *reported incidents*, respectively. Four *dispatching strategies* that require the *dispatcher* to guess an available unit's position using statistical averages are *center-of-mass* strategies. (See Table 3.2.)

Command
An area or region comprising several *sectors* that is administratively distinct, usually having a station-house used as a base of operations. Often called *precincts*, districts, or areas. A patrol officer is usually assigned to one command for a period of time. *Dispatch assignments* are nearly always intra-*command* assignments.

Complaint clerk
A police emergency telephone operator.

Complete barrier
An impediment to travel cutting through an entire *sector*, with one crossing point, possibly corresponding to a river with one bridge in the sector.

Coverage function
A function which indicates the relative amount of *preventive patrol* attention to be given to various points within a *sector*.

Cumulative distribution function (cdf)
A function indicating the probability that a certain random variable assumes an experimental value less than or equal to the argument of the function.

Dispatch
Usually the same as *dispatch assignment*. Occasionally refers to a *dispatch assignment* of a unit on *preventive patrol*, while *reassignment* refers to a *dispatch assignment* of a unit completing service at the scene of a previously *reported incident*.

Dispatch assignment
A directive by the *dispatcher* to a *patrol unit* assigning the unit to respond to the scene of a *reported incident*, or *call for service*.

Dispatch error
Refers to assigning other than the closest available unit to a *reported incident*.

Dispatch policy
A set of rules regarding the immediate assignment of *patrol units* to *reported incidents*. It specifies the conditions under which a *reported incident* of a particular *priority* from a particular location is entered into a *queue* of waiting *incident reports* or is handled immediately by an assigned *patrol unit*. Also see *reassignment policy*.

Dispatcher
An individual who has responsibility for assigning radio-dispatchable *patrol units* to *reported incidents*.

Dispatcher queue
A collection of *reported incidents* to which no *patrol unit* has yet been assigned. Physically, the *dispatcher queue* comprises a number of *incident reports*, which are either hand-completed tickets or data elements in an array in computer storage.

Dispatching strategy
Usually the component of the *dispatch policy* pertaining to distance estimation techniques.

Division
A collection of contiguous *commands* which comprise the next higher administratively distinct unit. In several cities, each *dispatcher* has responsibility for all radio-dispatchable units within a *division*.

Dynamic programming
A mathematical optimization technique that recursively finds the maximum (or minimum) of some function. The computations are usually carried out on a computer.

Effective travel speed
That speed that, if constantly maintained over the path of a response journey, would result in the same *travel time* as that actually experienced by the responding *patrol unit*.

Emergency response system
The system which is activated whenever a citizen (or alarm system or other detector) communicates the need for on-scene police service to the police communications center (or command and control center). Comprises *complaint clerks, dispatchers,* radio-dispatched *patrol units*, and related devices and methods.

Euclidean distance
The straight-line distance between two points, "as the crow flies."

Event-paced
A type of computer *simulation* in which the simulation clock, when requiring update, is advanced to the time of the next simulation event.

Fluid patrol
A method of patrol deployment with no fixed *sector* boundaries. One or more units are assigned to particular regions as the need becomes apparent, and these assignments can change dynamically over the course of a tour.

Flying
A police term referring to frequent cross-sector or *intersector assignments.*

Geographical atom
A region or area within the city that is sufficiently small so that all *spatial distributions* over the region can be approximated to be uniform.

Global repositioning
A type of intersector cooperation in which one or more available *patrol units* are temporarily reassigned to areas in other *commands.*

Hazard formula
A summation of crime statistics, geographical statistics, and other factors thought to be important in determining the need for *patrol units* in a region, each factor multiplied by a weighting indicating its subjective importance. Also called workload formula.

Home sector
The sector in which a *patrol unit* is assigned to perform *preventive patrol.*

Incident report
A hand-completed ticket or a data element in computer storage containing pertinent information describing a *reported incident.*

Intercept probability
The likelihood that a patrolling unit will pass (and perhaps detect) a crime while in progress.

Intersector assignment
A *dispatch assignment* to a *sector* other than the unit's *home sector.*

Local repositioning
A deliberate change in the position or patrolling strategy of an available unit in anticipation of incidents which may be reported from one or more *sectors* whose *patrol units* are temporarily unavailable. All movements are confined to be intra-*command.*

Multiserver queue
A *queue* in which each customer is serviced by one of several possible servers, or attendants (for example, *patrol units*).

Overlapping sectors
Sectors that at least partially share common regions or areas.

Overlapping tours
Tours that share one or more common hours of occurrence.

Partial barrier
An impediment to travel that extends part way into a *sector*, possibly corresponding to a park or cemetery.

Patrol allocation
The entire process of determining the total required number of *patrol units*, their spatial and temporal assignments, and rules governing their operation.

Patrol deployment strategy
A set of rules specifying the spatial distribution of available *patrol units*, including *sector* and *command* design, *patrol coverages*, and *repositioning.*

Patrol frequency
The number of times per hour that a patrolling unit passes a particular point.

Patrol status
The condition of a *patrol unit*, particularly pertaining to dispatch availability. In some police departments the dispatch status of a *patrol unit* is restricted to one of two possibilities: available or unavailable; in others, finer distinctions are made, including such possibilities as meal break, auto maintenance, patrol initiated action, station-house, or type of incident currently being serviced.

Patrol unit
A footpatrolman; or an assigned pair of footpatrolmen; or a patrol car, scooter, or wagon and its assigned police officer(s). Occasionally the term patrol car is used as a substitute for this more general term.

Point-polygon method
A procedure for determining whether a particular point is within a polygon specified by its clockwise-ordered vertices.

Precinct
Used interchangeably with *command.*

Preemption
Interruption of one activity in order to undertake another more important activity, such as *preemption* of a *patrol unit* completing a report of a past burglary to assign it to a robbery in progress.

Preventive patrol
An activity undertaken by a *patrol unit*, in which the unit tours an area, with the officer(s) checking for crime hazards (for example, open doors and windows) and attempting to intercept any crimes while in progress.

Priority
Order of preference based on urgency and importance, such as the *priority* placed on a particular *call for service.*

Probability density function (pdf)
A nonnegative function for which the probability that the corresponding random variable lies between x and $x + \Delta x$ (Δx small) is approximately equal to the function evaluated at x multiplied by Δx.

Quantized mileage
The trip mileage recorded from odometer readings, which results in one-mile or tenth-of-a-mile quantizations.

Quantized time
The duration of an activity recorded from time-stamp clocks or other mechanisms which approximate time at the quantization level of one minute or one-one hundredth of an hour.

Queue
A waiting line, as of customers before a checkout counter or *incident reports* before a *dispatcher.*

Random patrol
A *preventive patrol* in which the patrolling unit selects unpredictable patrol paths.

Reassignment
A *dispatch assignment* of a unit completing service at the scene of a previously *reported incident.* (See *dispatch.*)

Reassignment policy
A set of rules specifying how a unit completing service at the scene of a previously assigned incident is reassigned to a nearby unserviced incident or to *preventive patrol* duty.

Redeployment
The movement of available repositioned units back to their *home sectors* and usual patrol patterns. (See *global repositioning*.)

Reported incident
Same as *call for service*.

Repositioning
The deliberate movement of one or more available *patrol units* to cover for busy units or to relieve congestion in other areas. (See *global repositioning* and *local repositioning*.)

Right-angle distance
The sum of the total east–west and north–south distances between two points, given that the directions of travel are oriented east–west and north–south. Also called metropolitan distance, rectangular distance, and Manhattan distance.

Screening
The process of carefully questioning callers about the details of an incident or service request and eliminating from further police processing those calls that are found not to require on-scene police assistance.

Sector
Same as *beat*.

Sector coverage time
The time for the *patrol unit* to pass at least once every point in its *sector*.

Sector identity
A term applied to an officer's personal commitment to maintain public order and provide effective police service within his *home sector*.

Simulation
A method of replicating the operations of a system with a computer model that incorporates the same statistical behaviors as found in the actual system.

Spatial distribution
The relative allotment of some quantity (for example, *reported incidents*) to each region of the city.

Spatial Poisson process
A two-dimensional random process that distributes points in a plane (possibly corresponding to a city) independently according to some *spatial distribution*. If the *spatial distribution* is uniform, then the process is homogeneous.

Stacking
A police term referring to the deliberate delaying in *queue* of relatively un-important *incident reports*.

Standard deviation
The most common measure of the dispersion of a distribution about its mean or average value.

Street density
The number of street miles per square mile.

Temporal distribution
The relative allotment of some quantity (for example, *patrol units*) to each time of the day.

Tour
A shift of continuous duty, usually lasting 8 hours.

Travel time
The time required for the dispatched *patrol unit* to travel to the scene of the *reported incident.*

Utilization factor
The fraction of time a *patrol unit* is unavailable to respond to dispatch requests. Sometimes it is assumed that a unit can only be unavailable because of call-servicing duties. Sometimes called utilization rate.

Waiting time in queue
The time an *incident report* is delayed in the *dispatcher queue* or the time a telephone caller spends waiting for a ringing telephone to be answered by a *complaint clerk.*

Workload
Some measure of the time spent by a *patrol unit* on a number of prescribed duties, particularly *calls for service.*

Annotated Bibliography

Bard, M., 1970.
Training Police as Specialists in Family Crisis Intervention. Washington, D.C.:
U.S. Government Printing Office.
This report summarizes a 2-year experiment in Precinct 30 in New York City,
in which 18 police volunteers were trained as specialists in family crisis situations requiring police assistance. At least one radio patrol car was continually
staffed by the volunteers, and it was dispatched on all calls for service that
could be predetermined as involving a family disturbance. The car responded
to calls anywhere in the precinct without regard to sector boundaries. Evaluation included a neighboring control precinct and focused on the total number of family crisis interventions, the number of homicides and assaults,
the number of injuries to officers, and implications for mental health, law
enforcement, and the community.

Beck, R., 1970.
*The Application of a Teleprinter System to Law Enforcement Communica-
tions.* Phoenix, Arizona: Phoenix Police Department.
The experimentation with teleprinters discussed in this report utilized a squad
of 10 patrol units on a 24-hour basis for a period of 30 days in a geographical
area covering approximately 15 square miles. Evaluation considered officers'
subjective attitudes and opinions, as well as the technical performance of the
equipment. The report's value is enhanced by a rather thorough history and
description of the dispatch-patrol system in Phoenix, indicating for instance
a rather novel procedure for assigning two patrol units to each beat. R. Beck
was the project director.

Bergstrom, K. R., 1966.
The Fluid Patrol System. Traffic Police Paper prepared for Administration
Training Program, Traffic Institute at Northwestern University, Chicago,
Illinois.
This report was written by Bergstrom while he was a sergeant of the Tucson
Arizona Police Department. It describes a patrol allocation method (fluid
patrol) that does not use traditional fixed sector boundaries, but that al-
locates personnel dynamically, as the need develops.

**Blumstein, A., L. Curtis, J. Kiernan, R. C. Larson, J. Navarro, M. Schankman,
J. Taylor, and E. Webb**, 1968.
*A National Program of Research, Development, Test, and Evaluation on Law
Enforcement and Criminal Justice.* Prepared for Law Enforcement Assistance
Administration, U.S. Department of Justice, at the Institute for Defense
Analyses, Arlington, Virginia.
This report was funded by the U.S. Justice Department to follow up on the
general recommendations of the Science and Technology Task Force. It
details ongoing research projects and outlines promising future projects.

Blumstein, A., and R. C. Larson, 1967.
"A Systems Approach to the Study of Crime and Criminal Justice." In *Op-
erations Research for Public Systems*, P. M. Morse and L. W. Bacon, eds.,
Cambridge, Massachusetts: The M.I.T. Press, pp. 159–180.

This is an overview of some of the authors' work while they were members of the Science and Technology Task Force of the President's Commission on Law Enforcement and Administration of Justice.

Bryant, J. W., M. L. Chambers, and D. Falcon, 1968.
Patrol Effectiveness and Patrol Deployment. Lancaster, England: University of Lancaster, Department of Operational Research, Report on Home Office Project in Lancaster Division of Lancashire Constabulary.
These authors have been formulating some of the patrol problems related to the Lancaster Division of Lancashire Constabulary. One of their models, the readiness model, may be of interest to readers of this book. Apparently they observed in the Lancaster Division that a large fraction of time that a patrol unit was unavailable was caused by patrol-initiated activities. Thus, their readiness model, which predicts unavailability probability, incorporates a parameter indicating the rate at which a patrolling unit will engage in patrol-initiated activities.

Capaul, J., N. Heller, and E. Meisenheimer, 1970.
"A Stochastic Model for Allocating Police Patrol Units to Districts which Reflects each District's Rates of Injury, Property Loss, and Fear." Paper presented at 38th National Meeting of the Operations Research Society of America, 28–30 October, 1970, Detroit, Michigan.
St. Louis data from 1967 are used with a simulation model to illustrate how queuing concepts applied to resource allocation can be adapted to incorporate the relative importance of various types of calls.

Casey, P. J., 1968.
Determining Police Patrol Car Requirements by Computer Simulation.
M.S. Thesis, Dept. of Engineering, Arizona State University, Tempe, Arizona.
This is a preliminary simulation study of the police patrol force.

Chaiken, J. M., and R. C. Larson, 1971.
Methods for Allocating Urban Emergency Units. R-680-HUD/NSF. New York: New York City Rand Institute.
This report is a survey of ongoing research on allocation in municipal emergency service systems, with the emphasis on police patrol units and fire engines and ladders. In addition, it attempts to provide a general structure for a number of allocation problems commonly shared by many urban emergency service systems.

Chapman, S. G., 1964.
Police Patrol Readings. Springfield, Illinois: Charles C Thomas, Publisher.
This book contains numerous articles concerning various aspects of the police patrol force and presents an excellent tour of more traditional approaches to police patrol problems.

Chicago Police Department, Operations Research Task Force. 1968, 1969
Quarterly Progress Reports. Chicago, Illinois.
A. Bottoms, E. Nilsson, and D. Olson directed the work of the Chicago Police

Department Operations Research Task Force for 12 months during 1968, 1969. The work was federally funded and was reported in quarterly progress reports.

Cohen, B., 1970.
The Police Internal Administration of Justice in New York City. R-621-NYC. New York: New York City Rand Institute.
As one part of a study examining the selection, assignment, promotion and reward procedures in the New York City Police Department, this document deals with complaints against police officers and procedures employed to manage police misconduct. The study analyzes in detail the career history of nearly 2,000 officers who entered the department in 1957.

Eastman, G. D., and E. M. Eastman, eds., 1969.
Municipal Police Administration, 6th ed. Kingsport, Tenn.: Kingsport Press.
This is a classic text in police administration, prepared for police administrators, educators, and students. Focusing on general aspects of police organization and management, it provides few quantitative guidelines to assist police administrators in improving operations. However, it provides a comprehensive treatment of issues pertaining to organizational principals, changes in police service during the 1960s, general police functions, police-community relations, personnel management, and certain auxiliary services.

Elliott, J. F., 1968.
"Random Patrol." In *Law Enforcement Science and Technology II, Proceedings of the Second National Symposium on Law Enforcement Science and Technology,* Chicago, Illinois: Illinois Institute of Technology Research Institute, pp. 557–560.
Elliott quotes some results from search theory and attempts to estimate the probability of space-time coincidence of crime and patrol.

Folk, J. F., 1971.
Municipal Detective Systems: A Quantitative Approach. Technical Report No. 55. Cambridge, Mass.: M.I.T. Operations Research Center.
This report examines two types of problems found in a detective division of a municipal police department. First, viewing the detective division as a multiserver queuing system with saturated resources, it studies the effects of various strategies for assigning cases to detectives, particularly those that would reduce delay until a detective starts working on a case and those that allow a minimum acceptable amount of investigation time on each type of case. Second, viewing the actual work on solving a case as a sequential decision process, it structures the sequence of decision alternatives and uses Boston Police Department data to estimate various parameters of the model.

Frese, R. and N. Heller, 1970.
"Measuring Auto Theft and the Effectiveness of Auto Theft Control Programs." Paper presented at 38th National Meeting of the Operations Research Society of America, 28–30 October 1970, Detroit, Michigan.
This paper uses data on over 7,000 auto thefts that occurred in St. Louis in

1967 and examines various cost components of auto theft, including car-days lost, the cost of stripping and damage to vehicles, the cost of unrecovered vehicles, and the cost of the unavailability of stolen vehicles.

Gass, S., 1968.
"On the Division of Police Districts into Patrol Beats." In *Proceedings of the 1968 ACM National Conference*, Princeton, N.J.: Brandon/Systems Press Inc. Gass applies a heuristic algorithm first used for political redistricting to divide police districts into patrol beats (sectors). The suggested method is applied to the city of Cleveland, apparently resulting in a very satisfactory beat structure.

Graper, E. D., 1921.
American Police Administration. New York: The Macmillan Company.
This is one of the early texts focusing on police organization, personnel management, and supervision and control. The chapter on patrol provides interesting historical insights: Vollmer's "novel system" of automobile patrol in Berkeley, California is cited as a "radical departure from the ordinary methods of patrol," indicating "that in some cities at least, new methods are being tried and attempts are being made to lift police service to a higher state of efficiency." (p. 133) Footpatrol on linear or "straightaway" beats was the most prevalent type of patrol at that time.

Gray, Paul, 1971.
"Robbery and Assault of Bus Drivers." *Operations Research* 19: pp. 257–269.
Motivated by the sharply increased rates in robbery and assault of bus drivers in the United States during the 1960s, this study by operations researchers and social scientists examines the circumstances surrounding bus robberies and alternative methods to reduce the threat of such robberies.

Greenwood, P. W., 1970.
An Analysis of the Apprehension Activities of the New York City Police Department. R-529-NYC. New York: New York City Rand Institute.
Performed during 1968, this study analyzes New York City Police Department programs for apprehending serious criminal offenders. Using New York City data, it argues strongly for replacing clearance rates with more reliable arrest and conviction rates in order to evaluate the effectiveness of investigatory work.

Heller, N., 1969a.
1967 Service Time Histograms for Police Patrol Activities in St. Louis.
St. Louis, Missouri, Computer Center, St. Louis Metropolitan Police Department.
This valuable reference provides histograms for the total time spent by a patrol unit on a call for service (including travel time, on-scene service time and any additional time spent for report writing, arrest processing, and so forth) for each of 145 types of calls. It provides similar histograms for various types of patrol initiated activities that remove the patrol unit from dispatchable status and that are reported to the dispatcher; these include

building check, car check, meal, notification to a citizen, and auto repair. These data are illustrative of the type required to implement the techniques of this book and to provide a basis for comparative analysis of operations among various cities.

Heller, N., 1969b.
Proportional Rotating Schedules. Ph. D. Dissertation, University of Pennsylvania, Philadelphia, Pennsylvania.
Heller devises some easily implemented algorithms for assigning patrolmen to tours in such a way that all patrolmen are treated equally and that the total assignment at any time equals a desired prespecified number. He is presently continuing his work in conjunction with the St. Louis Police Department.

Heller, N. B., and R. E. Markland, 1970.
"A Climatological Model for Forecasting the Demand for Police Services." *Journal of Research in Crime and Delinquency* 7: pp. 167–176.
This paper provides a methodology for determining correlations between rates of calls for service and meteorological variables such as average daily temperature and hours of daylight. Data from St. Louis, Chicago, and Detroit indicate high correlations that may prove beneficial to police planners for scheduling patrol deployments and officer's vacations.

Hoover, J. E.
Crime in the United States, Uniform Crime Reports. Printed annually, Washington, D.C.: U.S. Government Printing Office.
This annual reference provides the most complete picture available of serious crimes reported to police in the United States. Emphasis is on index crimes: murder and nonnegligent manslaughter, forcible rape, robbery, aggregated assault, burglary, larceny $50 and over in value, and auto theft. In addition to reported crime rates, this document includes analyses of arrests, clearances, convictions, police employees, criminal careers, and demographic factors.

International City Management Association, 1971.
The Municipal Year Book 1971. Kingsport, Tenn.: Kingsport Press.
The International City Management Association publishes this very valuable reference annually. It contains extensive data describing recent trends in city management techniques; forms of municipal government; infusion of science and technology into municipal services; police, fire, and emergency medical services; functions of city agencies; municipal finances and manpower. Regarding municipal police departments, it focuses on inventories of police equipment, police-conducted educational programs in public schools, special juvenile programs, civilian employees, salaries, and equipment expenditures.

Kakalik, J. S., and S. Wildhorn, 1971a.
Aids to Decisionmaking in Police Patrol. R-593-HUD/RC. Santa Monica, California: Rand Corporation.
This paper reviews the allocation algorithm and simulation model described here in Chapters 5 and 6 and discusses further necessary development, test,

and evaluation of these tools. It suggests the incorporation of additional criteria, focusing on crime prevention and deterrence and criminal apprehension, and recommends experimentation to discover how these criteria relate to alternative police allocation strategies.

Kakalik, J. S. and S. Wildhorn, 1971b.
Aids to Decisionmaking in Police Patrol: Survey Response. R-594-HUD/RC. Santa Monica, California: Rand Corporation.
This report contains the results of a 5-month study of police patrol, sponsored by the U.S. Department of Housing and Urban Development. The report contains detailed responses elicited by questionnaire and personal visits to six participating police departments (Los Angeles City, Los Angeles County, Phoenix, St. Louis, and two major municipal police departments who requested they not be identified). Information is provided on costs, manpower usage and deployment, patrol tactics and operations, deployment methodology, the demand for patrol services, data and computer systems, research projects, and the police view of important problems.

Larson, R. C., 1967.
Operational Study of the Police Response System. Technical Report No. 26. Cambridge, Mass.: M.I.T. Operations Research Center.
This report details the author's work with the Boston Police Department during 1966, 1967. It is a revision of a Master's thesis in electrical engineering, supervised by Prof. Alvin W. Drake, M.I.T.

Larson, R. C., 1968.
"Hourly Allocation of Complaint Clerks, Dispatchers, and Radio-Dispatchable Patrol Personnel." In *Law Enforcement Science and Technology II, Proceedings of the Second National Symposium on Law Enforcement Science and Technology*, Chicago, Illinois: Illinois Institute of Technology Research Institute, pp. 247–254.
This paper summarizes Larson, 1967.

Larson, R. C., 1969.
Models for the Allocation of Urban Police Patrol Forces. Technical Report No. 44. Cambridge, Massachusetts: M.I.T. Operations Research Center.
This report was the predecessor to this book. The report is a revision of a Ph. D. dissertation in electrical engineering and operations research, supervised by Prof. Alvin W. Drake, M.I.T.

Larson, R. C., 1970a.
"On Quantitative Approaches to Urban Police Patrol Problems." *Journal of Research in Crime and Delinquency* 7: pp. 157–166.
This paper discusses in nonmathematical language the general approach taken in this book, the insights gained by modeling operations, and the types of results that may be obtained.

Larson, R. C., 1970b.
"On the Modeling of Police Patrol Operations." *IEEE Transactions on Systems Science and Cybernetics* 6: pp. 276–281.

This paper provides a brief introduction to the types of models developed in this book.

Larson, R. C., 1971.
Measuring the Response Patterns of New York City Police Patrol Cars. R-675. New York: New York City Rand Institute.
A 2-week sample of patrol car activities and response patterns for Division 16 in Queens is analyzed. Included is an hour-by-hour breakdown of activities by category: dispatch assignment, station house assignment, auto repairs and maintenance, fuel, meal break, preventive patrol, patrol initiated action. For each dispatch, initial and final patrol car positions and odometer readings are recorded, as well as the time required to respond to the scene. Some of the models developed in this book are tested for validity (for example, fraction of dispatches that are intersector dispatches).

Law Enforcement Assistance Administration, 1969.
First Annual Report of the Law Enforcement Assistance Administration. Washington, D.C.: U.S. Government Printing Office.
This first annual report of LEAA concerns the details of the program, authorized by the Omnibus Crime Control and Safe Streets Act, to help reduce and prevent crime. It contains a complete list of the financial assistance given by LEAA, whose fiscal 1969 budget totaled $63 million. Grants were provided to state and local governments, research and assistance projects, and an education program for law enforcement personnel.

Law Enforcement Assistance Administration, 1970a.
LEAA 1970. Washington, D.C.: U.S. Government Printing Office.
This is the second annual report of LEAA. During fiscal 1970, LEAAs budget totaled $268 million.

Law Enforcement Assistance Administration, 1970b.
LEAA 1970. Grants and Contracts. Washington, D.C.: U.S. Government Printing Office.
This document contains a detailed list of LEAA grants and contracts during fiscal 1970.

Law Enforcement Science and Technology I, Proceedings of the First National Symposium on Law Enforcement Science and Technology, 1967.
Chicago, Illinois: Illinois Institute of Technology Research Institute.
This and the next two references contain hundreds of papers from practitioners, manufacturers, and analysts. Along with the President's Commission reports, these present an excellent overview of current interest in the field of criminal justice and law enforcement.

Law Enforcement Science and Technology II, Proceedings of the Second National Symposium on Law Enforcement Science and Technology, 1968.
Chicago, Illinois: Illinois Institute of Technology Research Institute.

Law Enforcement Science and Technology III, Proceedings of the Third National Symposium on Law Enforcement Science and Technology, 1970. Chicago, Illinois: Illinois Institute of Technology Research Institute.

Leahy, Jr., F., 1968.
A Literature Review of Police Planning and Research. Interim Report to the Connecticut Research Commission. Hartford, Connecticut: The Travelers Research Center, Inc.
This is probably the most complete literature review of police planning and research available (as of July 1968). (F. Leahy, Jr., was the project director.)

Leonard, V. A., 1951.
Police Organization and Management. New York: The Foundation Press.
This book relies more on the scientific method than most other classic texts on police organization and management. The chapter on patrol recommends statistical procedures to help distribute the patrol force more effectively both geographically and chronologically. The suggested methods rely heavily on the works of Vollmer and Wilson.

Leonard, V. A., 1970.
Police Patrol Organization. Springfield, Ill.: Charles C Thomas Publishers.
This short text deals with organizational and management issues pertaining to small patrol forces, ranging in size from one to seventy-five officers.

McCormack, Jr., R. J., and J. L. Moen, 1968.
San Francisco's Mission Police District: A Study of Resource Allocation.
Berkeley, Calif.: Center for Planning and Development Research, Institute of Urban and Regional Development, University of California, Berkeley.
This report involved the analysis of a 1-week sample of radio dispatches from the San Francisco Mission Police District. The authors were both law enforcement officers supported as Office of Law Enforcement Assistance Fellows.

McEwen, J. Thomas, 1968.
"A Mathematical Model for Prediction of Police Patrol Workload," presented at the TIMS/ORSA Joint National Meeting, San Francisco, California. Available from the St. Louis Police Department.
McEwen documents several of the details of the St. Louis deployment scheme in this paper.

Maltz, M. D., 1971.
"Evaluation of Police Air Mobility Programs." *The Police Chief*, April 1971: pp. 34–39.
This article reviews recent experiences of police departments employing helicopters in day-to-day crime-related work and proposes several methods for improving evaluations of programs incorporating helicopters.

Misner, G. E., and R. B. Hoffman, 1967.
Police Resource Allocation. Working Paper 73. Berkeley, Calif.: Center for Planning and Development Research, Institute of Urban and Regional Development, University of California at Berkeley.

This paper discusses in a very general way some economic and demographic considerations relevant to the problem of police resource allocation.

Nordbeck, S., 1962.
Location of Areal Data for Computer Processing. Lund Studies in Geography, series C. General and Mathematical Geography, no. 2, The Royal University of Lund, Sweden, Department of Geography. Lund, Sweden: C. W. K. Gleerup Publishers.
This is an excellent reference for a number of techniques useful in the processing of geographical data, including the point-polygon method.

President's Commission on Law Enforcement and Administration of Justice, 1967a.
The Challenge of Crime in a Free Society. Washington, D.C.: U.S. Government Printing Office.
A summary of the work of the President's Crime Commission is contained in this report. Chapter 11 summarizes the work of the Science and Technology Task Force.

President's Commission on Law Enforcement and Administration of Justice, 1967b.
Task Force Report: Science and Technology. Washington, D.C.: U.S. Government Printing Office.
This is the summary report of the Science and Technology Task Force.

Revelle, C., D. Marks, and J. C. Liebman, 1970.
"An Analysis of Private and Public Sector Location Models." *Management Science* 16: pp. 692-707.
This paper reviews recent algorithmic approaches to the problem of locating fixed-position facilities, such as warehouses, fire stations, hospitals, and police precinct houses.

Rosenshine, M., 1970.
"Contributions to a Theory of Patrol Scheduling." *Operational Research Quarterly* 21: pp. 99-106.
Rosenshine models an urban street grid as a flow network, where the rate of flow on an arc corresponds to the rate of police preventive patrol. Several results are obtained, including a linear program that computes that feasible set of flows which satisfies constraints with minimum total patrol effort.

St. Louis Police Department, 1968.
Allocation of Patrol Manpower Resources in the St. Louis Police Department, vols. 1 and 2. St. Louis, Mo.: St. Louis Police Department.
The St. Louis Police Department has been applying queuing models and exponential smoothing (for demand predictions) to the allocation of patrol personnel to police districts since about 1965. This report and Shumate and Crowther, 1966, and McEwen, 1968, summarize this work.

Shumate, R. P., and R. F. Crowther, 1966.
"Quantitative Methods for Optimizing the Allocation of Police Resources."
Journal of Criminal Law, Criminology and Police Science 57: pp. 197–206.
This is an early paper describing the St. Louis effort.

Smith, Bruce, 1949.
Police Systems in the United States, revised ed. New York: Harper & Row,
Publishers.
Another classic text on police organization and management, this book has a
broader scope than most in that it addresses the history of U.S. police, the
probable future roles of police, general aspects of crime in the United States
and abroad, and the relationship of police departments to other governmental
service agencies.

Smith, R. D., 1960.
Random Patrol. Washington, D.C.: Field Service Division, International Association of Chiefs of Police.
This paper by Smith (an accomplished administrator with a law enforcement
background) applies in an elementary way some of the ideas of game theory
to illustrate the need for randomness in patrol procedures. To the best of my
knowledge, it is the first paper that uses the term random patrol applied to
police problems.

Smith, R. D., 1964.
Computer Applications in Police Manpower Distribution. Washington, D.C.:
Field Service Division, International Association of Chiefs of Police.
Smith discusses a preliminary computer algorithm for the geographical as-
signment of police manpower.

Tenzer, A. J., J. B. Benton, and C. Teng, 1969.
*Applying the Concepts of Program Budgeting to the New York City Police
Department.* RM-5846-NYC. Santa Monica, Calif.: Rand Corporation.
This paper illustrates an application of program budgeting to the New York
City Police Department, including a detailed program and cost structure, a
cost-estimating method, a comparison to conventional methods, and a com-
puterized cost model.

Vollmer, A., 1930.
Survey of the Police Department, Minneapolis, Minnesota. Publication
authorized by the Minneapolis City Council. Minneapolis, Minn.: Minneapolis
Police Department.
This is one of the early studies by Vollmer who introduced (with Wilson) the
ideas of equal workload, scheduling, and so forth.

Wildhorn, S., 1969.
Public Order Studies in New York City. P-4250. Santa Monica, Calif.: Rand
Corporation.
In this report, Wildhorn reviews some of the early work performed for the
New York City Police Department by the New York City Rand Institute.

Wilson, O. W., 1941.
Distribution of Police Patrol Force. Publication 74, Chicago, Illinois: Public Administration Service.
This is Wilson's original document explaining his allocation procedures now out of print. The material is contained in O. W. Wilson, 1963. His scheme (sometimes in modified versions) is the most widely used procedure for allocating police patrol manpower.

Wilson, O. W., 1963.
Police Administration. New York: McGraw-Hill Book Company.
This is probably the best known book on police administration. Wilson's allocation method is included.

Wiseman, F., 1969.
"Law and Order." Boston, Mass.: Zipporah Films.
Frederick Wiseman rode in Kansas City, Missouri, police cars for about 250 hours during 5 weeks of filming in one of the city's high crime districts in order to make this edited 81-minute film. The film was commissioned by the Public Broadcast Laboratory and first shown over educational television (WGBH, Channel 2 in Boston) in March 1969. The film provides an excellent sample of the police activities we designated as answering a call for service. Included are picking up a drunk from the street, breaking up a family quarrel, settling an argument over a taxi fare, comforting a lost child, arresting a man charged with stealing a car, assisting a young woman injured in an auto accident.

Index

Activity indicators, 33, 36–39
See also Hazard formula
Algorithm: patrol allocation to commands, 10, 149–169
dispatching, 94
grid sector design, 112
Ambulance, 3, 28–29, 70–71
Atoms, geographical, 174

Barriers, 102–106
Bellmore, M., 210
Boston Police Department, 17, 23–26, 41

Call for service, single sector example, 8
Car location, simulated, 184–185
Car locator system, 12–13, 26, 99
intersector dispatching, 249–250
in Simtown, 66–69
simulated, 185, 212–214
technology, 211–212
Center-of-mass dispatching, 89–100
comparison with closest-car dispatching, 206–209
with local repositioning, 255
in SPRINT, 26
Chapman, S. G., 31 n
Chicago Police Department, 85, 134
Chicago Transit Authority, 211–212
Cincinnati Police Department, in 1888, 32
Clock, for simulation, 177
Closest-car dispatching, 86, 205–241
Clumping, of busy patrol units, 88
Clustering, of independently patrolling cars, 241
Cobham, A., 153–155
Command judgment, 6
Command and control center
See Communications center
Command saturation, 259
See also Dispatcher queue
Communications center, 15
Complaint clerk, 3, 16–17
Complaint ticket, 18
Computer: assisted call processing, 18–19
real-time simulation, 50–51
See also Algorithm; Simulation, SPRINT
Constraint, 149
code, 157–158
equations, 155–157
Cost, 3, 12, 33
budget, 47
of car locator system, 206
of delay, 150
of error, 17–18
of preventive patrol, 131

Cost effectiveness, 12–13, 55, 206
Coverage: for global repositioning, 263
function for preventive patrol, 135–141
Crofton's theorem, 81
Cross-sector dispatches
See Intersector dispatches

Dallas, Texas, 73 n
Data collection, 114–125
Data truncation, 120–125
Demand sequence, 194
Deterrence, 33
Difference function, 90–91, 220, 239–240
Dispatch error probability, 33
linear sectors, 215, 220–221
in Simtown, 52–54, 58–59
simulated, 198–200, 222–224
See also Dispatcher; dispatching strategy
Dispatcher, 6, 18–26
intersector dispatches, 85
in Simtown, 47–48
See also Dispatcher queue; Dispatch error probability; Dispatcher queue delay; Dispatching strategy
Dispatcher queue, 19, 23–26
analytical models of, 232–238
relation to intersector dispatching, 250
in Simtown, 48, 56–59, 61–64
simulated, 180
See also Dispatcher; Dispatcher queue delay; Dispatching strategy
Dispatcher queue delay: in Boston, 24–26
equation in allocation algorithm, 150–151, 153–155
in Simtown, 56–64, 66
simulated, 193, 202
two causes, 19–20
See also Dispatcher; Dispatcher queue; Dispatching strategy
Dispatching strategy, 19–20, 22–26
center-of-mass, 87–99
closest-car, 86, 206–240
in Simtown, 47–48, 56–64
simulated, 173, 178–180, 184–186
See also Dispatcher; Expected modified center-of-mass; Expected strict center-of-mass; Modified center-of-mass; Strict center-of-mass
Dispatching zone
See Division
Distance traveled between patrol passings, 139–140
Division, 22, 44, 57, 62, 174
Domino effects, 262
Drake, Alvin W., 8 n